D0322234

'Race' and Sport

Critical race theory

University of

Chester

Warrington Campus

University of Chester Library
Tel: 01925 534284

Critical race theory provides a framework for exploring racism in society, taking into account the role of institutions and drawing on the experiences of those affected.

Applied to the world of sport, this framework can reveal the underlying social mores and institutionalised prejudices that have helped perpetuate those racial stereotypes particular to sport, and those that permeate broader society.

In this groundbreaking sociological investigation, Kevin Hylton takes on the controversial subject of racial attitudes in sport and beyond. With sport as his primary focus, Hylton unpacks the central concepts of 'race', ethnicity, social constructionism and racialisation, and helps the reader navigate the complicated issues and debates that surround the study of 'race' in sport. Containing rigorous and insightful analysis throughout, the book explores key topics such as:

- The origins, applications and terminology of critical race theory
- The meaning of 'whiteness'
- The media, sport and racism
- Antiracism and sport
- Genetics and scientific racism

The contested concepts that define the subject of 'race' in sport present a constant challenge for academics, policy makers and practitioners in the development of their ideas, policies and interventions. This innovative and challenging book is essential reading for anybody looking to fully understand this important subject.

Kevin Hylton is a Senior Lecturer in Sport and Recreation Development in the Carnegie Faculty of Sport and Education, Leeds Metropolitan University. He has been heavily involved in community sports development, working with marginalized groups in different settings. Hylton's research has focused on diversity, equity and inclusion, and in particular, racism in sport and leisure.

'Race' and Sport

Critical race theory

Kevin Hylton

01935100

LIBRARY

ACC. No. 36073692   DEPT. PS

CLASS No. 306.483 HYL

UNIVERSITY OF CHESTER
WARRINGTON CAMPUS

Routledge
Taylor & Francis Group

LONDON AND NEW YORK

First published 2009 by Routledge
2 Park Square, Milton Park, Abingdon, Oxon, OX14 4RN

Simultaneously published in the USA and Canada
by Routledge
270 Madison Avenue, New York, NY 10016

Routledge is an imprint of the Taylor & Francis Group, an Informa business

© 2009 Kevin Hylton

Typeset in Goudy by
Keystroke, 28 High Street, Tettenhall, Wolverhampton
Printed and bound in Great Britain by
TJ International Ltd, Padstow, Cornwall

All rights reserved. No part of this book may be reprinted or reproduced
or utilised in any form or by any electronic, mechanical, or other means,
now known or hereafter invented, including photocopying and recording,
or in any information storage or retrieval system, without permission in
writing from the publishers.

British Library Cataloguing in Publication Data
A catalogue record for this book is available from the British Library

Library of Congress Cataloging-in-Publication Data
Hylton, Kevin, 1964-
'Race' and sport : critical race theory / Kevin Hylton.
p. cm.
1. Racism in sports—History—20th century. 2. Discrimination in sports
—History—20th century. 3. Sports—Social aspects—History—20th century.
I. Title.
GV706.32.H95 2008
796.089—dc22   2008002088

ISBN10: 0–415–43656–7 (pbk)
ISBN10: 0–415–43655–9 (hbk)
ISBN10: 0–203–89367–0 (ebk)

ISBN13: 978–0–415–43655–7 (hbk)
ISBN13: 978–0–415–43656–4 (pbk)
ISBN13: 978–0–203–89367–8 (ebk)

Contents

Figures and tables

Figures

Tables

Foreword

At a recent conference for black parents and educators, I shared the platform with a colleague who leads a youth advocacy programme. In the midst of a discussion about institutional racism and the education system's perpetual ability to define black young people as 'less able', 'less motivated' – as just plain 'failures' – a delegate argued that the youth shared some of the responsibility because of their 'low aspirations'. My colleague begged to differ: 'there are a lot more brain surgeons than pro basketball players in the world, but the boys I work with still want to be in the NBA [National Basketball Association]. It would actually be *easier* to be a brain surgeon but they're sold the dream . . .'

The point was well made. Racism operates in multifaceted and complex ways. Sport provides a highly visible area where the prowess of black athletes (built through training and dedication) can simultaneously offer an apparent site of 'success' while supporting the crudest of racialised stereotypes. The endless hours of commitment and struggle are magically reinscribed as a 'natural' talent or gift by teachers who view black bodies as fit for physical rather than academic excellence. The racial structuring and commodification of sport – not least as a multi-million-pound enterprise – provide a vitally important context where racism works (sometimes subtly, sometimes more crudely) to protect particular interests while maintaining the racial status quo.

In this landmark study Kevin Hylton makes a powerful, sophisticated and original contribution to critical scholarship on the racialised dynamics of sport. The book deserves a wide readership, not only within its specialist field but also more generally, because it represents one of the first full-length applications of critical race theory (CRT) in the UK.

CRT is a movement of activist scholars who seek to expose and resist the workings of racism in contemporary society. Its origins lie in US law schools and the ground-breaking work of writers such as Derrick Bell, Richard Delgado, Kimberlé Crenshaw and Patricia Williams. Since the late 1980s, CRT has expanded and now finds a place in numerous disciplines including economics, anthropology, sociology and education. In each of these fields critical race scholars are asking radical questions that trouble the accepted assumptions and push for action to resist and reshape race inequities. Although CRT started in the US, it is increasingly international in its reach. Indeed, as CRT matures it may be that scholars working outside North America will become particularly influential in helping identify strengths and weaknesses in the perspective as an overarching theory of race and inequity. This book certainly offers important insights that will benefit critical race theorists internationally.

After a careful and wide-ranging review of key conceptual debates, Hylton outlines his view of CRT and perceptively reflects on its exclusion from certain debates and contexts that seek to define the theoretical highground – especially in Europe. He shows the utility of CRT, and this book is likely to help establish the approach as an important dimension in contemporary theorising about sport and social inequity in the UK. As the study unfolds, the reader is taken on a fascinating journey that challenges preconceptions and highlights the fundamental role of racism in questions concerning the nature of research, whiteness, the role of the media and the praxis of antiracist struggle.

David Gillborn
Institute of Education
University of London

Acknowledgements

Love and best wishes to Pia, Milli, Lukas and Lauren for bearing with me over the period of this work!

I would also like to thank Dr Ian Law at the Centre for Ethnicity and Racism Studies at the University of Leeds for his support from the inception of this project and Rachel Thornton for her sterling administrative efforts.

Thanks also to the 'critical mass' of staff at Carnegie for their support.

Chapter 2 is based upon a paper published in the *Journal of Leisure Studies* (Hylton 2005). Chapter 4 is based on a paper published in *Leisure Studies* (Long and Hylton 2002).

Chapter 1

Introduction – defining key terms

> Temperament, sexuality, athletic ability, aesthetic preferences and so on are presumed to be fixed and discernible from the palpable mark of race.
>
> (Omi and Winant 1994: 60)

Our capabilities in sport are often described in physical or psychological terms, 'natural' differences. These 'gifts' are often identified as the difference between those who are likely to succeed in a given sport and those who are not. This discourse of superiority and inferiority in sport is not dissimilar to other debates in wider society which revolve around genetics and intelligence, and ultimately underpin imperialist ideologies (Goldberg 1993, Essed and Goldberg 2002, Omi and Winant 2002). There is a popular perception in sport that our genes and to a degree our cultural background dictate the prowess of an individual sportsman or woman. This discourse of advantage and of course disadvantage in sport is invariably reduced to 'harmless' racial differences, a reduction that suggests, however, a more sinister undercurrent: 'race' logic (Coakley 2001), racial discourse (Goldberg 1993), racial formations (Omi and Winant 1994), raciology (Gilroy 2000) and racialisation (Murji and Solomos 2005). The preconceptions we have of Others act as a kind of shorthand for who they are and where they are located in social hierarchies. As Others speak they are gendered, classed and raced in a reflexive moment and beyond that the reality of their circumstances takes much longer to emerge. Omi and Winant (1994) suggest that often people are expected to act out racial identities, and where this does not occur it can be a source of confusion. Athletes such as the African American 400 metre runner Michael Johnson and Garth Crooks, the African Caribbean ex-footballer, contradict crude stereotypes of themselves when offering articulate and cerebral questions and answers on media panels. Oliver Skeets, the African Caribbean show jumper, Darshan-Singh Buller, the Asian contemporary dance choreographer, Tiger Woods and of course all of those white men who can jump, and those Asian women who can Bend it like Beckham, hint at the reality and very real contradictions of the diversity in wider society. The racialised social structures of sport therefore contribute to the way we shape and experience our own and others' identities.

This chapter examines why 'race' and racism are so powerful as concepts and processes that when they are the point of debate, especially in public policy, they remain unproblematised. That is, we need to appreciate more fully what 'race' means in sport (signification in a discursive practice) and then, on the basis of this meaning, how sport (social structure) is organised (racially, racial hierarchy). Sport could be described as a racial formation according to Omi and Winant (1994), who are concerned with how racial categories are created over time, lived, transformed and negated in such institutions. A racial formation is a process that can be described as a series of interrelated but historically situated *racial projects* where *racialised* people and social structures are organised and represented (Omi and Winant 1994). The complexities of racial projects can be encapsulated in the idea that they could be a representation of racial dynamics. In the same moment a racial project could be an interpretation or an explanation of the same racial process resulting in an allocation of resources based upon a racialised premise. There is no one interpretation of how these dynamic racialised processes work as the intricacies of these issues exercise the minds of many committed to furthering our understanding of racism in sport. This chapter considers the utility of the concept of 'race' because its use as an analytical concept implies a clear association with ethnicity which is often articulated in a reductionist black/white binary. The term 'race' is used by critical race theorists, as we shall see in Chapter 2, but it is emphasised here that the use of critical race theory (CRT) does not imply that the term 'race' is being applied without caution. In addition, there is no attempt to deny difference, individuality or identity in *'Race' and Sport: Critical Race Theory* by not consistently referring to ethnicity, as it is recognised here that we experience racialisation and racism(s) in different ways. It would also be fallacious to talk of a common experience, and of a monolithic phenomenon of 'race', racism or even blackness or whiteness (hooks and West 1991, Collins 2000, Long and Hylton 2002, Harris 2003, Frankenberg 2004). We will see in this and the following chapters that the irony of 'race' is that talking about it is still problematic even after the customary caveats have been expressed and parentheses denoting dissonance around it and related concepts such as the 'Other', 'black', 'minority ethnic' have been elucidated. When W.E.B. DuBois asserted that the problem of the twentieth century would be the problem of the colour line I wonder whether he anticipated how stirring those words would continue to be in the twenty-first century for so many (Bulmer and Solomos 1999, Alexander and Knowles 2005). The relationship between 'race', racism, racialisation, ethnicity, identity and nation in sport will be explored further on in this chapter and effectively used as the starting point for the many debates over the next chapters. As many writers have stated over the years, any discussion of 'race' effects what Gilroy (2000) describes as a perpetuation of everyday raciology or, as others such as Lee and Lutz (2005b) would suggest, a racial ideology. Certain attributions and associations are made with racialised practices that result in a system of representation that structures racial ideologies. It is evident that those with power and influence in societies defend and fix these ideologies in the form of racialised discourses (Goldberg 1993, Lee and Lutz 2005a, b). For Armstrong and Ng (2005: 35) 'race is the social construction, but the act and effect of this construction (racialisation) have produced actual divisions between people'. In hard populist terms what 'race' often boils down to is physical differences, and in particular physiognomy. Whereas many believe that they can tell the difference between people born in continents and countries across the world, the ability to distinguish social groups according to this notion of 'race' is beyond the most advanced minds and computers, the truth being we are as much collapsed into one 'race' as pieces in a jigsaw: we all may look different but we all fit together to make the one picture. Malik's (1996) argument that humanity is not a Dulux colour chart with everyone falling into discrete categories is reiterated here.

The problematic of 'race' thinking for many in sport is its endemic omnipresent discourse. The popularity of 'race' thinking is historically located in multifarious assumptions, and deeds that reinforce the legitimacy of 'race' and therefore physical differences in sport. Assumptions that have endured are those that argue humans could be divided into a few biologically and phenotypically detached 'races'; the similarities within these groups could be reduced to ability, behaviour and morality; these differences would be naturally passed from one generation to the next; and racial hierarchies exist with white people at the top and darker 'races' at the opposite end (Fenton 2003). The 'Jack Nicklaus syndrome' typifies the example of this unconscious, benign acceptance of differences in sport premised upon biology or psychology. In 1994, before Tiger Woods had established himself as the best golfer in a generation, Nicklaus was reported to have argued that African American golfers could not succeed at the highest level of golf because of their muscle structure (Hatfield 1996). The 'Nicklaus syndrome' has been evident at all levels of sport, and its related impacts replicated internationally. St Louis (2004) accepts that this racist orthodoxy exists while positing that the perception of racial Others as being particularly strong in motor rather than psychological terms, and that evidence of conspicuous success in high-profile sport is evidence of this, provides for many a *prima facie* case for the existence of racial physical propensities. These racial differences that emerge from a flawed social Darwinism begin and end in a biological reductionist morass. They give support to Younge's contention that these views (2000: 24) suggest that if (black) people are naturally talented at sport then they are naturally less equipped intellectually. The ability to generate stereotypes of this kind in itself points towards the insidious prejudices, 'race' thinking and social positioning of dominant hegemonic actors within sport and academe (Long *et al.* 1995, 1997, 2000). Turning to popular culture, in 1993 Jon Turtletaub's film *Cool Runnings*, the story of the Jamaican bobsleigh team competing in the Olympic Games, was written as a comedy that was underpinned by the conception and stereotype that black people cannot do winter sports, they do not like the cold and are quite superficial characters. Also, in Jon Shelton's *White Men Can't Jump* (1992) where the narrative is even more obvious, the film carries still a benign subtext that not only has the white man who couldn't jump, jumping, but shows him managing it only when he needs to and only after a lot of hard work! Here racial stereotypes prevail again with many racialised ideologies, concepts and stereotypes remaining intact and unchallenged. What was not considered in any respect was the corollary of these arguments which Coakley (2001) alludes to in his examination of race logic in sport as he points to the unlikelihood of commentators explaining the achievements of Swiss skiing from a biological viewpoint. This racial thinking in sport is perpetuated by four weak theoretical propositions (St Louis 2004: 32):

1 Sports are based on theoretical principles of equality.
2 The results of sporting competition are unequal.
3 This inequality of results has a racial bias.
4 Therefore, given the equality of access and opportunity, the explanation of the unequal results lies in racial physicality.

This race logic can be propagated by anyone from any social background. According to Williams (1977), Hargreaves (1986) and Sugden and Tomlinson (2002), the pressures and limits of a given domination or subordination are experienced and internalised by individuals and groups. This has the effect of power minorities, that is, individuals or groups in society, reinforcing or challenging their own subordination in a system that can alienate and disenfranchise them. A lived hegemony is always an ongoing process: it is not a passive form of dominance as it has got to be continually renewed, recreated, defended and modified. Goldberg (1993: 94) would argue that biology is not the only predicate of racial constructions. By this he is suggesting that, although the history of racial oppression has been marked by attempts to subjugate the Other through 'commonsense' scientific and folk arguments, there are other devices that are more readily invoked owing to their relative acceptance. These include cultural racism, nationalism and whiteness processes explored further during the course of 'Race' and Sport: Critical Race Theory.

The salience of 'race' in sport and society

In the public sector, underlying the development of equal opportunities policies and the 'race relations industry' since the 1950s has been a worldview that draws its reasoning from a racialised, race-biased discourse (Nanton 1989). The recent reports in the UK by Cantle (2002) and Ouseley (2001) on the disturbances in Bradford, Oldham, Burnley, Leicester, Southall and Birmingham were all heavily tinged with racial overtones and the subsequent reports spoke in particular of communities differentiated by 'race'. In legal terms, where a citizen's rights have been flouted in relation to racism there are sanctions in law, steps to be taken, to indemnify each individual. What Lee and Lutz (2005b) recognise with this approach is that the naturalness of 'races' is not questioned or disturbed in any way. This discourse has as its basic principle an oversimplified reductionist tenet that reinforces biological arguments, homogeneity and universalism (Harris 2003). In sport and leisure the lexicon of policy makers has promulgated a vocabulary that legitimates rather than challenges the notion of 'race', monolithic racial identities and the black 'Other' (Gilroy 1987, Cross and Keith 1993, Goldberg 1993, Back *et al.* 1999, Thomas and Piccolo 2000, Leeds Metropolitan University 2003). Approaches like these are 'unable to transcend their own complicity in the production and reproduction of racism' (Lee and Lutz 2005b: 9).

Omi and Winant (2002: 123) contend that '"race" is a concept which signifies and symbolizes social conflicts and interests by referring to different types of human bodies'. 'Race' is constructed and transformed using everyday assumptions, and it is viewed as the most powerful and persistent group boundary by Cornell and Hartmann (1998), hence the general tendency for politicians and sports practitioners to take cognisance, and to varying degrees consider the policy implications of 'race' regulations. Gates's (1986) observation that 'race' is the ultimate trope of difference because it is so arbitrary in application supports these constructionist views of the concept, even though it is well documented that 'race' is socially constructed (UNESCO 1978). The fiction and fallacy of 'race' as a cultural construct have been the source of much controversy (Husband 1984, Gates 1986, Miles 1989, Terkel 1992, Montagu 1997). Miles's (1989) view that the idea of 'race' was derived from nineteenth-century scientific theories has much support. Goldberg (1993) describes how racialised discourses emerge as ideological and conceptual conditions conflate over time. The nineteenth-century ideas that emerged from the racial science of the day have found their way into our public and private spheres (Husband 1984, Ben-Tovim *et al.* 1986, Anthias and Yuval-Davis 1993, Verma and Darby 1994, Haney-Lopez 2000, Solomos 1995, Guillaumin 1995, Parker 1998, Macpherson 1999). Unfortunately, clearly articulated positions have emphasised the spurious position of natural differences in sport and society and emphasised the 'othering' discourse of 'race', and we are still unable to halt the flow of folk concepts and definitions that maintain these fundamentally racist ideologies. In the wake of these essentialist conceptual and theoretical claims racism is propagated, is perpetuated and remains a cancerous aspect of social life. Racism by definition reinforces human differences and privileges some over others. It is on the basis of this controversial, but well documented, debate that in democratic, cosmopolitan societies discourses of 'race' are perpetuated, and 'race' equality no longer raises any eyebrows.

Society maintains the habit of reifying 'race' in sport and other institutions, and a critical analysis of racism and therefore antiracism needs to challenge any 'race' schema, commonsense views and other hegemonic impositions (Outlaw 1990). Most people in society accept the importance of 'race' whilst at the same time being revolted by its outcomes. The state, as a major sponsor of the notion of 'race', regularly endorses its value as a social and political boundary between groups. The state often utilises 'race' through the law in its implementation of statutes such as in the UK the Race Relations (Amendment) Act (2000), and the contested issues of affirmative action in the US. The discourse of 'race' is also used extensively in the context of race relations in the social, political and biological sciences (Miles 1989). Miles supports the idea that through a process of signification the utilisation of 'race' attributes social groups with physical and cultural characteristics and meanings. This racial differentiation is common and not unusual in everyday discourses. This 'commonsenseness' is what Miles (1989) finds unhelpful as 'race' is reified and given the status of a scientific concept.

Racialisation

In so far as there is an imperative to name and contest the notion of 'race' in its categorical sense, as an analytical or theoretical concept it is less useful and poorly equipped to explain the processes that privilege and limit people on account of their heritage and related social background. Similarly Rattansi (2005) is convinced that the term 'racialisation' is important as a concept that somehow unclutters the term 'racism'. The term 'racialisation' is used to expunge the notion of biology and other corporeal differences. It acts as a conceptual magnet drawing together other less useful concepts into one that fashions a more acceptable discourse for sociologists and other critics alike. It has been said that by naming this process it enables a sharper focus on the past and present utilisation of racial categories, both implied and explicit. This shifts critics from a mere acceptance of 'race' to a more critical analysis of the outcomes of racialisation. A more accurate picture of the processes that subjugate and oppress racialised people in the many contexts that constitute the many racisms is more likely to give antiracists a clearer picture of the interventions necessary. Not only do strategies become clearer but so does the vocabulary of resistance, so that the rather 'flabby' use of the terms 'race' and 'racism' through its many incarnations, whose use is understandable for many reasons, becomes synonymous with 'racialisation' which is dynamic, dialectical, transhistorical and reflective of a diverse post-structural society in a postmodern time.

Barot and Bird (2001), Miles (1989), Omi and Winant (1994) and Murji and Solomos (2005) have been influential in the way racialisation has been understood and mapped over the years. They agree that one of the earliest uses of the term is credited to Fanon in 1967 although Miles (1989) points out that Banton was the first to use it systematically and coherently in relation to 'race' structuring public perceptions. According to Barot and Bird (2001), racialisation is sometimes used as a synonym for racial or racist meanings or a description of the process through which the meanings are implied. This is the case with Miles (1989), where 'racialisation' is often the replacement for 'race'. Miles reiterates how he sees the delineation of group boundaries and people according to biological or ascribed traits to be part of this ideological process of racial categorisation. Miles (1989: 75) goes on to conclude that he uses the term 'racialisation' to

> refer to those instances where social relations between people have been
> structured by the signification of human biological characteristics in such a

way as to define and construct differentiated social collectivities [. . .] the concept therefore refers to a process of categorisation, a representational process of defining an Other.

Some of the earliest work on racism in sport focused narrowly on the stacking thesis which examined how racial thinking leading to stereotypes was expressed in the way individuals were positioned in sports teams. The result of much of this work was to find that racialised Others were less likely to be viewed as important, thinking, central players but more likely as physical, unintelligent, peripheral players. This disproportionate allocation of players to particular positions has led to the emergence of well known sayings such as 'he's black, he's fast, he's on the wing' and 'white men can't jump'. Here practice reinforces discourse, discourse reinforces practice. So from an early point in the sociology of sport, although this was not explicitly theorised, it was clear that sport was a racialised arena and that as a contested arena it required more critical exploration and examination. The use of the term 'racialisation' has reached the stage where it has been applied conceptually and descriptively to a plethora of social phenomena that range through statistics, the body, institutions, landscapes, technologies, the environment, images, cultures, religion, art and of course sport (Omi and Winant 1994, Barot and Bird 2001, Durrheim and Dixon 2001, King 2004, Woodward 2004, Murji and Solomos 2005).

Sport, racialisation and space

More recent work on racialisation has suggested a more contested use of spaces that are encoded by individuals and communities in complementary and divergent ways. Lefebvre's (1991: 292) view that the 'illusion of a transparent, "pure" and neutral space has permeated Western culture' is one of the main reasons offered by van Ingen (2003) for the lack of research in this area. Clearly the mapping of an area by planners and policy makers is but one crude vision of a space that offers little insight into the dynamics of those spaces and the meaning of the spaces and the activities practised in and around them. There has now been a significant volume of activity in this area in relation to the city (Cross and Keith 1993), urban planning (Thomas 2000) and well-being (Dines et al. 2006) that has explored the ways that people experience and attribute meaning to space in the city. In sport sociology this work has been complemented by other work focused on interpreting how space is structured in relation to the social and cultural practices of communities (Williams 1994, Carrington 1999), racial groups in South Africa (Durrheim and Dixon 2001), gender and sexuality and 'race' (van Ingen 2003) and sports (Andrews et al. 2002). Van Ingen in particular utilises a triad of concepts from Lefebvre (1991) to offer a dynamic insight to how spaces are *perceived, conceived and lived*. These ideas present a view of sport that systematically challenges functionalist orthodoxies with respect to how sport can be used to integrate social groups, as this dialectical model suggests that our lived spaces (spaces of representation) are instrumental in how we imagine other spaces (conceived spaces) and how we manage our spatial practices (perceived space) so that we may see them as formal or informal bounded spaces for sport and recreation (van Ingen 2003).

Our conceptualisation of a critical theorisation of sport and social relations would benefit from incorporating the complexities of spatiality and intersectionality in relation to racism as there is a dearth of policy and critical academic analysis in this area. The racialisation of spaces is commonly considered in relation to our lived spaces ('black', 'Asian', 'Hispanic', 'Chinese', 'white' areas (cf. Andrews *et al.* 2002, Lacy 2004) and we know too little about how spaces are conceived of or imagined by social groups. Further the creation, (re)creation and contestation of public spaces in terms of how our spatial practices structure how we experience sport (passively and actively) is underresearched and under-examined. In Chapter 6 counter-hegemonic resistance and spatial contestation make up part of the discussion in relation to formal and informal antiracism in sport. However, Murji and Solomos (2005) use the term 'racialisation' to describe processes by which racial meanings are attached to specific issues as one of the central issues that define a 'problem'. By this token they use the term as a 'lens' through which race-thinking operates, not in relation to space but there are clear areas of complementarity. So the racialisation of tennis (bounded spatial practice), through the descriptive reference to the white middle class (raced or classed groups) that make up its core player base and its administrative structure juxtaposed with the emergence of Serena and Venus Williams (racialised, classed, gendered, spatially located), has reignited at least on the surface a challenge to social relations within the game (Schultz 2005). The discourse that follows Serena and Venus Williams is one of novelty and awe, but ostensibly a raced, classed and gendered one underpinned by their working-class roots and African American heritage which often trivialises their achievements when they are described as 'natural athletes' and therefore 'physical' rather than 'cerebral' beings (see Chapter 5).

Rather than speaking of racialisation per se, Goldberg (1993) refers to racialised discourse and its various racialised expressions. These expressions can be philosophical or ethical, practical, and institutional acts. Goldberg's use of expressive or discursive objects is broad enough to include racism as one, as well as analytical accounts of 'race' and racism, like this one, as another. He therefore describes how racialised discourses can be disaggregated into two 'texts' the *enunciative* and the *analytical*. Goldberg's (1993) analysis is different from that of Miles (1989) and Darder and Torres (2003) in that racialisation is not necessarily the result of a racist ideology. Racism is but one outcome of a racial discourse. This process is most significant in the way the state manages social relations using 'race' and ethnicity as 'real' and fixed categories through which the lives of social groups are mediated, signified and represented. Departments of immigration, employment, education, crime, health and sport have all relied upon the racial and ethnic categories and the consequent racialised statistics collected to inform policy agendas. In a society that disadvantages Others because of their social or perceived differences, steps have to be taken to combat these prejudices and discrimination. However the imprecision of these categories, their static or, reductionist nature and the lack of ownership by the social groups they purport to represent presents other important issues about the effectiveness of such a process. It is also a significant issue for antiracists who themselves have been accused of being vague in their approach to the subjects of their resistance.

Barot and Bird (2001) adumbrate the nature of the 'race'/racialisation problematic as it has consistently rated a debate amongst critical theorists in its overall utility or damage in the consideration of social relations defined or understood through racial processes. They pose some of the key writers against each other, such as Omi and Winant (1994, 2002), Winant (2001) (pro the use of 'race'), and Banton (1998) and Miles (1989) ('post-race'). It is generally accepted in the sociology of sport and beyond that 'race' as a concept is purely used as a socially constructed category that has no credible use beyond this reference to denote any real biological or psychological differences between groups in society. The difficulty with adopting and defending the reasoned choice of the utility of 'racialisation' over 'race' as a sociological concept is highlighted here by Barot and Bird (2001: 601) who, even after their systematic analysis of the genealogy of the concept 'racialisation', concluded that:

> 'Race' still remains as part of the lived experience of people . . . and it is this problem of the lived experience of people on the one hand and uneasiness of sociology with the concept on the other, that seems to account for the current popularity of racialisation.

Racism

Although in most critical arenas it is necessary to clarify key concepts and terms, it often seems that little progress is made in the theorising of problematics owing to the ambiguous nature of key debates. Bulmer and Solomos (1999: 3) describe the time spent on reimaging terminology as 'somewhat abstract and unsatisfactory'. Fredman (2001, cited Bhavnani et al. 2005: 15) conceptualises racism as a process that can be recognised by its penchant for stereotyping which may lead to violence if not prejudice. In Italy's top football leagues Carroll (2001) observed incessant racist chanting, crowd violence and racism on the pitch resulting in an institutional ambivalence that effectively condones this behaviour through a lack of action. (The decision not to act is not unusual in relation to racism in sport organisations and is a significant consideration in Chapter 6.) This then leads to cycles of inequality and disadvantage that finally negate the culture of the groups concerned. For Anthias and Yuval-Davis (1993: 2) racisms need to be recognised as 'modes of exclusion, inferiorization, subordination and exploitation that present specific and different characters in different social and historical contexts'. Racism is often articulated in a plural sense (racisms) as in policy terms it is acknowledged as negatively impacting specific social groups at different levels, but also because we experience racism in often quite different ways. Racism is often described as operating in the dialectic between individual, institutional and structural forms (Miles 1989, Mason 2000). Although any of these racially motivated discriminations can be direct or indirect, against individuals or groups in society, it is institutions like sport that legitimate these actions and embed them in what seemingly become benign practices. When institutions like sport become complicit in institutionalised racist acts it no longer takes the efforts of rogue actors or right-wing organisations when racism is intentionally or unwittingly perpetuated. Institutional racism is often marked by its more subtle covert incarnation as opposed to the more overt expressions of behaviour by individual actors (Wieviorka 1995). Structural- or societal-level racism reinforces the pervasive embedded nature of racism in the major arenas of our social lives. The interconnectedness of these domains – education, employment, housing, health, policing, legal system, politics – leads us to a chronic disempowering of some social groups that marks their existence in a way that requires more of a contest with the system for them to succeed, often despite the system. These processes lead critical race theorists to support the view that racism is effortlessly reproduced and perpetuated in society.

Racism is a highly emotive, complex and perplexing concept. For many it is an existential experience that despite its multifarious incarnations is 'known' and shared by populations with perceptions of group identities to the point that an empathy exists between individuals and groups, so much so that the exact nature of these experiences are commonly left unexamined. As a result racism means different things to different people: for some racism is something that is perpetrated by white people on black people; for others 'racist' is a popular adjective that describes a stigmatising process, or 'racism' is a noun that puts a name to outcome(s) of these stigmatising processes. Racism becomes shrouded in conceptual ambiguity when in political, media and other discourses it becomes associated with behaviours that range from hubris to ignorance of other cultures (Mason 2000, Omi and Winant 2002). Racism is further considered as a popular analytical concept that many imbue with little credibility in its potential to interrogate the social and historical reasons for the developed hierarchies and transhistorical advantages accruing to particular socio-economic groups. Armstrong and Ng (2005: 37) propose that racism differs across time and space as a result of the intersecting and historical differences that individuals have and develop over their life cycle. This has a consequent effect on the racisms in any society, so they argue: 'In every instance, we have to interrogate how racism actually operates and what kinds of divisions it creates. As well we have to examine how it intersects with other axes of power and difference.'

In sport this can be seen in terms of how people have been racialised and their opportunities to work or play restricted and how today those same standards would be deemed out of place and unacceptable. For Goldberg a racialised discourse involves more than racist expressions: he also argues that racial discourses are structured in terms of shared views on racial hierarchies, an acceptance of power privileges and institutional regulations. For example, in the case of the baseball player Curt Flood in the late 1960s, racism in the US was located in a different era from the 2000s. In the 1960s the civil rights movement was at its zenith, Jim Crow segregation was active even at a micro level in sport and even between team mates, and in the 1968 Olympic Games the athletes Carlos and Smith promoted the Black Power movement to a global audience. Given this backdrop, Flood's challenge to the baseball authorities to change their reserve system was a radical move to counter the racism and class relations of that time (Lomax 2004). The racism(s) occurring across sports, and clubs, in some states and for diverse individuals meant that in this time, in these places, for these people racism needs to be understood in this situated context. These were times of paradigm shifts in social relations in the US and, although the processes of racialisation and outcomes of racial projects can be witnessed in other places, the social factors that made these times unique are particular to this situated place. Flood's confidence to fight for equality for all players, but in particular African American players, could occur only after he felt empowered once he became financially sound. Most players do not achieve this position, and in the 1960 or 1970s a black player would have had to endure other 'race'-related indignities to compound this fact. Social commentators like Goldberg (1993, 2002), Solomos and Back (1995) and Skellington (1996) are critical of the well known disparities between those who have and those who do not have the blend of social, cultural and economic capital that keep some on the inside of sport and others out. Thus sport has a role challenging social closure even if its role in this task is perhaps not as clear as the state's. However, a cursory reading of the related sports literature in the UK identifies an institution repeatedly accused of advantaging white people as players, spectators and employees over those from Other backgrounds even in those sports where success amongst these groups is more conspicuous (Jarvie 1991a, Back *et al.* 2001, Carrington and McDonald 2001, Long and Hylton 2002, Swinney and Horne 2005).

Ethnicity, nation and new racism

Solomos and Back (2001) suggest that more recent conceptualisations of racism have shifted debates in a more positive direction. They argue that earlier work zealously overlooked the status of 'race' as a social construct and often reinforced the notion of 'race' and its implicit meanings for themselves and racialised others in their enthusiasm to tackle racism (cf. Cashmore and Troyna 1982). The emergence of whiteness critiques and other metonymic analyses in the new racism debates, media investigations and other influential racial formations have helped to move narrower static conceptualisations of racism into more fluid and critical descriptions and analyses of social relations in diverse and late .modern times. Importantly, an analysis of racialisation processes would not be complete without a consideration of ethnicity and identities and their contribution to the way racism is constructed and experienced and the way racial ideologies are (re)created. Ethnicity is a term often used in the social analysis of sport, and has been presented as a more palatable alternative when considering human diversity (Mason 2000). What 'race' and ethnicity share are boundary making properties that are socially constructed, can be self-imposed or externally imposed or both, and can be rooted in explanations that can be reduced to territory, culture, biology or physiognomy. Cronin and Mayall (1998: 4) posit key questions in the application of the notion of ethnicity to the context of sport. They ask us to consider: (1) whether ethnicity is formed and then imposed by outsiders; (2) whether it is a self-forming process by a group; (3) what role does resistance play to ethnic identity (antagonism); (4) whether ethnicity is 'natural' or 'constructed'; and (5) whether ethnic identity is 'fixed' or 'fluid'. 'Ethnicity' is not without ambiguity but its common usage in everyday life has perpetuated its more divisive potential through narrow political categorisations of majority and minority populations intranationally and internationally. For many, ethnicity is the source of much rancour and is often used as a ploy to question the identity of individuals and populations, not least their national identity where belonging and inclusion issues are a heightened source of nation-state interest. The term ethnicity can be further seen as a paradox as it remains a source of both inclusion and exclusion.

Traditionally, ethnicity for many influences the norms and practices of individuals in different settings (Kew 1979), reinforces boundaries (Barth 1969, Anthias and Yuval-Davis 1993) and reinforces group consciousness and collective action (Ratcliffe 1994) despite the free movement of people between them. For Weber (1997) political categories of ethnicity are influential in forming ethnic identities but they do not necessarily constitute an ethnic group as critiqued by Law (1996), Jenkins (1997), Ratcliffe (1994) and other writers on this topic. In attempting to define ethnicity, Law (1996) and Jenkins (1997) identify models for understanding it. Both agree that ethnicity involves a process of differentiation, with Law emphasising the common cultural bonds of a shared diasporic 'home', language, religion, behaviour, diet, dress and tradition. In addition to Law's caveats that these boundaries are never clear and should be used with caution, Jenkins (1997) recommends that our understanding of ethnic identities must recognise the ongoing process of give-and-take between similarity and difference between groups, based on a social identity characterised by metaphoric or fictive kinship (Eriksen 1997: 39).

Jenkins's (1997) description of the dynamic nature of ethnicity is not uncommon amongst social scientists, and for good reason. Ethnicity is often used uncritically in vernacular and political parlance and as such they imply clear objective boundaries between groups. On one hand they reinforce the differences between people that can on the one hand lead to the xenophobic, nationalistic, and racist behaviour evidenced in sport and wider society over recent years (MacClancy 1996), and on the other hand assume static incarnations of ethnic groups that remain as defined and identifiable from generation to generation (Mason 2000, Jenkins 1997). The categorical nature of ethnic identities proposed in political discourses is but one use for group boundaries especially as separate settings might call for 'separate selves' or even the 'performance' of ethnicity as a mechanism to mark group unity, resistance, inclusion or possibly exclusion (Alexander 1996, MacClancy 1996). There is much evidence in sport today that ethnic identities are fluid, strategic, and under constant revision. Jenkins (1994: 198) usefully summarises this problematic:

> Ethnicity is not an immutable bundle of cultural traits which it is sufficient to enumerate in order to identify a person as an 'X' or a 'Y' or locate the boundary between ethnic collectivities. Rather, ethnicity is situationally defined, produced in the course of social transactions that occur at or across (and in the process help to constitute) the ethnic boundary in question.

In sport any examination of ethnicity like those of Burdsey (2004a), King (2004), and Ismond (2003) is welcome, but the message is 'proceed with caution'. Mason (2000) is unequivocal that ethnicity is situational and as such it is not surprising that we can draw upon multiple strategic ethnic and national identities. It is not uncommon for the same people to support the Brazilian football team, West Indian cricket, New Zealand rugby union, UK athletics, Washington Redskins NFL and Leeds United (championship football at its best). We will also see in Chapter 5 that it is also not uncommon for individuals to be conflicted when torn between media discourses of 'us' and 'them', especially when 'they' look like 'me'. It is also not unusual for allegiances to switch in public and private spaces dependent upon the situation. Although moves in the 'wrong' direction can cause some antagonism for emergent groups in sport. McDonald and Ugra's (1999) study of sub-county-level cricket in Essex revealed the difficulties that minority ethnic teams and players can have where they behave in a way that is different from the socially accepted 'traditional' behaviours of the leagues. For example, many of the Asian heritage players felt that they were not accepted because of the perception that they would not participate in the culture of post-match drinks. In some cases players felt it necessary to tolerate this culture to become accepted in sports club culture (King 2004). It can be argued that fuller explanations of ethnicity in sport need to shift from essentialist descriptive categorisations that perpetuate these stereotypes to ones that consider the flow of bodies across imagined and political communities so that a sense of hybridity and situationality becomes part of any analysis (Cohen 1999).

Tiger Woods's description of himself as a 'Cablinasian' (Caucasian-black-Indian-Asian) is one example of this hybridisation, and the more banal Lord Taylor of Warwick's description of himself as an 'Afro-Saxon' takes some beating. However, Burdsey's (2004a) analysis of Anglo-Asian football players synthesises an argument that explores the situatedness (cultural assimilation) and issues of hybridity (dual ethnicity) of 'Asianness' on Anglo-Asian players being accepted (cultural capital) into the institution of football. As in Lacy's (2004) analysis of middle-class black Americans' 'strategic assimilation' with their self-identified 'black' and 'white' repertoires, Burdsey's (ibid.) view that players 'deprioritise' their identifiable 'Asian culture' has serious ramifications for the identities of Asians in football, sport and wider society. There is evidence from other writers that these strategies are being strategically employed. In King's (2004: 26) case he explored how black football players developed a 'performance, a certain socially delimited role, tailored to the fluctuating demands of white coaches and managers'. What is clear here is that the constructed and dialectical nature of hybridised ethnicities presents a more realistic picture of contested ethnic identities than the categorical, fixed, static political constructions of ethnicity that are so commonly referred to. Ethnic identities are as contested across established social boundaries as they are within them as there are also implications for how we view ethnicity in relation to time, space, location, situations and other more complex social factors. Globalisation's impact upon this process of hybridisation is extended further in Chapter 5 where the media's influence is considered in more detail.

The subtleties of ethnicity and racism have led to the coining of a new term: 'cultural racism', in some cases 'new racism'. This term is often used by those decrying particular racialised populations where little recourse is made to explicit biological differences. Solomos and Back (2001) argue that this type of racism is often categorised by 'metonymic elaborations' as a consequence of racisms being effected through coded signifiers. In this case references to cultural differences reify distinctions between powerful and less powerful groups that present an argument for exclusion, prejudice or hatred. Excluded groups are therefore not the victims of more traditional and overt racism but more subtle incarnations of even more insidious practices. In sport these discourses have been used as a majoritarian device to set newer communities apart from others by questioning national allegiances through cultural and civic preferences. A constant aspect of this new racism is its ability not to be recognised as the explicit or overt racism of the past as it transforms itself into debates about citizenship, immigration, nationhood. A 'safe' distance emerges for these discourses from the more identifiable biological or phenotype explanations of racial hierarchies and inferiority or superiority, and results in amorphous types of racism that are difficult to detect and much easier to deny. The imagined communities as exemplified by Anderson (1991) become a property that is then defended, resisting any perceived differences that would come only from those who have been described in the past as ultimately different in essentialising biological terms. In some cases, whom people cheer for when their country of residence plays their country of family origin is an acid test for many public figures. In the UK this has been labelled the 'Tebbit test' after Lord Tebbit, who challenged Asian communities to stand with English national teams against the country of their heritage as a test of their social integration, citizenship and loyalty to the nation. In this one 'test' debates on immigration and xenophobia become metaphors for a debate on 'Britishness' and nationhood.

Conceptual boundaries?

To reiterate, just as 'race' is a social, often ideological construct, ethnicity is socially constituted and draws upon the linguistic and cultural practices in sport and society that Harvey (1990) and Bulmer and Solomos (1999) suggest generate practices that produce a dynamic sense of contested but collective identity. Cornell and Hartmann's (1998) analysis of the overlaps between ethnicity and 'race' offers some explanation as to why one is often used as a shorthand for the other, and 'Other' by the state and influential institutions. Although this conflation is not helpful (as it conflates already ambiguous categories), the reality of the outcomes of institutionalised racial processes exacerbates and reinforces these very real circumstances. The result of the exclusion of racial and ethnic groups owing to their status as the 'Other' initiates similar responses in their experiences. Responses to material differences, political activity and the conceptual deliberations of these alienating processes have mutual ground. There is a 'naturalness' attributed to socially constructed, sometimes shared categories that sets up arbitrary boundaries. The conflation of ethnicity and 'race' continues as both concepts are often used to differentiate the white community from Others. These differences are often designated as a mix of phenotype and culture, and act as significant boundaries between those labelled as minority ethnic or black and 'white' (Mason 2000). Intuitively most people understand that there is a relationship between 'race' and ethnicity which they struggle to explain fully. Fenton (2003) argues that the mutual ground between 'race' and ethnicity is shared at least by them both relating to descent and culture communities. These are essential points of convergence for 'race' and ethnicity in essence. However, racial references tend to diverge from ethnicity as biological categories are often what is used to distinguish populations, in addition to other physical markers. Ethnicity often refers to a national subset that differs culturally rather than physically, and is regularly (incorrectly) used to distinguish numerical minorities from numerical majorities in a nation.

This merging of concepts is what oppositionist writers work to demystify and to resist (see Wallman 1988). However, some writers have been pragmatic in their research where 'race' and ethnicity are concerned as they are sometimes used as synonyms owing to the disruption of the boundaries between the biological and cultural. Gunaratnam (2003) uses 'race' and ethnicity together and separately to make this point and to emphasise *racism's two registers of biology and culture*. 'Race' however is often *the* primary social category for Harvey (1990) as it always implies ethnicity; ethnicity becomes racialised in social or cultural terms, 'Either by reducing linguistic or cultural identity to biology, or by naturalising linguistic or cultural identity within a fixed hierarchy of "social traits"' (Harvey 1990: 157). Solomos and Back (2001) conclude that the semantics of 'race' act as a catalyst for a racial narrative to be hidden in debates on culture and nation, thus naturalising racial formations in terms of 'race' and ethnicity. This view is reiterated by Gunaratnam (2003) and other researchers and writers mentioned in Chapter 3 who emphasise the problematic of doing research and writing around 'race', racism and ethnicity in sport. The social categories that we use need to be clear, rational, and able to reflect the politics of the balance of harm and good in making these contested choices. This and related questions are considered later.

The concept of a nation, what qualifies as a nation and who constitutes that nation (and of course who does not) have been contentious for many (Hutchinson and Smith (1994). Gilroy (1993) is convinced that sport discourses shape national identities and in particular our racialised identities. Consequently a critical reading of 'race' and racism in sport requires recognition of 'socially produced, heterogeneous and dynamic processes of *being and becoming*' (Gunaratnam 2003: 4). Where national identity is concerned, sport has become a high-profile testing ground for bringing into sharp relief those who are included or excluded, integrated or separated, 'us' or 'them'. We also exercise a level of agency in which nation(s) we identify with and how strategically or reflexively we do this. National and cultural *identification* are also opportunities for resistance where nation states have demonstrated an inability to provide social justice in the main social policy arenas like housing, employment, education, immigration, health and the legal system (Skellington 1996, Jones 1996, Mason 2000). There is further contention as to which form of collective identity takes primacy over the others: for example, ethnicity, gender, class, 'nation'. Further to Fenton's (2003) earlier convergence/divergence model of 'race' and ethnicity, he adds the concept to what now becomes a 'race'/ethnicity/nation tripartite. Each of the three concepts is still united by connections to descent and culture communities; however for Fenton (2003) a 'nation' is generally 'associated with a state or state like political form'. The ambiguity of what defines a nation has not prevented the restating of criteria for unified nations from politicians to sportspeople and their followers alike. This ambiguity has been observed by many commentators on nation and nationalism, not least Benedict Anderson (1991: 6), whose definition of a nation as 'an imagined political community [. . .] both inherently limited and sovereign' tends to sway key writers on this topic. The notion of an imagined community emerges from the fact that although it is impossible for all members of a 'nation' to meet, in their minds they imagine the constitution of this community. It is this notion of a united, loyal community that enables the relatively small step from national imaginings to nationalism (Carrington 1998b, Garland and Rowe 2001). It is this view of a nation created within political spheres and national media that is so persuasive at times of high national interest. For some this imagined nation is not the nation state of residence, which ultimately becomes problematic at these times. For others, especially at times of global competition such as the Olympic Games or the football World Cup, the shift from an appreciation of nations to nationalism can occur in a heartbeat and becomes one of the most disturbing aspects of these competitions. It is this sometimes over-zealous primacy of nation over other collective identities that suggests the power and autonomy of the unity and identity behind nation and subsequently nationalism. This blurring of differences across socially stratifying factors has demonstrated that sport can unite as well as divide very diverse people (Cronin and Mayall 1998). The force of nationalism can define a nation – according to Gellner (1994: 64) 'it is nationalism that engenders nations, and not the other way round' – and sport is able to evidence many examples of this in its many cosmopolitan settings.

The conception of 'nation' can be extended through the increasingly tenuous nature of the concept. Unlike the biological nature of 'race', the description of a nation is not static and can turn upon social and political whim and be bound up with other ideological factors (Geertz 1994). Both social and civic identities, which include rights of citizenship, affect notions of nationhood and who should be 'supported' and integral to a nation. In the case of sport, players can play for different national teams if they 'find' a great-grandparent from another nation, or if they stay in a country long enough to become 'naturalised', which is the equivalent of a form of political assimilation. The issuing of a passport has some administrative authority to name citizens of a nation state but it does not have the power to shift those included in these constructed communities. Gilroy's (1987) view of citizenship being 'more than a passport' has some resonance here. Imagined communities can be strategic as they are nebulous and ambiguous. Where they become compelling is in those contested spaces where this imagined social identity does not equate with the social identity of individuals with shared citizenship (internal conflict) – or cross-nationally where Orwell's description of sport as war minus the shooting is conspicuous in international competition. The task of defining a nation perplexed Hobsbawm (1992) in his seminal text *Nations and Nationalism* to posit that he would prefer not to start with a defini-tion of a nation because to limit a definition to consciousness or choice would not truly reflect the complex nature of the process individuals go through to define or redefine themselves. Some writers adopt this view as they recognise the political and constructed nature of group identities and would prefer to encourage a rigorous interrogation of any racialised definitions. Solomos and Back (2001: 354) argue that this approach 'seeks to decipher the meaning of racialised identities without attempting to prioritise one classification as more legitimate than another'.

The politics of 'blackness'

We will see in Chapter 6 the difficulties that antiracists have had in defining terms and therefore their response to racism. For example Grant Jarvie (1991a, 1991b), like Gramann and Allison (1999) and Modood (1988, 1994), is sceptical about any uncritical usage of the term 'black' as it can itself obscure cultural identities through their consequent relegation and negation. Anthias and Yuval-Davis (1993) also use 'black' critically as a signifier of those targeted by racism. These superficial inherited characteristics draw the prejudice, discrimination and dis-advantage that often preclude the politics of assimilation or integration into mainstream society. Therefore thanks to these oppressive racialised processes this signifier is used to unite individuals with common social experiences and needs. Over the past few years there has been some agreement by racism critics that the term 'black' should be used to describe all those who because of their colour are unfavourably treated. Anthias and Yuval-Davis (1993: 142) have explored how 'black' has been used in two main ways: (1) black people sharing a common origin and culture and (2) black people sharing a common experience (destiny) of racism. Still, the concept 'black' is contested, and there have been many battles over the ownership of suitable identifiers for social groups and names that suitably describe groups of individuals in society. In particular, the Asianness hinted at by Burdsey (2004a, b), it is argued, is being smothered by a narrow, reductionist, one-sided politicised conception of a social group that assumes unity and identification with the term by its members (Modood 1994). Modood (1997) furthers this debate in arguing that this black/white binary is not only alienating Asians and augmenting an antipathy towards them; it also has a deleterious effect on antiracism as this situation means a 'racial dualism rather than a rainbow diversity'. As important as these debates are, conceptual discussions should not act as obstacles in the pursuit of the analysis and contesting of racism. Hall (1997) and Cohen (1999) support this view as they reiterate that a positive connotation of in this instance, the word black, could only be so if there was some form of problematisation of it (Cohen) and black-consciousness resulting in an organised struggle and resistance to subjugation and oppression in society (Hall 1997). In agreement with Hall, Anthias and Yuval-Davis (1993) and Jarvie and Reid (1997) concede that the 'Other' in a racialised discourse may adopt its content to identify itself positively. So those marked as the 'Other' accept that they are at least socially 'raced', 'black', 'minority ethnic' and so changing an evaluative content from a negative to a positive. The discourse is therefore subverted and made oppositional (Miles 1989).

Polley's (1998) observation of Kenny Dalglish (then the Liverpool FC manager) trying to quell the media fervour behind John Barnes's transfer into the Liverpool team in 1989 is an interesting issue for this section to consider as an introduction to some of the main issues in the following chapters. In defence of the signing of Barnes, who at that point became the most significant black player ever at Liverpool, the manager Dalglish offered a response to the media that has become familiar in liberal-minded political discourses (see Chapter 5). On the other hand, Dalglish, who had played with and against some of the best black players in the world, made a statement which we can only guess he had heard before and honestly believed in its sentiments when he stated that 'He [Barnes] is not a black player, he's a player' (cited Polley 1998: 135). As suggested by Gilroy (1987) in the classic *There Ain't No Black in the Union Jack*, being black and British is often too much for politicians to reconcile: in fact the coupling becomes naturally separated as oil and water, as Ali found in the US on his return from winning Olympic gold in Rome (1960). There are at least two readings to this. In Dalglish's case, Barnes's being black *and* a footballer was an awkward coupling, causing

Dalglish to trivialise Barnes's African Caribbean heritage, as others did with Ali's African *American* status. At this point in the 1980s, monkey chants along with banana throwing were commonplace in UK stadiums. In fact one of the iconic images of football in this period was John Barnes back-heeling a banana skin off the pitch whilst playing for Liverpool. Dalglish's comments need to be considered with this backdrop and also need to be understood as reflective of the experience of black sportspeople over the years. A second reading sees Dalglish as wanting to transcend racialised discourses that he has seen mar football so that we can accept Barnes for the person that he is rather than what his marked body symbolises.

This racialised marking of difference through sport has become constitutive of a global discourse of difference and othering resulting from racial and ethnic background. I would concur with Song (2004) and Omi and Winant (2002) in arguing that what these processes reinforce are racial hierarchies that can be seen played out on the fields of Eton, East Ham and East Leeds just as they play out in the corridors and classrooms in equivalent places all over the world. Further, sport has been seen by many as an arena where the meanings attached to 'blackness' are socially constructed, reified, fixed and sharpened (Polley 1998, Campbell 1995, Hall 1990, Carrington 1999, Carrington and McDonald 2001, Ismond 2003) (see Chapter 4). To extend this analysis, inclusions in sport discourses are as important as absences in gauging perceptions of social groups in the UK. The inclusion of those from an African heritage is as conspicuous as the marginalisation of those from a UK Asian or US Hispanic background. Fleming's (1991: 53) critical analysis of Asians in sport and education presented a view that 'sport is a vehicle for the expression of antagonism and racial tension' that is further emphasised by a number of authors (Bains and Patel 1996, Coakley 2001, Carrington and McDonald 2001), not least Jas Bains (Bains and Johal 1998, Bains 2005). Bains and Patel's (1996) ironically titled work *Asians Can't Play Football* was a critical attack on the English football authorities for their lack of commitment to include Asians in their infrastructure. The professional and amateur game was a target for Bains in pointing out the institutional barriers that precluded the development of Asian players and coaches. Nearly ten years afterwards an even more critical Bains (2005) has seen little change in the work of the Football Association even after a number of further events have highlighted this problem in rigorous and robust ways. Kick It Out (Long *et al.* 2000) identified racism in sport as a significant factor in the experience of African Caribbean and Asian players and coaches from the grassroots game through to semi-professional and professional levels. Long *et al.* (2000) found that all black players stated that they had experienced racism whilst involved in grassroots football. This racism was not restricted to the pitch as it was also coming from spectators, referees, league administrators and sometimes even team mates. There have even been high-profile race equality initiatives in professional clubs where the clubs themselves were openly accepting that there was a problem within their industry. Bains's (2005) response was to present the football authorities with a strategic framework from which they could build in order to increase opportunities for Asians in football, identify good practice and outline ways to tackle the barriers that are still 'Part of the Game' (Long *et al.* 2000) (see Chapter 6).

The absence of some social groups in the writing of sport literature is not only raced but also gendered, as sports writers have failed to include black women in their analyses. Writers such as Scraton 2001, Watson and Scraton (2001), Birrell (1989) and Hargreaves (1994) have been critical of social science's recidivism in this area. In particular, sports feminists have been reticent in engaging with the leisure lifestyles and sporting experiences of black women and as a result we know far less about black women than we do about black men in sport. Black women are invisible in sports writing in academic and everyday contexts. Where women are given attention in either academic or even sports feminist writing, then the focus is mainly reflective of a white perspective about (white) women in general (Mirza 1997). Writing on 'race' and ethnicity has made the black male as conspicuous in sport as the white woman in mainstream gender theorising, therefore making our understanding of the black woman's leisure and sporting lifestyles a mystery (Scraton 2001, Birrell 1989). These hierarchies in our epistemologies are reflective of wider raced, classed and gendered power processes that seek to structure our knowledge and intellectual development (Goldberg 1993) (see Chapter 3). Goldberg (1993) recognises the bias of discourses and their ability to normalise vocabularies, thus privileging some whilst marginalising others. The view that sports feminists have regularly dealt in stereotypes of women in sport as white, middle-class and heterosexual is further emphasised in Mirza's (1997) work on black feminism which alerts us to this marginalising process in sport theorising.

> The invisibility of black women speaks of the separate narrative constructions of race, gender and class: it is a racial discourse, where the subject is male; in a gendered discourse, where the subject is white; and a class discourse where race has no place.

Exceptions to this become evident when superstars already famous in the media become a fair topic for a critical lens. The high profiles of Serena and Venus Williams in tennis, and Marion Jones and Denise Lewis in athletics, have been the focus of work recently which has generated some critical writing in this area (Billings and Eastman 2002, Spencer 2004, Schultz 2005). However, these women cannot be seen as typical of the majority of black women of whom we struggle to gather a coherent picture. Hargreaves (1994) argues that what is written about black women still conforms to stereotypes, as the esteemed athletes above are testimony to in that they are often described as 'natural', 'flamboyant', 'quick', 'strong' and 'powerful'. Birrell's (1989) suggestion is that what is needed in sports writing is a black ontology that centres the experiences of a heterogeneous black people, where before it had been at the margins of such work in sport and leisure. Others have led calls to writers in sport and leisure studies to locate the black presence so that the community is viewed as comprising purposive actors in their own 'real worlds' as opposed to passive victims in increasingly pathologised stories (Hylton 2005, Singer 2005a) (see Chapter 2). For example, Cashmore's (1982) seminal text on black sportsmen vilified the black family of the 1970s in that it was interpreted as being dysfunctional, regularly 'broken' and without support networks. This, Cashmore (1982: 79) went on to argue, was reflective of 'many black sportsmen growing up in broken homes'. A reading of this influential text would result in a view of the black family through not only sport that gave the impression that it was careless in respect to its young people but also painted a harrowing picture of many young people in search of adult role models that could be found only outside the family through coaching and other sport networks. The ambivalent picture of the black family is captured in discussions around their cynical behaviour when their inertia is broken after the child demonstrates that he or she can succeed in their chosen pursuit. Of course the black child is described by Cashmore as needing sport as a vehicle for social mobility and career progression. So the centrality of sport to the black child makes it a doubly hard journey on which to embark as racism, and the family militate against the child. In comparison, Ismond's (2003) more recent ethnographic study, which reflected upon elite sportspeople from Cashmore's (1982) era, generated a counter-story that adopts a more critical black perspective. On Viv Anderson and Cyrille Regis, Ismond gathers information about their childhood that sketches a completely different story of familial support and love and two intelligent young sportsmen putting great store in career planning and education. What we do get from Ismond is an image of a diverse black community that is raced, classed and gendered and therefore not a narrow homogeneous experience about sport and those wishing to pursue it.

Given the significance of 'race' and racism and the contested arena of these debates in sport, another paradox emerges to challenge the critical sociologist, the antiracist, student and practitioner. The paradox is, can we really ignore 'race', as much as we may want to? Can we somehow reject it out of hand to somehow begin the process of debunking it as a form of social categorisation? If we do this, then how can we effectively transform racialised relations of power structured by racial projects underpinned by reductionist 'racial' thinking? Given the imperative to resist racism, how can we do this without recourse to the lexicon of 'race' even with the warnings of those advocating racialisation as a possible way forward? For even with a racialisation framework we still must revert *with caution* to 'race', racial signification and representation in sport to challenge racism. 'It is impossible to organise, maintain, or transform social structures without simultaneously engaging in racial signification' (Omi and Winant 2002: 128).

Chapter 2

Critical race theory

> The success of any standpoint on 'race' and racism must depend on its ability
> to offer resistance to racism(s).
>
> (Goldberg 1993)

This chapter explores critical race theory (CRT) as an ontological starting point for the study of sport today. CRT has been described as exciting, revolutionary and an intellectual movement (Roithmayr 1999). It can be summarised as a framework from which to explore and examine the racism in society that privileges whiteness as it disadvantages others because of their 'blackness'. CRT also confronts 'race-neutrality' in policy and practice and acknowledges the value of 'the black voice' that is often marginalised in mainstream theory, policy and practice. CRT challenges past and present institutional arrangements in sport that racially discriminate, subjugate and oppress (Nebeker 1998, Delgado and Stefancic 2001). CRT has also been described as a hybrid discipline as it draws from a number of necessarily relevant disciplines to incorporate a transdisciplinary approach to the development of theory and praxis in relation to racism in society (Stovall 2005). Like the law, sport is an institution deemed to lessen or eradicate racist dysfunction when it rears its head within this hallowed cultural construct. Research agendas dominated by what could be viewed as an elitist Eurocentric social science are a target for part of this transformation as critical writers such as Goldberg (1993) reiterate how the success of any standpoint on 'race' and racism must depend on its ability to offer resistance to racism(s). CRT has the potential to interrupt and transform social structures and racial power to further an agenda of 'racial emancipation' (Roithmayr 1999: 1).

CRT can also be seen as a configuration of alternative accounts in sport that challenge orthodoxies, canons and dogma. The utility of CRT in our analyses of sport can be drawn analogously to Mirza's (1999) critique of liberal 'race' reform in the US. Here Mirza's frustration with the discourses of assimilation, integration and 'colour-blindness' can be equally levelled at sport where few sports or sport theorists have taken a proactive, radical stance to the construct of 'race' and racism in their arenas of expertise or influence. In agreement with Mirza (1999: 112), racial inequality in sport, as in the law, is often seen as 'exceptional and irregular rather than routinely ubiquitous and deeply ingrained'. In this respect *'Race' and Sport: Critical Race Theory* continues the tradition of CRT, which itself emerged out of critical legal studies (CLS) as a hybrid that rejected some of the assumptions of CLS. As theoretical standpoints do not appear out of the ether it is important to restate that this work owes much to the author's grounding in critical sport and leisure studies. However, sport and leisure theorising have been ultimately viewed as limited in their liberal incremental nature and inability to consistently centre 'race' and racism as a result of their marginalisation of processes of racialisation and racism (Delgado 2000, Gardiner and Welch 2001, Hylton 2005). This situation is analogous to the moments that moved critical race theorists to emerge from CLS and is likely to be the precursor for a version of CRT to emerge out of the study of sport and leisure (Peters 2005).

An outcome of using a CRT perspective is its potential for resistance to the passive reproduction of established practices, knowledge and resources that make up the social conditions that marginalise 'race' logic and racialised processes as core factors in the way we manage and experience our sport and leisure; mainstream agendas and epistemologies are therefore simultaneously transformed (Birrell 1989, Messner 1992, Layder 1994, Rowe 1998, Collins 2000). There are three sections to this chapter, which concludes with a vision for academics, writers, researchers and policy makers to centralise 'race', racism, and racialisation in their everyday considerations. Section one contrasts CRT and 'race' critical theory and rationalises their mutual transformative social capacities. Five precepts of CRT are then outlined as a framework to consider as an emergent development in sport and leisure theorising. Section two maps out the parallel developments of critical theory in sport and leisure sociology and the more advanced critical legal studies experience, which gives an insight into what can be achieved when writers develop a critical 'race'-centred approach. It further introduces a critical 'black' consciousness that has many supporters in the study of sport such as Henderson (1988), Hemingway (1999) and Scraton (2001), although few active in advancing theoretical frameworks from which to challenge dominant paradigms and epistemologies in the study of sport or related areas such as Birrell (1989), Anthias (1998) and McDonald and Birrell (1999). After sketching out these theoretical links, the implications for the study of 'race' and racism in sport are spelled out in section three. More importantly, critical race theory is advanced as a theoretical framework from which to interrogate issues of 'race' and racism, and to refocus the theoretical lens on to anti-oppressive theory and practice, in sport and leisure studies.

Stanfield II (1993) encapsulated the need for writers to engage with 'race', identity, equality, and policy in sport, when he wrote, 'There is a great need to begin to treat racial and ethnic studies as a serious area of inquiry, worthy of epistemological and theoretical reflections and innovation' (Stanfield II 1993: 6). It has been generally agreed that critical race theory is a theoretical framework that has emerged from the writing predominantly of black scholars in North America (Crenshaw *et al.* 1995, Delgado 1995, 2000, Nebeker 1998, Parker

1998). CRT has come out of a particular struggle by scholars who in challenging one of the most symbolic bastions of white privilege and power, the legal system, have developed a transdisciplinary tool from which to oppose the hegemonic influence of the Eurocentric and predominantly white establishment. The legal system embodies a conspicuous site of struggle that says as much about who has power and who is privileged in society as about who has not. It is also this arena in which battles are fought that have a massive impact upon the way we engage with society on an individual and collective basis. Not only does CRT have the potential to shape the discourses of minds closed to racism-centred perspectives, it also wishes to influence the lethargy in liberal critiques of those debates. CRT writers argue that: 'Racism has been ingrained through historical consciousness and events, and that racist ideologies have directly shaped the law, racial cate- gories, and racial privilege' (Parker 1998: 45). Haney-Lopez (2000) emphasised that a critical 'race' consciousness is necessary to uncover the assumptions and presumptions implicit and explicit in the way structures in society work. Sport, just like the law, can be observed as a key tool in the subjugation of black people and the magnification of the place of 'race' as a major mediating factor within society; in sport many have made these connections (Lapchick 2001, Carrington and McDonald 2001, Marqusee 2003). Sport, like the law, is supposed to be a 'level playing field'; however there is a body of knowledge to suggest otherwise. Sport is another racially contested arena which is used as a 'ring to wrestle' for academics, participants and policy makers. As much as our cultural background is mediated by the intersection of gender and class, critical sport sociology is beginning to focus on these and other more conventional fronts concerning racial formations and related processes around gender, identity, nation, racism(s) and policy (Marqusee 1994, 2003, MacClancy 1996, Watson and Scraton 2001, Carrington and McDonald 2001); racism(s) (Shropshire 1996, Polley 1998, Long 2000, Lapchick 2001); and policy (Horne 1995, Swinney and Horne 2005, Gardiner and Welch 2001, Hylton 2003).

Societies are constituted of individuals who have internalised the dominant worldviews and hegemonic practices that have found their expression in key institutions such as education, politics, health, housing, law and the arts, and sport is not exempt from this. However, legitimation of the racial inequalities and assumptions in these institutions can still be open to resistance and emergent ideas. Roithmayr (1999) identifies the classroom as one site of struggle and resistance where racial power (in sport) can be disrupted. CRT is being presented here as an oppositional voice to the worst excesses of sport that propagates and perpetuates racism and the related processes it engenders as we know that sport has the same issues in relation to racialisation and racism as other institutions in society do. 'Race' and Sport: Critical Race Theory supports Singer's (2005a) view that a dialogue should be encouraged with academics, students, practitioners and policy makers to think beyond their everyday opinions and ideologies. In relation to 'Race' and Sport: Critical Race Theory, CRT offers an alternative way of knowing and an alternative vocabulary and discourse from which to understand research

(Chapter 3), whiteness (Chapter 4), the media (Chapter 5) and antiracism (Chapter 6) (Singer 2005a: 466).

Singer (2005a: 467) contends that CRT positions thinkers to challenge the social order, of which he has identified whiteness as the optimal status criterion. Although whiteness is the focus of Chapter 4, its significance as an agenda for critical race theorists is reinforced by Singer's (2005a) illumination of the processes that help to maintain the dominant hegemony of key institutions, commonly described as 'white' owing to the preponderance of white people (predominantly males) privileged by their practices. This has the result of power networks, knowledge formers and influential others having a level of influence over opinions, attitudes and ideals that become the unquestioned norms from which other things are judged. The need for CRT is reinforced by the urgency to challenge power relations structured by racism that will not necessarily be disrupted voluntarily. CRT offers an agenda for social transformation with whiteness a key target of this effort.

Birrell's (1989) optimistic view of the sociology of sport as a field of study moving purposefully to a more critical theoretical position is one worthy of further consideration. Her argument that a black ontology would centre the experience of the racialised Other, where before it had been at the margins of such work in sport and leisure, has merit. This would ultimately result in the location of black people and their relations being viewed in a different light (as noted in Chapter 1): *purposive actors in their own 'real worlds' as opposed to passive 'victims' in increasingly pathologised stories.* This is accomplished by ensuring that the experiences of marginalised groups emerge clearly in the stories disseminated by and to research and policy communities. A critical black theoretical standpoint challenges social scientists to (re)interpret the black experience, racial formations and processes in the deconstruction of 'race', racism, and antiracism therefore generating a more liberating and emancipatory discourse. Collins (1990) exemplified this debate when she accused white social science of struggling to maintain the credibility of being the most appropriate viewpoint from which to study 'race' and racism in society. However, the Eurocentric knowledge of social science would be far more difficult to maintain were emergent themes, ideas and perspectives reflecting black experiences in sport more evident (Goldberg 1993, Carrington 1998a, Gramann and Allison 1999, Jones 2002).

Authors such as Stanfield II (1993), Twine and Warren (2000), Coates (2002), Gunaratnam (2003) and Bulmer and Solomos (2004) argue that researchers and writers need urgently to centralise 'race' and racism(s) as core factors in the study of wider social relations. Such actions improve and enhance the bodies of knowledge pertinent to 'race', racialisation and racial formations, as they 'challenge and transform' epistemologies and ways of thinking about the world (Gunaratnam 2003). This has the effect of questioning the everyday assumptions about socially constructed groups that often become the foundation for myth and folklore. Stanfield II's (1994) challenge is that we *all* should establish new lines of inquiry whilst criticising traditional epistemologies, rather than acquiescing to their hegemony. As Leonardo (2005, xi) contends, CRT writers explore social issues with 'race' (and racism) as 'the point of departure for critique . . . not the end of it'.

Critical race theory and 'race' critical theory

The juxtaposition here of CRT and 'race' critical perspectives is a practice that Essed and Goldberg (2002) argue is not a regular enough occurrence in the social sciences. They are critical of what they see as academic parochialism; they see CRT applied only to socio-legal issues. CRT is, however, a pragmatic perspective that engages a theoretical framework that has been applied as effectively to education as freely as it has been rigorously applied to US law (Parker 1998, Ladson-Billings 2003). In addition, Tate IV (1999) also acknowledges an extensive but not exhaustive list of the diverse traditions that inform and exercise the application of CRT. He identifies Marxism, post-structuralism, critical studies, liberalism, cultural nationalism, critical race feminism, critical white studies and LatCrit amongst others. The unapologetic but strategic focus on 'race', racism and anti-subordination translates the best of what is seen as theory from late modernity while pragmatically sponsoring the anti-essentialism of post-structural and postmodern ideals. According to Valdes *et al.* (2002: 3): 'The trick is to forge a potent theory and praxis through a critical and self-critical melding of identity-conscious analysis, anti-essentialist politics, and anti-subordination principles.'

The agendas and foci of critical race theory and 'race' critical theory are complementary; however they have been the subject of some conflation and misinterpretation even though there is more to unite than separate them. Seidman's (2004) analysis of critical race theory is one such example of the misplacing of 'race' critical theory and critical race theory. In considering the work of Molefi Kete Asante, Cornel West, bell hooks and Kwame Appiah he suggests that there is a tacit acceptance by those who write critically about racism that they, firstly, accept terminology in relation to 'race', and, secondly, accept a CRT framework. Implicit in Seidman's (2004) analysis is the notion that the term CRT can be used interchangeably with 'race' critical theory. One point of departure for race critical theorists such as Appiah (1992), Miles (1989) and Gilroy (2000) from those others who explicitly identify themselves as CRT writers has been the centring of racism but in particular 'race' so leaving CRT writers open to accusations of being essentialist or deterministic. This fundamental CRT standpoint on 'race' and racism is a topic for re-examination by CRT writers: it is explored in Chapter 1 and is indulged further in this chapter. 'Race' as ideology and theories of 'race' are useful theoretical explanations for its use in critical studies (Anthias and Yuval-Davis 1993, Guillaumin 1995). Many critical scholars on 'race' accept and acknowledge the flawed science and racist ideology underpinning racial categories but are convinced that it is unhelpful to suggest ignoring it as a social category of some import and should not be 'ruled out of court'

(Anthias and Yuval-Davis 1993: 1). However, in the social constructionist tradition, to *acknowledge* the social and physical differences that make up these 'races', as CRT does, is not the same as *agreeing* that they essentially determine intellectual, social or physical attributes (Lewis 1998). Chong-Soon Lee (1995) warns writers that 'race' is defined not by its inherent content but by the social relations that construct it. She challenges Appiah's (1992) view that 'race' has no ground to give it meaning apart from where there is racist intent. Appiah's argument that ethnicity or culture should replace 'race' is a belief that does not fully recognise the institutionalised discourse of 'race' and therefore the trans-historical cultural markers that go with it. Chong-Soon Lee goes further to add that Appiah's condemnation of 'race' fails to recognise the social nature of the concept, neither does it consider the subtleties of biological racism and cultural differentialism that Hall (2000: 223) and Gunaratnam (2003) characterises as racism's two registers. In each case of racism biology and culture are 'in play'. The 'racialisation' or meaning attached to relations in sport will not disappear and neither will its racial projects. Sport fulfils a number of roles in society that fixes and sharpens our views that define

> the already established boundaries of moral and political communities; to assist in the creation of new social identities; to give physical expression to certain social values and to act as a means of reflecting on those values; to serve as potentially contested space by opposed groups.
>
> (MacClancy 1996: 7)

The importance of approaching 'race' neither as an illusion nor as a fixed entity draws agreement in the literature from critical writers on 'race' and racism and amongst critical race theorists (Omi and Winant 1994, 2002, Haney-Lopez 2000, Hylton 2003, 2005). 'Race' is an aspect of our being, our identities that we learn to perform and decode (Alexander 1996, Dixon-Gottschild 2005). Omi and Winant (2002) talk of the 'commonsenseness' of 'race' as we consciously or not navigate our way through various racial projects. These racial projects are means through which we mediate the discursive or representational ways that 'race' is signified and further how it is organised and institutionalised in racial formations like sport. In considering these ideas Haney-Lopez (2000: 65) offers a progressive analysis of 'race' worthy of consideration as a dynamic concept fixed in neither space or time but nevertheless a viewpoint that is common amongst CRT writers and other racism critical writers.

> 'Race' is neither an essence nor an illusion, but rather an ongoing, contra-dictory, self reinforcing, plastic process, subject to the macro forces of social and political struggle and the micro effects of daily decisions . . . terms like 'black' and 'white' are social groups, not genetically distinct branches of humankind.
>
> (Haney-Lopez 2000: 65)

In any examination of racialised identities, Lee and Lutz (2005a, b) and Goldberg (1993) contend, is a transhistorical understanding of 'race', racisms and antiracism due to the changing social, cultural and political landscapes that we inhabit. The meaning of 'race' changes over context and time; therefore the opportunity for 'race' to be redeployed by critical race theorists to assert the power of social groups is one worth taking. Using the term 'race' in critical race theory is to use a powerful metaphor and to reject it out of hand is to deny a potential political vehicle (see also Haney-Lopez 2000). Chong-Soon Lee's pragmatics argue for a critical navigation of the definitions of 'race' and a focus on its related social processes, rather than becoming stymied by unceasing debates and their limiting outcomes. In achieving political outcomes a critical application of these conceptual and theoretical debates needs to be in operation in the discourse of 'race', racialisation and racism in sport and leisure. Goldberg (1993) reiterates how the success of any standpoints on 'race' and racism must depend on their ability to offer resistance to racism(s). Writers from any standpoint need to be careful in their use of terminology: these are caveats that hold not just for CRT theorists but for any critical actors. Gilroy's (2000) call for us to transcend 'race' is not without its rewards; however the politics of 'race' is such that oppressed groups, advocates and academics have used the language of 'race' to their own ends as a tool to challenge racists, to deflect abuse, to unify and as a source of pride.

In theoretical analyses, writers sometimes have to acknowledge that these debates are ensuing; at the same time we must accept a theoretical frame from which to be critical if racism in society is to be the ultimate focus of our energies. Hence this book's predilection for the strategic use of 'race', especially since its power as a social category is still persuasive for many others; similarly, blackness as a core signifier of political unity is utilised strategically here (Husband 1984, Cornell and Hartmann 1998, Essed and Goldberg 2002, Ward and Lott 2002). As noted in Chapter 1, many, like Brunsma and Rockquemore (2002) and Modood (1994, 1998), contest the use of 'black' as a political unifying concept as they doubt its capacity to effectively incorporate the fluidity of changing identities and circumstances among those traditionally viewed as constituting this group. Brunsma and Rockquemore's (2002) doubts arise from recent changes in ethnic monitoring across a number of countries that has meant that 'black' is but one hyphenated category amongst many reflecting the real diversity of individuals and social relationships today. The methods used by Brunsma and Rockquemore (2002) in this case is confusing because of the 'objective' measures they are using. 'Black' is used here and in most conventional 'race' critical studies politically and not objectively or empirically. In fact efforts put into such projects to categorise populations empirically by racialised boundaries are likely to do more harm in reifying 'race' than the use of 'black' as a political identity. As a political umbrella term 'black' is dynamic and generally signifies racialised Others disadvantaged by racist processes.

The reality for Gilroy (2000) as it stands for many CRT writers is that racialised discourses are the mutual ground for antiracist activity, race regulation and policy.

The subversion of racist discourses is not without some compromise in establishing resistance or 'oppositional identities' which Gilroy (2000: 16) understands are not likely to be given up easily. The solidarity of racialised groups is not to be given up unless those who wish us to transcend 'race' engage with them with an acceptable, alternative discourse that they can identify with. To conclude this section, it is argued here that writers should navigate the topography of racialised discourses, but in addition should bias their efforts toward transforming the targets of these competing accounts. CRT writers begin from this realist standpoint that racism is part of sport and the society we live in and that as an all-pervasive social construct 'race' (warts and all) is a reality for many.

In relation to Seidman's second point, although many approaches are shared by both CRT writers and those who write critically about racism in terms of terminology, social justice and their challenge to orthodoxies, Seidman's critique of 'race' critical writers implies their explicit adoption of a CRT framework, which his writers have not adopted; even though the work of hooks and West, in particular, has been instructive in the development of critical 'race' perspectives in the US. By not clarifying a CRT framework, which will be outlined shortly, from which to locate these theorists Seidman consequently presents the views of 'race' critical theorists as critical race theorists.

Over the years 'race' critical theorists have, according to Goldberg (1993) and later Essed and Goldberg (2002), been critical of CRT as its global impact has been reduced, firstly because of its primary focus over the 1980s and 1990s being with the law and, secondly, because they would like to see a more 'generous . . . acknowledgement of the conceptual debt to the wider history of racial theorising in the critical tradition' (Essed and Goldberg 2002: 4). However, in excluding the work of CRT writers such as Patricia Williams, Lawrence Parker, Kimberlé Crenshaw, Richard Delgado and Gloria Ladson-Billings, Essed and Goldberg's (2002) prospects of incorporating the best of 'race' critical writing over recent history became flawed when they responded to their critical second point (above) by excluding CRT writers from their text *Race Critical Theories*. An opportunity was missed to draw together key forms of 'race' theorising that would have allowed readers to see the overlap between these two complementary theoretical areas, although the benefits are not ignored here. As an umbrella concept 'race' critical theory embraces CRT; however CRT embraces 'race' critical theory only where some of the basic tenets such as the centring of 'race', racism and transformatory politics, outlined below, are seriously considered. Finally in response to Seidman it can be concluded that CRT is necessarily 'race' critical theory although the five precepts outlined below give an indication that 'race' critical theory is not necessarily CRT.

Five precepts of critical race theory

This chapter supports the principles maintained by a CRT framework. A CRT perspective as outlined below acts as an umbrella for a range of views. The points discussed here are presented as a foundation for approaching the following chapters in this book. This chapter engages constructively with anti-essentialist ideals and significantly, rejects the canons and beliefs that have afflicted the work of some writers such as those critiqued by Seidman and Chong-Soon Lee, such as Appiah (1992), who deny the efficacy of 'race' as a social category. It is useful at this juncture to point out that CRT perspectives should be as fluid and dynamic as the problems they attempt to tackle. To present an overview of CRT five significant aspects are drawn out of the main ideas of CRT writers such as Crenshaw *et al.* (1995), Parker *et al.* (1999), Solórzano and Yosso (2001, 2005), Delgado and Stefancic (1995, 2000, 2001) and Ladson-Billings (1998, 2003).

The *first tenet* involves centralising 'race' and racism at the same time as recognising their connection with other forms of subordination and oppression (Gordon *et al.* 1990, Ladson-Billings 1998, Parker 1998). For example, class cannot be theorised in isolation from 'race', as Marxists might wish, as 'race' must be central to the theorising of class relations from a CRT viewpoint (Nebeker 1998). It has further been argued that, although there is some recognition amongst writers and researchers that 'race' and racism are a significant area of study, they have done little more than acknowledge this as they wander on to more familiar theoretical terrain (Anthias 1998). Stanfield II (1993) also asks researchers to consider less the question of methodology but more the notion of an epistemology that gives a more accurate picture of the black experience in society. Back *et al.* (2001) are keen to follow this advice as their investigations into racism in football demonstrate the need for innovation and diversity to show how racism is a 'multiply inflected and changing discourse . . . this involves understanding how forms of inclusion and exclusion operate through the interplay of overt racist practice and implicit racialised codings' (Back *et al.* 2001: 6).

In *'Race' and Sport: Critical Race Theory* racism is defined and processes described and critiqued with a view to highlighting systems of oppression and negative power relations in sport. Solórzano and Yosso (2005) argue that we should do this as it is important for us to move beyond theorising 'race', valuable as this process is, so that the focus on racism becomes an activist project (Singer 2005b, Tate IV 1999). Tate IV (1999) agrees with this initial premise of CRT but advises caution on how a CRT viewpoint is presented, as the politicisation of such a view is clearly necessary but not to the detriment of denying that progress is being made elsewhere. Further, such a realist position could be a clarion call to accept the racial status quo because of the intractable position we find ourselves in. Has history taught us that this is the way it will always be or can CRT present an emancipatory and liberating discourse that inspires rather than dejects? The careful centring of 'race' and racism in our analyses of sport should engage a thoughtful consideration of racial processes that explore and examine further, past and present processes and practices in sport that are neither inevitable nor accidental. Rather, they can be seen as part of a cycle of activity that can at the very least be broken or disrupted. CRT can develop a political lexis that can heed the advice of Tate IV (1999) and others that is conscious of the clumsy use of systemic racism as a beginning and end in a world that cannot be reduced into homogeneous experiences and polemic binaries. For example, when the talented young golf prodigy Kiran Matharu stated that she had been the victim of racism at golf clubs where she was refused membership, she clearly had grounds to base such an assumption as other less successful juniors were being admitted (*Guardian* 2007). However we will see further when we explore the fifth tenet of CRT how it encourages us to explore such issues even further as an intersectional analysis of racialisation and racist acts. In Matharu's case as a young Asian woman from a working-class background, her exclusions from these clubs could be due to a mix of racial discrimination and/or golf's gender relations which have been the subject of many controversies owing to its patriarchy. In addition golf has been accused of its membership policies relying on social networks and cultural capital as criteria for entry. Peters (2005) has witnessed CRT become an inclusive and pluralistic framework that resists racism in complex, multidimensional ways. The intersections of 'race' and culture, gender, class, space, whiteness, politics, history, community, identity and nation, for example, have ensured a more sensitive theorising of social issues. McDonald and Birrell (1999) see many benefits to moving from single-issue theory and debates to a critical theoretical approach that converges issues and relations of 'race', class, gender and sexuality. Similarly a reading of the experiences of Serena and Venus Williams on the tennis circuit would be bereft of its various complexities without a consideration of racialisation, racism, gender, sexuality, class and whiteness (Spencer 2004).

Secondly, CRT challenges traditional dominant ideologies around objectivity, meritocracy, colour-blindness, race-neutrality and equal opportunity (Nebeker 1998, Solórzano and Yosso 2001, Gardiner and Welch 2001). Two founder proponents of CRT, Richard Delgado and Jean Stefancic (2001), identified patterns of criticism of CRT in relation to meritocracy and the challenge to objectivity. The challenge to dominant ideals and philosophies is not a pointless one. The need to separate positive forward-looking practices from those that reinforce racism and hegemonic power relations is a challenge acceptable to Solórzano and Yosso (2005) and others adopting a CRT perspective. In effect sport as a racial formation becomes the subject of many challenges across its many racial projects. The academy, practitioners, policy makers, the media and the law join sport in the contested racialised arena of society, each maintaining dominant viewpoints, racial hierarchies, racial inequalities and 'truths' open to reinterpretation. These are typical sites of struggle for those adopting a CRT lens, and one of the strategies for resistance is to challenge viewpoints and ideologies created and maintained by those who do not, cannot or will not represent counter-views because of the nature of their fundamental assumptions. An alternative reading of sport and its history for example is likely to challenge the existing orthodoxies surrounding it of cultural pluralism, fairness, integration, racial harmony, colour-blindness and other social benefits. Just as the law, policing, education, health, housing, social welfare and politics cannot afford to be colour-blind, neither can those in sport as managers, policy makers, the media or academics.

Chapter 6 makes clear links between CRT ideals, policy and practice, especially in the way that the colour-blind state, in the belief that being neutral is a necessity, perpetuates even further the historical and material advantages and disadvantages that have accrued to members of the community dependent amongst other things on their racial background (Cross and Keith 1993, Goldberg 2002). Colour-blind racism revolves around issues of liberalism or ambivalence to matters of racism; the mechanism of cultural rather than biological arguments to support prejudicial views or racial projects that maintain recruitment and employment patterns, sports participation, sports policy exclusions; the utopian ideal that owing to effective opposition over the years racism is now a marginal or insignificant issue (Bonilla-Silva 2002). This colour-blindness takes a more sophisticated strategy to expose and tackle for 'race' critics as the nature of these issues is so divisive because they can seem so innocuous. There are numerous examples in sport where some racialised groups have a higher level of acceptance than others and in some instances are held as exemplars of successful integration. Colour-blindness, like the new racism noted in Chapter 1, is a device that maintains dominant hegemonies and social hierarchies by regularly ignoring discriminatory factors.

Similarly, a CRT examination of employment practices in sport management, media, education, sport participation and spectatorship reveals parallel findings to those in CRT and education where the notions of meritocracy and colour-blindness are much more closely aligned to a defence of the status quo and racist practices that many would want to distance themselves from. In Chapter 6 the work of Horne (1995), Hylton (2003) and Swinney and Horne (2005) is drawn upon to develop further an understanding of the injustices of a neutral state and even of notions of 'equal opportunities'. Delgado and Stefancic (2000, 2001) identify writers who disagree with this anti-meritocracy stance because in their experience if people from one social group can succeed then so should others with similar life chances. In sport this criticism could be forwarded as we can see examples of success from a range of racialised Others across all levels. The two African American head coaches in Superbowl 2007 will 'prove' to many that there is no racism in a sport that has six out of 32 black head coaches when 70 per cent of the players are black. Perhaps a more critical lens would produce an analysis that would provide a more insightful conclusion to these contradictions. The argument that holds as a rejoinder to these criticisms is that often for certain social populations they succeed *despite* the system. We will see in Chapter 6 that in sport where institutions do monitor for ethnicity they are often apologetic in regards to their recruitment and employment histories, their administration in relation to racism, the concentration of racialised Others below senior management positions and the diversity of spectatorship in professional sport. The challenges to the liberal idea of meritocracy must continue if repetitive cycles are to be broken.

The *third tenet* posits that CRT has a clear commitment to social justice that incorporates elements of liberation and transformation (Solórzano and

Yosso 2001, 2005). With Bernal (Solórzano and Bernal 2001), Solórzano posits that the core variant of transformational resistance is social justice. For a politics of social change to have any value, the praxis of CRT must culminate in a process of social transformation which in sport might result in radical employment practices that value black people in sport management whether it involves professional clubs or local authority providers; practice in each of these arenas has been woefully inadequate in the UK and North America. Similarly, racism occurs at every level of sport ranging from innocuous exclusions at local clubs to discrimination in sports policy and practice and racist behaviour in the stands and in our living rooms when watching, listening to or reading media sources. CRT's emphasis on social justice in terms of policy aligning itself with radical, proactive forms of policy discourses that would cite racism, amongst other concerns, as the cause of the need for the manipulation and redistribution of resources (Parker 1998). The short-term impact of these policies on some people over others may seem inequitable but are necessary if ahistorical conceptions of provision and the concept of a level playing field are to be rejected and the material differences between those disadvantaged in society are thought through in terms of how they are balanced out, leading to a 'de-cloaking' of colour-blind ideologies and institutional arrangements.

A critical ontology ensures that where writers or researchers are conscious of the crucial social processes that structure their worlds they take those ideas forward as their starting point. That is, where racism and the distribution of power and resources disproportionately marginalise the racialised Other and their position in society, sport, local government and any other major social structures, then they will ensure that those issues stay at the centre of their investigations, or lens, rather than at the comfortable rim. West's (1989) starting point is that black consciousness should be a focus for a challenge to Eurocentric, patriarchal (homophobic) agendas. So, for example, as a critical black theorist, he considered postmodernist debates not so much for their emancipatory content but more to find out the context, actors and location of these arguments as an opportunity to position antiracist opposition to the hierarchies of power.

The *fourth tenet* reflects this centralising of the marginalised voice that is often tabled as a significant contributory aspect of CRT but is also seen as a potential weakness by some according to Delgado and Stefancic (2000). CRT encourages us to explore what sport means to those whose experiences and identities are inadequately represented in the various conceptions of sport policy and practice. The 'lived experiences' (Hylton 1995, 2003, Solórzano and Bernal 2001) of those voices rarely heard in sport, such as black academics, black spectators, black referees, Asian darts players, African Caribbean swimmers, Latina managers and white people talking about whiteness in sport, are highly valued. A criticism of this approach is that the recognition of the black voice has an essentialising effect on the black experience. It suggests that views from racialised individuals somehow represent the experiences of all black people and is open to conventional criticisms around validity, reliability and representativeness. CRT encourages counter-storytelling methodologies such as the centring of a black or racialised 'voice' seen as 'race'-centred research tools that can effectively voice the marginalised experiences of the Other in a bid to present different or competing versions of reality that is often the prerogative of white social scientists (Delgado and Stefancic 1995). Henderson (1998) offered a post-positivist critical framework to be utilised by feminists, or writers with other social agendas, to explore the meaning of leisure from the perspective of Other individuals in the social system (see Aitchison 2000) – that is, to centralise the experiences of women or racialised Others in such a way that any engagement with marginalised or alienated groups becomes a political one. In Chapter 3 it is further considered how authors therefore embrace the grounded values of the researched and researchers that are often ignored or frowned upon in mainstream research. CRT is an empowering framework that encourages Others traditionally excluded from the dominant perspectives to put forward views that have not been heard before. Lorde's (1979) assertion that the *master's tools will never dismantle the master's house* is thought-provoking in the extreme as she encourages us to challenge tradition with different viewpoints and methodologies, and not be afraid to present experience as valid resources and knowledge to supplement and challenge established epistemologies. The 'voice' aspect of CRT should be viewed as 'an asset, a form of community memory, a source of empowerment and strength, and not as a deficit' (Villalpando 2004: 46). Henderson (1998) supports this as a major thrust of enlightened meaningful social analysis. A CRT viewpoint allows us to get a clearer understanding of the major structures involved in the organisation of sport, which is crucial when racism is the ultimate target. An emergent counter-narrative helps us to focus on experienced power processes, white hegemony, racism and equality that have been consistently ignored by mainstream theorists.

The *fifth element* posited by CRT writers involves the transdisciplinary nature of CRT. In the spirit of challenging dogma and orthodoxies it is incumbent on CRT advocates to adopt a resistance to ahistorical, unidisciplinary models of analysis (Crenshaw *et al.* 1995, Delgado and Stefancic 2000, 2001, Solórzano and Bernal 2001). As much as CRT, sport and leisure studies are necessarily multidisciplinary, it is argued that they, like CRT writers, should be wary of utilising a familiar and/or narrow multidisciplinary straitjacket that might constrain them in explaining modern (or historical) phenomena (Coalter 1998, Delgado and Stefancic 2001). A criticism angled at CRT, according to Delgado and Stefancic (2001) and reinforced by critical Marxists Darder and Torres (2003, 2004), is whether CRT has taken enough account of globalisation, and economic democracy. Darder and Torres rely on a critical Marxist analysis that effectively subsumes all oppressions under those of class that traditional Marxists attempted many years ago. The view that racism is integral to the accumulation of capital and that racialised populations that benefit the least from globalisation is one that they would argue generate, little attention from social scientists. This lack of attention to global racialised processes confirms their argument that some racism theorising can be parochial in nature and reductionist in perpetuating a dominant black/white binary in the centralising of 'race' as an analytical category. Darder and Torres (2003) go on to accuse 'race' critical writers of considering class too superficially and almost in passing. Their reference to CRT writers who emphasise the need to consider the intersections of oppressions does not bring class into sharp enough relief for them and they see this as a failure of CRT. The notion of intersectionality is also seen by them as a smokescreen for avoiding class as a central issue of racism theorising. A weakness of presenting 'race' as a central political construct, and therefore ignoring 'the class struggle', is to separate the two spheres – 'A move that firmly anchors and sustains prevailing class relations of power' (Darder and Torres 2003: 248). Darder and Torres's (2003, 2004) fear is that ahistorical, apolitical, classless analyses of homogeneous rather than culturally pluralistic societies prevail, thus presenting narrow and static views of racism and racialised politics. Delgado and Stefancic (2001) suggest that these criticisms are justified to a degree. However I have yet to see a theoretical framework that has satisfactorily tackled all of the crucial issues of its time. CRT is clearly metamorphosing in North America in terms of critical subjects ranging from critical race feminism and whiteness to Latino/a critiques (Lat/Crit) which emphasise crucial issues for our time, or for specific racialised populations. In some places like Europe, CRT is only just emerging as a valid framework and so it is not extraordinary that some important questions are yet to be fully explored (Gillborn 2005, Hylton 2005). Delgado and Stefancic (2001) add that this situation reflects the resources and emphasis to date but things change as CRT's ability to offer important contributions is only strengthened by external and internal reflections.

The need to draw ideas from multiple disciplines will assist this process of growth for CRT, and so in their cultural analysis of sport McDonald and Birrell (1999) go as far as to describe transdisciplinarity as 'anti-disciplinary'. For want of a better term they attempt to emphasise the need for writers to engage constantly in an intellectual project to broaden their theoretical and methodological frames. CRT draws on necessary critical epistemologies to ensure that their social justice agenda intersects to highlight related oppressive processes or the 'multidimensionality' of oppression that affect gender, social class, age or disability (Harris 1999). In this respect, CRT challenges orthodoxies and dominant ideologies congruent with critical approaches to complex social issues. Where this, albeit limited, transdisciplinary stance has been employed in sport and leisure, the strengths of critical 'race' analyses have been evident. Scraton's (2001) argument that 'race' cannot be added to other sites or discourses of oppression in a 'bolt on' fashion draws this aspect of the work of CRT writers into sharp relief. For example, the challenge to interrogate phenomena such as whiteness and racism in the historical and contemporary developments of sport and leisure, and how processes within sport and society conspire to reinforce or liberate oppressions, is one worth taking (Long and Hylton 2002). The *crossing of epistemological boundaries* forces us to shift from and ultimately 'unlearn' the domain assumptions and orthodoxies that many have in their 'home' disciplines and opens the door to other innovative ideas and worldviews.

Limited bodies of work have been successful in realising the potential of theorising sport phenomena through the strategic use of related critical perspectives such as critical cultural studies, sexuality, masculinity and feminist theory, class, 'race' critical theory, history, politics, discourse analysis and post-structural, postmodern and post-colonial analyses. Cultural analyses that have juxtaposed 'race', class, masculinity, politics, nation, identity and popular culture, evident in the work of Birrell (1989), Messner (1992), Gilroy (1993), Werbner (1996), Carrington (1998a, b, 2002a), Back *et al.* (2001) and Garland (2004), have, in addition to the work of other writers mentioned, demonstrated the potency and insight afforded by transdisciplinary techniques. A consideration of these issues is likely to assuage some of the criticisms levelled at leisure and sports studies writers accused of a narrow theoretical focus, although in the case of 'race' a concerted effort is required before an established body of knowledge can be formed. Taking this opportunity, critical leisure and sport studies could broaden out their foci and utilise further instructive epistemologies likely to illuminate the multiple intersections of 'race'. Consequently, critical sport and leisure studies will be more likely to consider 'race' and racism(s) with reference to converging social markers and processes such as power, gender, class, and how they play out in sport and leisure contexts. By employing such techniques common ground between CRT and core sport and leisure studies theory is likely to become more evident, especially where narrow disciplinary epistemologies are rejected.

As a result of transdisciplinarity theoretical resources evolve shared with poststructural and postmodern perspectives, of course with Parker and Lynn's (2002: 12) caveat that 'Justice can not be merely theoretical'. Omi and Winant (2002) are sensitive to the need for social theorists to be concerned with the development of critical social analysis and theory development but they never lose sight of the balance between the ivory tower of academe and the need for engagement with political struggles beyond its walls. The temptation for academics to propagate abstract academic debates in sport and other subject areas can compromise our capacity for social transformation. Similarly, CRT writers are anxious to avoid the ambivalence of postmodern perspectives by adopting a critical theoretical position on 'race' and stratifying structures and processes at the same time as they stress there are no canons, dogma or methodologies that embrace all CRT scholars. They attempt to use the necessary theoretical devices at their disposal to reinforce their challenge to the privileging mechanisms and accepted orthodoxies in place. Thomas (1993) refers to postmodernists as 'armchair radicals' as they regularly rehearse arguments that challenge traditional, established, modernist, structuralist ways of perceiving things, of which research and practice are two aspects. Their challenge to established grand theory is explicit and has ramifications for critical race theorists who support oppositionist views to structural racism. Hooks (1990) proposes that postmodernist insights should not be overlooked in the maelstrom of abstract, apolitical debates that themselves reinforce racial formations and power relations, even as they champion their 'master-narrative' of difference, otherness and heterogeneity. Hooks (1990: 30) goes on to reinforce this view by suggesting that 'to change the exclusionary practice of postmodernist critical discourse is to enact a postmodernism of resistance'. This postmodernism of resistance is one that West (1989: 91) identified as part of his 'black opposition to the hierarchies of power'. Maynard (2002: 112) also sponsors West's cautionary approach to postmodernist ideas as she considers the effect of over-emphasising difference, otherness or heterogeneity in feminist research 'which runs the risk of masking the conditions that give some forms of difference value and power over others'. In Chapter 6 it will be demonstrated how this can lead to the detriment of antiracist projects whose substantive agenda is 'race' and antiracism; thus the conditions that Collins (2000) argues are symbolic for uniting black women activists are those that strategically employ the notion of difference that could dilute their efforts if used uncritically.

Critical race theory and sports studies

Sport and leisure writers have been keen to emphasise their critical voices over the years (Rojek 1989, Hargreaves 1994, Jarvie and Maguire 1994, Polley 1998, Sugden and Tomlinson 2002). 'Race' and Sport: Critical Race Theory has acknowledged its debt to the critical theory of sports studies. Kellner's (1989) belief is that critical theory has as its fundamental underpinnings a critique of domination, and a liberatory focus. He is keen to recognise that under the umbrella of critical theory there are different versions, which have been adapted and transformed by social and historical events. These phenomena have been manifest amongst other things in the shape of research, social problems and intellectual insight. Harvey (1990) concurs that a critical approach is particularly concerned with attempting to make links between important social issues and wider structural and power relations. Such an agenda facilitates clearer connections with, and conclusions about, oppressive structural relations.

Critical social theorists have made the connection between critical perspectives and their use in research (Gramsci 1971, Habermas 1987, West 1989, Thomas 1993, Watson and Scraton 2001, Wray 2002) – that is, the experience and interests of the researcher or writer informing and being overtly part of the process of political liberation and emancipation. Forst's (1996) analysis of critical theory resonates with Watson and Scraton's (2001) and Wray's (2002) views on the leisure lives of Asian women as the writers offer an endorsement to this type of social research. They link the techniques for criticism with the ability of purposive actors to unravel the ambiguities of a constructed society with the 'actual' experiences of marginalised voices that offer up a story from a more gritty existence. This chapter adopts a critical 'race' perspective that aims to 'unearth and transform ideological and institutional arrangements' (Apple 1996, Nebeker 1998, Parker 1998) – that is, the basic standpoint that we live in an unequal society, where resources and power are unevenly distributed and are key aspects of a critical theorist's perspective on society. The need to demystify these social arrangements is a clear aim of critical theorists (Lenzo 1995, Sugden and

Tomlinson 2002). The message from 'race' critical theorists Essed and Goldberg (2002), which has met with agreement from sport and leisure writers over the years, is that we should all be concerned with positive social change and processes concerning structure, agency and power (see Sugden and Tomlinson 2002, Jarvie 1991 and Hargreaves 1986). The critical element of this type of inquiry engages political ideas that without it would render work tame and therefore unable to influence mainstream agendas. It is argued that critical researchers should be engaged in social and cultural criticism, that there should be recognition of inequality in society, that oppressive dominant forces should be laid bare and challenged, that oppression has to be tackled on more than one front and, significantly, that mainstream epistemologies and research agendas make up part of the forces of oppression. The principles of a CRT approach make up an essential framework from which to invite sport and leisure academics to reconsider their own positions on 'race' and racism. It can be seen later in Chapter 3 how research and writing that adopt CRT principles have been considered to be at the cutting edge of emergent critical black and cultural studies research (Stanfield II 1993, West 1995, Parekh 2000, Gillborn 2005).

Ladson-Billings (1998) goes further to make a crucial distinction between critical legal studies (CLS), critical theory and CRT. Although she has acknowledged that CLS and by default CRT are ostensibly grounded in critical theory, she argues constructively that critical (legal) theorists (like many in sport and leisure studies) have identified the processes and contradictions within institutions that reinforce oppressive social situations, for example discourses, ideologies and other related practices. However, she is critical of two aspects in particular that dilute critical (legal) theory, and for that matter much writing in sport and leisure studies, as a source for transformative action. The first point is that CLS, like sport and leisure studies and Hemingway's (1999; Hemingway and Wood Parr 2000) critical theory, fails to centre 'race' and racism as a starting point of its critique of social systems. CLS signifies that structures are inequitable; however the political 'race' focus, the emancipatory edge for black people, is not the starting point – yet this is a crucial element of CRT. The second point relates to strategies for transformation. CRT's aim is to give voice to racialised Others, and to make them and their views heard in the system where currently in sport they hold a marginal position. Their need for social justice and transformation, from a public policy perspective, is exemplified in a wish to move beyond slow and painful political gains as witnessed in the UK Race Relations Amendment Act (2000) and local government 'race' standards (Commission for Racial Equality 1995, 1999, Local Government Association 2001) to more sweeping radical action. In the UK, as in the US, there is a long history of human and civil rights gains, but for many the pace of change negates any meaningful transformations.

The target for CRT activists is not just the conservative right but also the liberal left who put their trust in a system with the vain hope that it will somehow ensure fairness. According to West (1995), CRT challenges both liberals and conservatives whose assumptions are such that they reconstruct white privilege.

Also, those seen as radicals who have marginalised or stayed silent on 'race' and racism in society are prime targets. This has serious implications for local authority sport providers who refuse to accept a collectivist perspective on race equality (Horne 1995, Clarke and Speeden 2000, Hylton 2003). In fact CLS writers and activists were concerned that the historical inequities and power differentials were continually being reproduced. In addition, actors from similar privileged backgrounds were replacing those making the key decisions. However, as Ladson-Billings (1998) argues, CRT emerged out of these critical ideas because of the feeling that CLS, which came out of a group predominantly made up of white writers, did not have enough of a focus on 'race'. CRT writers felt it significant enough to centralise 'race' and racism in their challenge to the way hegemonic power relations are constituted. The work of Jones (2002) in his analysis of the experience of black players and administrators in semi-professional football and Carrington's (1998a) study of black masculinity and cultural resistance in cricket are examples of this type of approach. This shifts 'race' from the margins to the centre and enables CRT principles to transform more orthodox approaches to critical sport and leisure developments. It is this shift that Henderson (1988), Birrell (1989), Gramman and Allison (1999) and others are advocating if sport and leisure studies are to accommodate 'race' adequately in their analyses.

Reflections on critical theory in sport and leisure studies

There have been a number of recent criticisms and debates amongst leisure and sports studies writers that challenge their own focus of study as narrow and myopic (Deem 1999, Coalter 2000, Hemingway and Wood Parr 2000). Their concern has been the limited research agenda (in which incidentally 'race' issues have been peripheral), where specific concerns were seen to have been played out too often in both the UK and the US. Of this Coalter (2000: 38) added that 'Leisure studies would benefit from a wider debate about some of the "domain assumptions", a greater plurality of perspectives and greater clarity in the meaning and relevance of certain widely used terms'. Clearly an agenda for change is being advanced by Coalter (2000), just as Deem (1999), Gramman and Allison (1999) and Hemingway (1999) are supporting a carefully constructed agenda that does not marginalise equity and issues of inclusion. Deem (1999), in reflecting upon gender and leisure studies, a relatively well documented body of knowledge compared to 'race' and equality issues, complained of a 'ghettoisation' of gender by other leisure researchers in their analyses. Deem's (1999) argument to locate gender in the mainstream is a question a long way off the slowly developing interests in the analysis of 'race' in sport and leisure in the UK. This systematic neglect of 'race' is of some concern (Floyd 1998, Back et al. 1999, 2001, Stodolska 2000, Carrington and McDonald 2001, Scraton 2001).

A cursory review of the literature that takes a critical view of 'race'-related debates would show that there are a number of categories in which similar viewpoints are expressed. Critical race principles can be observed in 'race' critical theory (Essed and Goldberg 2002), in critical cultural analysis (Williams 1997, Back *et al.* 1999, Owusu 2000, Garland and Rowe 2001, Lapchick 2001), in critical black studies (Solomos and Back 1995, Carrington and McDonald 2001) and in related fields (Ratcliffe 1999, Kivel 2002, Long and Hylton 2002). The few writers to engage with 'race' in informing leisure and sport research have been intent on working towards 'race'-centred approaches that would progress a critical theoretical understanding of epistemological approaches in sport and leisure (Floyd 1998, Gramman and Allison 1999, Scraton 2001, Watson and Scraton 2001). Some writers have been successful in raising the profile of 'race' in understanding sport and leisure contexts to the point where the efficacy of established paradigms is being challenged (Jarvie and Reid 1997, Floyd 1998, Henderson 1998, Back *et al.* 1999, Gramman and Allison 1999, Carrington and McDonald 2001, Long and Hylton 2002, Hylton 2005, Singer 2005a, 2005b).

However, in attempting to engage a critical theoretical viewpoint, today's leisure and sport writers in the UK and the US have reached a stage that critical legal scholars had in the US in the late 1980s and early 1990s. This has been exemplified by the recent work of Hemingway (1999) and Hemingway and Wood Parr (2000) as they argue for critical theory to be adopted to challenge the pseudo-scientism of established paradigms in sport and leisure studies – although in each case each writer misses the opportunity to outline techniques to reduce the chances of 'race' being subsequently marginalised or even ignored. This recent movement towards critical theory encourages writers in sport and leisure to do a number of things in different ways. Critical theory challenges leisure and sport writers to make their research political rather than neutral, transformatory rather than merely critical. It also urges writers to reject paradigms as dogma for more plurivocal epistemologies and methodologies. However, it was critical race theorists that forced a centring of 'race' that ultimately defined a new paradigm for legal scholars. This could be the next step for leisure and sport studies in the UK as writers such as McDonald (2002: 101) attempt what he calls a radical antiracist agenda in sport. He urges us to 'reconcile a commitment to progressive political change with sound sociological scholarship'.

Conclusion

Critical race theory has the potential to challenge sport and leisure theorising through its advocates' fundamental belief in its transformative capacity. CRT can be used effectively to generate a useful theoretical vocabulary for the practice of progressive racial politics in sport and leisure theorising, in addition to understanding the essential formations of racial power and ideologies. CRT rejects orthodoxies as a challenge to mainstream paradigms. In the study of 'race' and racism in sport it can be used to reject the notion of neutral objective detachment from issues for more personal political perspectives. Crenshaw *et al.* (1995) and sports writers such as MacClancy (1996) consider writing about 'race' and racial processes as a site where racial power can be reconstructed, therefore redefining it as an arena from which paradigms can be challenged. CRT facilitates analyses of sport and leisure phenomena from a starting point that is 'race'-conscious. From an example of policies that have had integrationist, assimilation, multicultural or colour-blind viewpoints, CRT shifts those paradigms to a 'race'-centred one. 'Race' and Sport: Critical Race Theory progresses from the standpoint that we live in a fundamentally racist and unequal society where processes systematically disenfranchise and limit the potential of black (and white) people. We therefore have a racist society that impinges on all aspects of our lives (Macpherson 1999, Parekh 2000). The academy is one such network that is affected by naturalised systems of order, often where research practice is flawed owing to epistemological (in)consistencies that make claims to the nature and order of things. Delgado and Stefancic (1995: 206) refer to this as a DNA-like process as knowledge bases have a tendency to replicate themselves endlessly, easily and painlessly – knowledge being one of those processes that is regularly modified and recreated through the hegemony of mainstream agendas. This is replicated in other key social institutions.

CRT applied to sport and leisure focuses on core social relations and processes of power. 'Race' and racism are central to any CRT focus, and its transdisciplinary nature ensures that disciplinary borders and conventions do not preclude appropriate methodologies or epistemologies from being applied. CRT's political agenda of challenge, change and transformation contributes to the ability of sport and leisure communities to re-examine critically how 'race', and racialised processes and formations are incorporated into their theory and practice. The CRT framework is presented here for serious consideration: whether or not Birrell's (1989) view of the sociology of sport (and leisure) is to be realised now is dependent upon what happens next.

Chapter 3

Researching 'race' and sport

Introduction

Social researchers are tasked with investigating and shedding light on phenomena that they have a sound grasp of; conceptual issues around 'race', racism and sport however are often elusive, ambiguous and requiring consistent clarification. Researching 'race' is fraught with a plethora of conceptual and theoretical problematics as raised in the previous two chapters. For example, can research be conducted that is divorced from its political context? How do we avoid being reductionist or universalistic or simplistic? And how are lived experiences valued over mediated accounts (cf. Gunaratnam 2003)? Bulmer and Solomos (2004), like Twine and Warren (2000) and Seidman (2004), among others, raise questions about what should be on an agenda for researchers of 'race' and racism. Ontologies, epistemologies, methodologies and ethical questions such as insider/outsider status, diversity and racisms, whiteness and the impact of researcher identities on the research process have been the source of many debates. Although there might be some consensus about the need for social transformations there are still tensions around the process of getting there.

This chapter centres on a series of three interviews with experienced researchers involved in researching 'race' and racism in sport and leisure who have approached their work with a critical 'race' consciousness, all with differing biographies and viewpoints. The interviews explore intriguing political, theoretical, conceptual and practical considerations for the working researcher that offer insight into the everyday concerns of those balancing the demands of critical academic writing and the often narrower contract research for governing organisations. In this chapter writer/researchers have taken their opportunity to share ideas with the research community by consenting to a public dialogue with me and a virtual one with each other; they were not together at any time even though they responded to the same questions. The responses are structured in a discursive or dialogic form enabling the respondents to enter into a 'conversation with' me in the style of bell hooks and Cornel West's themed conversations in *Breaking Bread* (hooks and West 1991). This chapter aims to replicate aspects of the *Breaking Bread* process by reporting back the three interviews of Professor

Jonathan Long, Dr Beccy Watson and Dr John Singer as an interactive, dynamic dialogue with myself and each other. Cornel West and bell hooks have informed my thinking as my and their ideas have changed over time. West's work in particular has been instructive because of his critical black consciousness and equanimity of response to the academy that he has challenged in ways that have forcefully stated a series of positions in relation to 'race' and 'race' matters that have provided leadership for academics like myself who are often lone academics in need of acknowledgement and reassurance from others confronted with similar questions about epistemologies, theory, power and racial politics in our field. Significantly, the three researchers accept their raced and social selves as tools within the research process and have written reflexively about the politics of research, 'race' and what Reinharz (1997) would describe as their 'multiple selves'.

The need to position the researcher within the research process is a practice that is particularly well rehearsed by feminist writers and a significant point to restate here (Lather 1991, Naples 1997, Reinharz 1997, Bulmer and Solomos 2004). This chapter also recognises how power is exercised epistemologically in the dual practices of naming and evaluating. This critical race theory position starts the process of focusing the theoretical lens so that, where leisure theory, policy and equality processes have been colour-blind (Gardiner and Welch 2001; Swinney and Horne 2005) and 'race'-neutral (Delgado and Stefancic 1995, 1995b; Solórzano and Yosso 2001), this work engages a critical black consciousness to centre it (Goldberg 1993: 150). Stanfield II's (1994) thesis concentrates on black researchers and writers and their need to urgently centralise 'race' and ethnicity as core factors in the study of social relations. Such actions improve and enhance the bodies of knowledge pertinent to 'race' and 'race relations'. This would have the effect of challenging everyday assumptions about socially constructed groups that often become the foundation for myth and folklore, e.g. identity, homogeneity. Stanfield II's challenge is that we should establish new lines of enquiry whilst criticising traditional epistemologies, rather than acquiescing to the hegemony of established epistemologies.

Researcher 1

Researcher 1, Dr Beccy Watson, is an active researcher in the Carnegie Research Institute, Leeds Metropolitan University, contributing to work on diversity, equity and inclusion. As a self-defined Leeds (UK) born white middle-class female, Beccy has been reflective of her researcher status since her doctoral research on the interrelationships between gender, 'race' and class. Beccy's more recent work has involved projects on ethnicity, identity and whiteness, changing cities and women, older women, leisure and young women, leisure and mass media. Beccy sits on the editorial board of the *Leisure Studies* journal. In her work on South Asian women Bhopal (2000) outlined three guiding themes for her methodology. They came from her alignment with feminist research principles that share a critical emancipatory project. Feminist research also has a clear application to the study of 'race' and black perspectives, especially as both perspectives have been struggling to develop methodologies within the constraints of a white, male research agenda. Bhopal's first two themes involved centring the subject – that is, making significant the experiences of women in her research where previously their views had not been sought or had been subsumed in other mainstream agendas. In addition there should be an acknowledgement by the research community that the research about women (or black people) is not just 'on women' but also 'for women'. But it is Bhopal's third point that reinforces the views of Ben-Tovim et al. (1986) and Stoecker (1991): the researcher should be part of the research process and their reasons for doing the research should not just be implicit in their work. This self-reflexive aspect of Beccy's work was emphasised as a crucial element of work on and for women (and of course black people). About her academic background Beccy stated that:

The appeal of leisure studies was that you could do all these different [multidisciplinary] topics and not least, for me at the time, work on the environment. But that coupled with – I'm very much a product of my time, the urban unrest in Chapeltown [multicultural inner-city area of Leeds], in the early 1980s, and then new age travellers, you know, fought with the police . . . so there's a whole sort of time frame for me and not least as I became a woman I also probably began to develop more of a feminist consciousness. So to get a degree course where you could look at all of these things was like, wow, it had a big wow factor for me! And because we did policy [studies] as well so you could look at, you know, debates about multiculturalism and democracy and those kinds of things, it was a good piecing together. Now that all gives you a framework to know if you go on to do a research degree, which I did, to think what I would look at and although I went specifically into looking more at gender and the feminist debates, issues of race and ethnicity were absolutely essential to my PhD, and that was a conscious decision that they would be . . . And in leisure studies and sports studies, although I've probably always tended to take more from leisure studies than sports studies, you know, there was just this thing that said, oh, it's [sport] all ethnocentric. But there didn't seem to be a great deal of empirical research that was doing anything to engage with that or challenge it. So from that, that's why I decided I would get more centrally involved with South Asian women.

Selected writings (Beccy Watson)

Watson, R. and Scraton, S. (2006) 'Ethnicity, ageing and gender: exploring the leisure lives of older South Asian women'. *Loisir*, forthcoming.
Scraton, S. and Watson, R. (2005) 'Leisure as a space for belonging'. Submitted to *Sociological Review*.
Watson, R. (2004) 'Exploring identity through shifting "leisure cultures"'. Paper presented at Leisure Matters, World Leisure 8th International Congress, 12–17 Sept., Griffith University, Brisbane, Australia.
Watson, R. and Scraton, S. (2001) 'Confronting whiteness? Researching the leisure lives of South Asian Mothers'. *Journal of Gender Studies*, 10(3), 265–277.

Researcher 2

As an able-bodied, heterosexual white male ensconced in the hierarchy of the academy Professor Jonathan Long has been instrumental in developing the work of the Carnegie Research Institute (CRI) at Leeds Metropolitan University in relation to diversity, equity and inclusion for many years. Fawcett and Hearn (2004) ask questions of academics with Jonathan's biography when they do work on 'others'. They wonder if it is too much of a challenge to conduct research into ethnicity and racialisation and intersecting social divisions such as gender, disability and class without experience points of identification of these or associated social constraints. The 'master narrative' often reinforces the position of dominant groups in the academy and, like McCorkel and Myers (2003), Jonathan has worked to decentre such processes through critical reflexivity and continually challenging these complex issues. Prior to joining Leeds Metropolitan University, Jonathan was Research Director at the Tourism and Recreation Research Unit and the Centre for Leisure Research in Edinburgh. He has extensive experience of managing external contracts, having now directed or jointly directed some fifty projects. Jonathan was also a founding member of the editorial board of the journal *Leisure Studies*, and has been its book reviews editor and managing editor. He is an Academician of the Academy for Learned Societies in the Social Sciences. Born in India, Jonathan remains conscious of his ethnicity throughout the work he conducts in the CRI. Reflecting on his early training Jonathan states:

Academically my influences were my initial training at Bristol . . . as I said . . . I was originally a geographer . . . geography as in the original multidisciplinary discipline. I was very fortunate in the time that I was at Bristol it was one of the leading departments in the country. It was at a very particular moment in that they had been at the forefront of the quantitative revolution in geography so I got taught all those techniques but they were also beginning to emerge out the other side before a lot of the others so that they were also questioning what that had all been about, you know, where are we now and what have we learnt from that? I got taught the techniques and I got taught the critiques and just that process of having a set of techniques that were introduced to you and explained to you and explained to you and you were encouraged to challenge those was an absolute Godsend for any researcher. I didn't appreciate it at the time but in retrospect it was hugely influential . . . it was the 'moment' that I benefited from.

Selected writings (Jonathan Long)

Long, J. and Wray, S. (2003) 'It depends who you are: on asking difficult questions in leisure research'. *Loisir et Société*, 26(1), 169–182.

Long, J. and McNamee, M. (2004) 'On the moral economy of racism and racist rationalisations in sport'. *International Review for the Sociology of Sport*, 39(4), 405–420.

LIBRARY, UNIVERSITY OF CHESTER

Long, J., Robinson, P. and Spracklen, K. (2005) 'Promoting racial equality within sports organizations'. *Journal of Sport and Social Issues*, 29(1), 41–59.

Spracklen, K., Hylton, K. and Long, J. (2006) 'Managing and monitoring equality and diversity in UK sport: an evaluation of the sporting equals racial equality standard and its impact on organizational change'. *Journal of Sport and Social Issues*, 30(3), 289–305.

Researcher 3

Of the three researchers John Singer is the only one adopting an explicit use of critical race theory in his work. This may be the case because he is the only black researcher of the three and the only one from North America, where we have seen that CRT has diversified into varying strands and fields. Basu (2001) argues that, for black scholars like John, being in a predominantly white institution leaves them open to accusations of being involved in less objective research and more of a 'racial crusade'. Their 'activism and challenge to the status quo are construed as displaying outright hostility to established paradigms of scholarship and the protocols of ascendancy in the academy' (Basu 2001: 26). In a broad sense, John's research and scholarship have been most concerned with the impact that 'race' and racism has on sport management research, teaching and education, and practice. He utilises elements of a CRT framework to understand and address Eurocentrism and how it has impacted (1) research concerns and approaches as scholars, (2) our consciousness, curricula and pedagogical approaches as teachers and educators, and ultimately (3) the impact that our research and teaching has on our students and the various stakeholder groups in the managed sport industry. John's research and scholarship focus on the following areas: 'race', racism, discrimination and diversity in sport management; the black or African American male as a primary stakeholder group in sport (particularly in the context of intercollegiate athletics); career aspirations and outcomes of marginalised groups (particularly athletes and students of colour). John is a member of the editorial board for the international *Journal of Sport Management*, and one of the few African American men writing in sport sociology today. Of his early memories John remembers:

I was an athlete in high school myself and I went to Michigan State University with hoop dreams and aspirations myself but I realised early on and thankfully I had the right kind of influences in my life where I realised that GPA (Grade Point Average) was more important than PPG (Points Per Game). So I was in that athletic culture but at the same time I valued academics. So having worked in the NFL [National Football League] and having worked with some of those athletes and working with those that had been through and coming back to college studying and looking at these athletes . . . a lot of them having aspirations to make it to the league whether it's basketball or football, it just kind of began to stir up a lot of questions. Especially if you think about how the literature sometimes talks about how young black males, black students, seem to gravitate towards a career in sport and have high aspirations. That's what kind of led me . . . especially being a black male myself, it was just natural for me to kind of gravitate towards that sector. So really those summers spent advising, challenging, disciplining and working with these athletes led me to become curious about research. So that led to me saying – you know what? The motor's running and I want to continue to pursue my studies. I think I'll take on a PhD in an area that I'm fascinated with in sport management, kind of like I'd heard of sport management a year or two prior to that, but the fact that I could get a PhD in that area focusing on my passion for sport and education was the perfect marriage . . . so that's what led me to the PhD and now what I'm doing today.

Selected writings (John Singer)

Singer, J.N. (2005). 'Understanding racism through the eyes of African American male student-athletes'. *Race, Ethnicity, & Education*, 8(4), 365–386.
Singer, J.N. (2005). 'Addressing epistemological racism in sport management research'. *Journal of Sport Management*, 19(4), 464–479.
Singer, J.N., and Armstrong, K.L. (2001). 'Black coaches' roles in the holistic development of student-athletes'. *Academic Athletic Journal*, 15(2), 114–131.

The research process is often viewed as an ethereal process that 'just happens'. This might be the case but on closer inspection we see that it happens for a reason: it may be rigorous but is open to subjectivities, and research projects often have internal and external politics that situate each researcher's everyday world. The situatedness of each researcher and their subjectivities enables insight into the assumptions, motivations and relations that inform their work (McCorkel and Myers, 2003: 200). In planning the questions for this series of conversations I drew on an emerging collection of research literature that focused on 'race', ethnicity and processes relating to social inequality. These relatively new studies contribute to the already established critical research literature but present a cutting edge in respect to the development of 'race'-related work. Ten years ago there was no such specific, sustained and substantive epistemological foundation for researchers with an interest in these topics, and for this I am grateful for the work of Bulmer and Solomos (2004), Gunaratnam (2003), Twine and Warren (2000) and Truman *et al.* (2000). However, there are few accounts in the research literature from researchers who openly consider the practicalities of being a social being who conducts research with all of our biographies, perspectives and imperfections.

The researchers

We can see above that the context for each of the three researchers is complex as their choices of career, research and politics when researching 'race' are informed by what Witkin (2000) labels macro, mezzo and micro considerations ('macro' context – their history and culture; 'mezzo' context – their academic

..utions and scientific communities; and 'micro' context – personal beliefs and values). The presumptions that have historically underpinned our societies find their way into research questions: these questions can often hide significant under-researched areas in sport that can obfuscate key social issues that use a traditional lens. Interest in racism in sport has often misdirected the focus of researchers because the questions asked by academics and policy makers in sport have too often turned from powerful institutions towards powerless racialised individuals or collectivities. Our interests, or the politics of our institutions, can often dictate research agendas and as such can marginalise what could be seen as less important questions. Hence in research-focused institutions the focus of research might remain on established rather than emergent questions because of the value placed on each in the academy. This is likely to reinforce the marginal status of critical 'race' theorising and research justified purely on the basis of spurious claims of established epistemologies and outcomes of research from the critical mass in each institution. In the United Kingdom this process is typified by the Research Assessment Exercise (RAE) while in other countries hegemonic forces in research communities exert their will in different ways.

KH: Ideally what do you think a research agenda on 'race' in sport should include?

BW: Mmm . . . a recognition of how ethnocentric . . . so that people are aware of the ethnocentrism in sport . . . because you can't separate sport from the cultures it's part of, . . . it's so institutionalised, that to do research within sport [we] would have to acknowledge ethnocentricity . . . that prompts me to think of the sport and leisure research as well. It needs to try and open up its doors to far more things towards various people's identities rather than it just being the doing and the functional aspect, because even leisure studies is in danger of that . . . where is it that a sense of who you are and what you think about comes from if it's not in your leisure time?

JS: if I was challenged as to how I feel, this whole idea of who we are, what we teach, who we teach and how we teach, I think certainly for me personally in the years to come, my research on race in sport has to deal with some of those questions, in the field itself.

BW: I think that people working certainly in the public sector, and I know the public sector is changing, so anybody loosely affiliated with a quango and local council should have the opportunity and be actively encouraged to come and make use of some of the work that we do.

JL: Well that point for a start . . . getting into the sporting institutions . . . *'because we've cracked racism in British sport haven't we, because there's not so much racist chanting at football matches?'* – that would be the public's general view. Well come on . . . we've got to find some way of leading people to a slightly more sophisticated analysis than that. There are some things that we have to seize on and make use of like the Stephen Lawrence Inquiry for example. But we're still trying to use that and that was eight years ago now? Where are the other things that are big in the chattering classes' perception that you can seize on that have happened that have had a similar impact and that can draw our attention to those other wider public forces? There's not a lot around . . . Occasionally you'll get very brave chief police officers saying that their forces are institutionally racist but that's an excuse sometimes as some people might say 'I'm not racist but there might be some institutional racism going on' but the people themselves aren't racist. You think come on please!

The background of each researcher here is made up of a very specific set of circumstances constituting their lives, identities, their selves. A reflexive researcher is able to draw on the knowledge generated by these attributes to enhance the quality of the research process. When Reinharz (1997) reflected upon her research in a kibbutz she identified three major ways in which she was able to categorise the identities that she took on at times during her work. It was this identification with herself as researcher and subject that enabled her to understand how as a 'tool of the fieldwork' she was able to operate effectively. Her multiple identities helped her to know when she was in a good position to get access to information and also when she might be better served to take a different tack with respondents. Her use of her 'three selves' developed the idea of a 'research-based self', a 'brought self' and a 'situationally created self'. In the context of this research, for me, Reinharz's three selves can be translated into the following. Research-based self – CRT researcher, sounding board, source of information; brought self – second-generation African Caribbean/black/British, male, 43 years old, parent, sports development/equalities background, local government/regional and national links, academic; situationally created self – author, advocate, critical friend. These multiple selves help to explain how dimensions of the 'research tool' (the researcher) can be displayed by researchers to reflect the situated identities that we utilise strategically.

> Once the social and dialectical nature of research is realized, its veil of neutrality parts to reveal researchers actively involved in constructing the social reality they discover. Like practitioners and policy analysts, researchers both reflect and shape the social landscape . . . Research thus becomes a form of social action and practice.
>
> (Witkin 2000: 208–9)

In Ratclifffe's work on the politics of social science research (2001) he introduced his contributors by establishing their collective ethos. His practice is replicated here as a starting point for Beccy, John and Jonathan as a suitable backdrop to explore their views and biographies. These include:

- A rejection of the view that 'races' exist in a scientific sense.
- A rejection of cultural or ethnic essentialism.

- A commitment to research which empowers.
- A commitment to redressing inequalities and a rejection of racism, prejudice and discriminatory processes.
- A rejection of Eurocentric notions of culture and ethnicity and a commitment to equality.
- In policy terms, an acceptance of the salience of 'difference'.

(Ratcliffe 2001: 8)

On the very first point identified by Ratcliffe (above) the three authors were enthusiastic about stating their own position on the work they do on 'race' and racism.

KH: Given that the concept of 'race' has been discredited, why research it at all?

JL: Well, you know, 'race' as a biological concept has been discredited but most of our research is about issues to do with racism of both the perpetrators and those who are experiencing it and issues to do with opportunities and inclusion as well as the construction of identities. I don't think that's a trivial agenda. It would be naive to think that because there isn't a biological race, people use those short cuts to allow them to operate in our society.

KH: Can we research 'race' without reinforcing reductionist categories?

JL: It's difficult, it is genuinely difficult and I think a lot of the time we do [reinforce reductionist categories]. I mean, I don't know what the perfect research is, I don't pretend to . . . I think that if you are prepared to ask questions of yourself and you're prepared to allow other people to ask questions of you then it helps to safeguard against that, (1) we as researchers have our failings and (2) we can't control how other people use our research. So yes we do slip into reductionist categories and reinforce them and we need to be alert to that and acknowledge that and allow people to challenge us. You can't be too defensive about your own research, you can't afford to be.

KH: When you say we slip into the reductionist categories are you saying you've done it and not been aware of it or you've done it and explained why you've done it?

JL: Oh . . . all of those I suspect! Sometimes it is not always possible to rehearse the debates every time you use a particular term.

KH: Well, in 'The end of anti-racism', and in a recent book called *Against Race*, Gilroy suggests that we should stop using the terminology, the label of race, and use racialisation or talk about specific issues (rather than generic racism) – so we're not talking about race per se and reinforcing those biologist labels,

BW: No, I don't think we can. I don't think that we can transcend gender – and I don't think we can transcend class. It doesn't mean to say that they're not massively problematic, and you know, if he was here [Paul Gilroy], he would make such a good job of explaining it . . . I'd go out of the room feeling inadequate! . . . but it's just like . . . everything has such a historical context that, even though you can't rake up that historical context every time you need to express something, you are a product of it and therefore it seems just a bit silly to me to try to pretend we can make it disappear, and we only end up with these products and processes, and unfortunately most of the human population is flabby and slippery, and not sure what it's talking about and so everybody's terminology for everything is questionable in some way. And a bunch of sociologists aren't going to make any difference by saying we're really going to have to stop using this [race] because this hasn't worked either.

JS: Well, in simple terms, because race still matters. As Cornel West reminded us some years ago . . . Is it possible? – well I don't know that in my lifetime that's really realistic. I'm sure a lot of the early scholars who were responsible for bringing CRT into education have talked a lot about how people have taken it and misunderstood it or misapplied it, kind of abused its usefulness or applied it incorrectly, whatever that looks like or whatever that means, but I've heard rumblings from some of my colleagues under the canopy of education, some of the CRT scholars in education have kind of moved away from CRT because of this. There's an article, I was going to say, when you asked why did I study race, the title of this article was 'We are still not saved, critical race theory in education ten years later', by Adrienne Dixson [Dixson and Rousseau 2006], I guess simply put, in 2007, race and its residual effects are how we became racialised in the first place. There are residual effects being felt throughout society, throughout many social institutions. A lot of people don't want to admit that, it's an uncomfortable thing to really grapple with, a lot of students that I deal with here, even at Texas A and M, are of the mindset that if we stop talking about race it will go away, and one of the problems is that we keep talking about it and that's why racism continues to exist – there's an old notion of colour-blind racism, right?

BW: It's interesting that we've been talking about race and you're asking me about race, because I've noticed somewhere, and I was going to comment on it, that I've increasingly been writing about ethnicity and less about race, but for me there is a premise that ethnic difference and differences of ethnicity that we see and that are lived out, whether and however they are marked by people, of people, for people, naming themselves or whatever, that ethnic difference results in racial inequalities in different ways. But I'd reached – I kind of reached that other conclusion in my PhD that – I mean I can go on to talk about some of the concepts and ideas that informed that – but certainly that, yes, that debate that raged was ineffectual had gone around for long enough. Therefore, let's not talk about race, let's talk about racism, and I think the contemporary political climate is such that you have got to talk about ethnicity more because it is more about identities and communities and who creates those identities, when they're made visible, when they're not made visible. There's something too crude about race and there's also something a bit scary about racism, the kind of so-called progressive scientific knowledge around gene-based research and stuff, it scares me a little bit. So a conclusion in the PhD was that maybe unpacking ethnicities is far more important. I think ethnicity has been discredited, a bit too, not weak, but a weaker concept because ethnicity didn't capture the real structure of race, the impact of race, and it's a bit like the stuff to do with gender, by the time I'd finished my PhD I had a problem naming patriarchy, patriarchal discourse, the impact of the fact that again to a lesser or more extent men have more power than women – I did think I'd noted a shift more towards talking about ethnicity and away from race.

Storytelling: unsettling dialogues

We can observe here a process of critical reflection that allows readers to see researchers 'open to unsettling dialogues with humility' (Back 2004: 211). Researchers often complain that they rarely get the opportunity to have an open dialogue with critical friends, to consider new approaches and techniques, and so the opportunity to reinforce good practice and to acknowledge each other's efforts and contributions is regularly missed. For me writers such as West, hooks, Collins, Williams have spoken in ways that other influential 'race' critical writers have not, and that is with a resonant narrative voice that delivers knowledge with authority and humility. These voices have kudos in the academy but, more importantly for those lost in its epistemological strictures, provided new ways of seeing and understanding. Their views challenge the reader to turn the kaleidoscope another time to explore patterns and ideas that were marginal or ignored and to turn the volume up on voices that were rarely heard. In the introduction to *Breaking Bread*, bell hooks talks about her conversations with Cornel West as having a 'quality of testimony'. She goes on to state that

> Indeed the purpose of testimony is not only to strengthen an individual's faith but also to build a faith of the community . . . We want to start with this sense of communion and breaking bread, of sharing fundamentally that which is most one's own . . . sharing the word.
>
> (hooks, cited hooks and West 1991: 1)

Fetterman's (1989) consideration of political research comes out of the ongoing debate between those who support critical research and those who may support other more traditional, less political 'objective' research methodologies. As a researcher the aim is to further the cause of those under the investigative lens at the same time as recognising the political capital that is being acquired as the research develops over time. Fetterman aligns this aspect of a research programme closely with the ontological starting point of a researcher. In effect he suggests that research of this nature is not 'just research': it becomes a stage of the life of the researcher and as a result there is an investment in the work which is professional, political and personal. On this note Frankenberg's (1993) assertion that the 'blank faced' neutral researcher is never really neutral is also a point of principle for Crompton and Jones (1988), who maintained the critical element of their work through keeping all of their consciousness 'switched on' rather than falsely 'switched off'. A black consciousness guides the work of CRT writers in an area that Raymond (1995) would consider a 'sensitive research topic'. For me as a black author, taking a critical lens to researching 'race' is not likely to fall into the 'neutral' category. In reality why would any researcher be neutral in an investigation, never mind one that focuses on these key areas? Witkin (2000) and Ben-Tovim et al. (1986) have argued that any research is political, in particular research concerning 'race':

> The tendency to divorce research from its would-be political context and to abstain from research based interventions in politics has only served to sanction the political status quo and in some instances no doubt to actually exacerbate inequalities themselves.
>
> (Ben-Tovim et al. 1986: cited Harvey 1990: 179)

KH: What is your motivation to do research on 'race' and sport?

JL: Well, motivations are relatively straightforward, a feeling of some sort of obligation to act as an advocate of the underdog . . . and that's allied to a sense of social justice. Now, I might get my interpretation of social justice wrong but I feel impelled to act in that way because I am quite a political animal. For my sins I have been a member of the Labour Party for the best part of thirty years and though I don't like where the Labour Party is now. But political debates are a part of me and what I'm about and my involvement in the Labour Party was because of this feeling to champion the cause of the disadvantaged and you try to secure social justice for them.

KH: Why sport/leisure?

JL: Well it was useful for me because I had a job doing it, you are driven and are constructed by where you are but I think more profoundly they are important because they are a cultural expression and they are where a lot of people come together, and increasingly, if occupational communities are no more, then social networks are built around alternative social forces, and sport, arts, culture, leisure are a major player in that. I see leisure/culture and sport being far from the trivial/ peripheral position that I suggested many policy makers and academics have seen it as historically being. I think that they are now slightly less dismissive of the functions that are performed in that arena.

BW: When I did an undergraduate dissertation I looked at feminist epistemology, and I'd already got ahead of myself and decided I couldn't possibly do empirical research because there were too many questions to be asked, so I would do the extended literature review on feminist theory. And so within that I got really caught up in the debates about difference, and identity politics and hierarchies, because how could you put gender in front of class in front of race in front of sexuality? So I really kind of tried to begin to engage with those debates, and then that informed wanting to go on to do a PhD, and in the PhD although gender was probably the main thrust I did decide that I wanted to look more at ethnicity and, like I say, made a conscious decision that half the participants at least would be South Asian women, so it's a study of young mothers and their leisure, and again that's a product of my generation and my upbringing, probably in multicultural schools in Leeds and what I saw going on around me, some of the debates about motherhood and moral panic, those kinds of things.

JS: Well I think a lot of it is rooted in the fact that right after leaving Jacksonville in 1996 after my internship, I really became conscious of race. I have a younger brother who played college basketball and he went through what I would consider to be a Malcolm X black experience. He was really the one that got me focused on race. He went through an experience where he, you know, converted. His religion became very focused on race and racism in society and religion, and the . . . and American society. And through his transformation, because we were so close, we were a year and a half apart, because we grew up playing sport together and doing everything together, his transformation led me to become curious about this race thing because prior to 1996 I had this thing that, sure I wasn't aware of race and its importance, but it wasn't a problem one for me. It was more peripheral. But seeing my brother's transformation and how that kind of impacted his life, it really kind of challenged me to dig into this thing called racism at that point, it was something that I really studied from an academic standpoint, from a social standpoint, it became a major, major point of my interest . . .

Similar to this, Dockery's (2000) view of conventional approaches to research supports the argument that the notion of absolute truths, neutrality and objectivity leads to discriminatory and exclusionary practices. Dockery is not afraid to 'take sides' where power and status is stacked against those groups that have been marginalised but could gain some advantage from his research process. His aim to reduce practices that exacerbate inequality are in step with the ontological perspective taken by critical race theorists. By engaging with research that is fundamentally political, as we have seen in Chapter 2 McDonald (2002), like many critical race theorists, challenges the concept of value-neutrality, positions himself within a cause and attempts to identify the criteria for the transformation of, in his case, the racist institution of cricket. Where McDonald differs from CRT writers is in his criticism of the 'researcher as activist' technique, which he sees as a separate albeit contiguous roles. McDonald's apprehension is one of traditional attachment/detachment rigour. However, the researcher as activist role has been utilised explicitly in innovative work in Ben-Tovim *et al.*'s (1986, 1992) ethnographic study, and advocated by CRT writers Crenshaw *et al.* (1995), Williams (1997) and Delgado and Stefancic (2000), who argue that the researcher should be part of the process and their reasons for doing the research should not just be implicit in the work. This self-reflexive aspect of Bhopal's work 'on and for' Asian women was emphasised as a crucial element of her work. Here these principles allowed Bhopal to 'examine and question the differences and similarities (in terms of gender and "race") which exist between the researcher and the researched and how this affects access, the influence of personal experience and power' (Bhopal 2000: 70).

One of the defining aspects of CRT since its emergence in North America in the 1990s is its use of storytelling, narrative and in particular 'counter-storytelling' as devices to challenge established epistemologies and accepted 'truths' and to centre the black voice where previously it had been ignored. Amongst other emancipatory techniques counter-storytelling is a CRT device that pursues colour-blind policy and practice in a way that lays bare single discourses or stories so that plurivocalism enables a more balanced view of phenomena, disrupting hegemonic power relations and challenging the myopia and complacency of liberal academia. Where discourses are reinforced through iteration and practice they can similarly be challenged through the same methods. Delgado and Stefancic (2001) emphasise the potential for the 'destruction' of narrowly constructed perceptions. In sport we have seen how media constructions, education and other social institutions influence how we experience it. Each proximate influence has a contingent effect on the other through each individual.

Williams's (2004) argument that CRT can 'reveal the gaps' in dominant cultural perceptions through the use of counter-storytelling illustrates this point succinctly and frames a contested arena in sport and leisure research that, like other disciplinary fields, has satisfied itself on its rigour and balance of argument, with a backdrop of objectivity neutrality and equity. Opinions, attitudes and ideologies change according to the force of new ideas; however counter-stories are named as such because they are marginal, ignored, trivialised, unconventional and therefore delegitimated. One benefit of counter-storytelling is to reinforce the cohesiveness of 'outgroups' as their alienation or counter-stories become part of a social network of others sharing similar experiences and therefore gaining strength from stories of retaliation, victories and strategies to transform negative social relations, just as 'ingroups' reinforce their superiority by telling their own stories. Delgado argues that dominant discourses are like

> eye glasses we have worn a long time. They are nearly invisible; we use them to scan and interpret the world and only rarely examine them for themselves. Ideology – the received wisdom – makes current social arrangements seem fair and natural. Those in power sleep well at night – their conduct does not seem to them like oppression.
>
> (Delgado 2000: 61)

Delgado and Stefancic (2001: 43) describe the act of storytelling and counter-storytelling as a proactive method of tackling preconceptions that 'marginalise others or conceal their humanity'. In legal circles the criminalisation of social groups and their racialisation must be a central focus of these lived realities offering what Montoya (2002: 243) would describe as a narrative economy of shared vocabularies for those engaged with anti-subordination projects. In sport the stereotypes and racial processes that affect the experiences of individuals and social groups rarely surface as the experiences of many and as such are relegated to the status of individual rather than collective issues.

Montoya (2002) identifies three benefits of using storytelling and counter-storytelling like those outlined here: *discursive subversions*; *identity formation*; and *healing and transformation*. Discursive subversions in sport and leisure challenge conventional thinking of politics and identity through standpoints such as feminism, post-structuralism and emerging critical black and white studies, contesting epistemologies and seats of knowledge (cf. Hylton 2003, 2005; Singer 2005a; Burdsey 2004b). In so far as knowledge is power there is an emerging trend of critique in the sport and leisure literature that at the very least propagates a racialised narrative into the sport and leisure literature that disrupts established patterns of thought and behaviour (Montoya 2002; Carrington and McDonald 2001; Scraton 2001; Wray 2002; Long and Wray 2003)

Challenges to identity formation in sport and leisure can occur through the use of Outsider stories which subsequently destablilise stereotypes and homogenising social processes (cf. Long and Hylton, 2002; Carrington 2002a; Watson and Scraton 2001; King 2004). All of us are affected by these experiences in our leisure time and sport, and recent work by King (2004), Long and Hylton (2002), Scraton (2001), Watson and Scraton (2001) and Carrington (2004b) has taken this challenge seriously not only by considering the complexities of 'race' and racialisation processes in sport and leisure discourses but also by rendering white-ness visible and consequently white identities and the white experience. Where Montoya (2002) emphasises the essential need to read Outsider stories, it must also be noted that Insider stories are often ignored and therefore rarely the subject of critique and evaluation where 'identity borders and boundaries are controlled' (Montoya 2002: 244). King's use of narrative in his exposition of whiteness in English soccer is a powerful reminder of how complex and subtly racism is perpetuated and whiteness is left uncriticised. King's analysis is one of the few attempts to imbue everyday situations with a critical 'race' perspective that persuasively attributes different meanings to common practices and behaviours in sport, thus unpacking subordinating forces and demonstrating to the academy the real emotional and professional costs of everyday institutionalised behaviours. Work such as King's helps to 'restory' the past and to 'reimagine' the future through our stories and counter-stories. CRT espouses a politics of change, liberation, transformation and conciliation, and as such Montoya's celebration of narrative stories becomes validated only where they stimulate emancipatory social action. The dangers of conducting an emancipatory agenda however must be considered further: the fact that there is emancipatory intent does not mean that this will be the final result of rigorous research. As Humphries (2000) states, we need to be constantly reflective upon our own interpretation of, and actions in, events in case as researchers we become more central to the cause than the alienated or marginalised groups the research is supposed to work with. This may result in reinforcing their marginality by perpetuating their distance from positions where they can instigate change on their own terms.

The three researchers were clearly conscious of their status within racialised societies and were able to articulate how they saw themselves and how others saw them in a way that clearly informed how they approached their research and writing.

KH: How would you describe yourself to someone who hadn't met you?

JS: That's interesting because I remember the first day of my first semester teaching here was just this past January, and whenever I introduced myself to the class, even though they'd seen me, I always introduced myself with my name, my racial background and my age. I'd always say I'm a 33-year-old black male. So simply, I know I was talking to a friend the other day and she asked me what was the first thing I noticed about a person and two things I'd say, I'd say I noticed their racial background, the clothing that they wear. That tends to be the first thing I'd notice about a person before anything else. For me, I would describe myself as a 33-year-old black American male.

JL: Well I wouldn't describe myself in ethnic terms, as you would know from the experiments and the work that we've done [alluding to work on 'race' and reflexivity with two other colleagues]. Professionally I would say that I am the Director of the Carnegie Research Institute and if we're going to meet at the station I would say that I am tall with a beard and that would be it . . . ethnicity would not enter into it. You and I know why that is, because of white people in society . . . so there would be no ethnic statement there.

KH: I think that's interesting because if the same person asked me that question I would describe myself as 'not as tall as Jonathan and with a beard' but that would have its own significance.

JL: Yeah, you'd be making your own statement about that.

KH: Yeah, Yeah.

JL: But if people wanted to know about identity, I'm with Billy Bragg on this, I think you ask people 'where you from?' I think that tells you an awful lot about what people see as being their identity. I've always found that a difficult one for me as I have lived in different cultures and was born in India but would never say I was from there as I left there when I was four and a half. When I was in Canada when people asked me where I was from I would say England, when in Edinburgh I would have started out by saying Yorkshire and then latterly I would say I lived in Edinburgh or I am British but I never say England or English. It is either British or a more local allegiance. When people say now 'where are you from?' I would say Leeds as I've lived here 20 years.

KH: Why wouldn't you say 'England'?

JL: . . . Well this is interesting, isn't it, because it's an emotional thing, an irrational thing. I don't say England because I don't like the way it seems to seek to portray itself internationally, I suppose partly because I was born in India I have this hang-up about things to do with the British Raj and all the rest of it. The Scots were hugely influential in determining the nature of the British Raj so it's not a rational choice of affiliation and I suppose it's partly because I did live for nearly 11 years in Scotland so it does leave its marker on you. If you set aside my four and a half years in India I have still lived for twelve and a half nearly thirteen years living outside England. So it does lend a different perspective . . . not from the outside but from a different viewpoint.

BW: That's funny . . . probably I'm a white middle-class woman from Leeds.

KH: So you'd *actually say* a white middle-class woman from Leeds . . .

BW: Yeah, because I know who I am now, I can't pretend to be unconscious of labels. But maybe that's because I'm an academic.

KH: So at what point then would you have made that shift where you would have described yourself differently?

BW: Yes, I think – part of that is bound up with – I was going to say youth, but also I flirted with a politics of resistance, so I would have had a period when I wouldn't have wanted to tell you anything because we do that whole thing of *you're not naming me and I'm not giving you any details about my identity*. Then I might have had a period when I was an outspoken single parent, and I might have said I'm a single mum. I might have put that identity first. And the whiteness bit, . . . I find a similar thing is sexuality actually . . .

KH: What you've just said reminds me of Gunaratnam's notion of being and becoming, in terms of racialised identities. And if somebody asks me to describe myself, then again it depends on whom I'm speaking to, if it's somebody I've never met before I've got to help them out, but if I'm going to Newcastle and they're meeting me to take me to work, for example, if I'm external examining or something, then I'd say I'm a six-foot-tall black guy. Because that's enough on Newcastle station!

BW: You could do some interesting research on that couldn't you . . .

KH: Yeah, if I just said well I'm about 6 foot, I've got a beard – then who would they be looking for – because they'd be thinking (1) I'm looking for an academic, (2) looking for a Dr Hylton, (3) an academic at Leeds Met Carnegie, (4) 6 foot with a beard, and you'd get that sense of them looking everywhere else before . . . me . . .

In North America, educational research has been criticised for ignoring marginalised groups, relying on biologically reductionist perspectives, or for using inappropriate theoretical tools (Parker and Lynn 2002). Similarly, as noted in Chapter 2 there have been a number of recent criticisms and debates amongst leisure and sports studies writers that criticise their focus of study as narrow and myopic (Deem 1999, Coalter 2000, Hemingway and Wood Parr 2000). Their concern has been the limited research agenda, in which incidentally 'race' issues have been peripheral, where specific concerns were seen to have been played out too often both here and in the US. Critical social theorists have made the connection between critical perspectives and their use in research (Gramsci 1971, Habermas 1987, Ohri and Faruqi 1988, West 1989, and Thomas 1993) – that is, the experience and interests of the researcher or writer informing and being overtly part of the process of political liberation and emancipation. Forst's (1996) comments reinforce this and offer an endorsement to this realm of social research. He links the technique of critique with the ability for purposive actors to unravel the ambiguities of a constructed society with the 'actual' experiences of marginalised voices that offer up a story from a more gritty existence. Recent experience of sport and leisure policy suggests a field that has yet to come to terms with colour-blindness, difference and diversity. Saggar (1992) notes with some displeasure how the policy studies literature has not reflected issues of 'race' and ethnicity. This he puts down to the area being overlooked, or to the underestimation of sociological change in the last three or four decades. White and Adams (1994) give a further reason to the debate surrounding the paucity of academic interest concerning 'race' and ethnicity in policy studies as officer and policy-maker values are examined further. They are of the mind that research into public administration per se is generally focused upon using positivistic explanatory research. The positivist techniques adopted by many involved in policy studies, which exclude or marginalise issues concerning 'race' and ethnicity, are used as a result of the dominant need for predictability and rational logic. There is a perception that the intricacy of issues surrounding equality are often so complex that emphatic, clear-cut solutions are unlikely because of practical or political expediency (Mason 1990, Jewson and Mason 1992). This tendency to try to predict solutions in the absence of a wider consideration of explicit community aspirations and needs is likely to result in misplaced resources and missed opportunities for black people, thus reinforcing their disadvantaged position in sport. A common argument for the lack of research and writing in relation to issues around 'race', racism and diversity is that there are too few black researchers, which in itself has been criticised as relying on a crude reductionism by suggesting that only people from the same social background can know and understand the issues in relation to 'their' group.

KH: Does it matter who conducts research on 'race' and racism?
JL: Yes, of course it does. Ideally everybody would be a researcher and everyone would do it. That's not going to happen . . . if it's going to be a select few then you want a few who are good and competent researchers. You and I also know that it matters also on the basis of people's own ethnic background and their cultural experiences and life worlds. But then suggesting only black people can do research on racism I think is really counter-productive. (1) There are so few black researchers in sport and leisure we're not going to get far anyway and (2) presuming that a piece of research on 'race' done badly by a black researcher is better than a piece of research on 'race' done well

by a white researcher is clearly not a tenable position. So I think one of the major advantages of the research we've been involved in is that we've got some fairly competent researchers around and we don't accept crap research and we have had teams of researchers comprising people from different ethnic backgrounds and I think that is the ideal. I don't think we should say we have only black or we've only got white researchers on staff, we're only going to have white researchers. The mixed composition I think is important. That is more important than a specific match – just those different perspectives to make sure the questions always get asked even within the research team. So it doesn't matter that you are doing a study that talks to people from different Asian backgrounds and the Asian researcher in your team is from Bangladesh, Pakistan rather than India and one of your researchers is African Caribbean. I think having those different perspectives helps you stop falling towards the immediate apparent explanation and to ask questions that help you get to a more detailed understanding.

JS: I got this question when I presented my paper on epistemological racism a few years back, of can white scholars do this kind of work? Why not? What other talent is associated with it? Jennifer Brody and I have talked about collaborative efforts in the future. She looks more at black feminism, looking at African American female athletes in the college, and I am very much impressed with the work that she has done to this point and many of her ideas and thoughts about race and sport, and what not, so to answer your question I certainly don't think critical race theory, or race-based scholarships, are in the domain of certain racial ethnic groups and not others. Even if you think what society and how the dominant group has been seen as the problem in many people's minds, that doesn't exclude the dominant groups from different contexts, from being able to do this kind of research in a healthy way.

BW: Yes, I think it does, in relation to the feminist – of course you don't have to be a woman to talk to a woman . . . people like Michael Messner who were arguing why they considered themselves to be pro-feminist, they are at least engaged with the debates, the epistemological debates that already existed . . . but you've got to have some certain intellectual training or something, because I think when I thought about that question on the face of it, if you don't have some kind of responsibility . . . I suppose it's about responsible research.

BW: I've got something to say about that, but I'll just give you an anecdote . . . when I got involved with a group for black and South Asian women in Harehills. It was one of the groups that was involved with my PhD. A great really outspoken Caribbean woman was in charge of the African Caribbean group and there was a South Asian woman in charge of a South Asian women's group, and I don't mean to be offensive by attempting bad patois, but I got something like 'You don't think you can come in here and make up for four hundred years and you're saying, sorry you want to do a bit of research now', so I go back out with my

tail between my legs . . . somebody else put me in my place and said
'you still a little white girl with a university education'.

Research challenges

This chapter utilises responses from researchers and writers engaged in researching
'race' and racism in sport and leisure, allowing them to reflect on the nature of
their realities in these enterprises. The process of reflection opens a window
on why they are doing their work and why they completed racialised projects as
well as their intentions for the future. A number of writers have been cautious in
their description of what qualitative research like this involves. Denzin and
Lincoln (1998) attempt to define qualitative research with the proviso that over
the last four decades it has meant different things to different people owing to the
shift in academic focus. They argue that the present time is typified by a questioning of previous worldviews, universal theories, methods and discourses. These
positions, as seen in Chapter 2, are not shared equally across academia. In fact it
is argued here that the catalysts for these dominant hegemonic positions have
systematically excluded other more marginal perspectives. Similarly, Denzin and
Lincoln (1998: 3) have argued that qualitative research focuses on things in their
natural settings, attempting to make sense of, or interpret, phenomena in terms
of the meanings people bring to them. What makes the work 'qualitative' stems
from descriptions of such research that incorporates the following characteristics:
interpretative, flexible, rich, reflexive, using context or settings (Mason 1996: 4)
and process, theoretically driven, challenging common assumptions, emic
(Silverman 1993: 29). Bulmer and Solomos (2004) and Truman *et al.* (2000)
advocate such a practical approach to researching 'race' and inequality owing to
the paucity of praxis-oriented debates in the cognate area. Their aggregated view
suggests that recent debates on 'race' and racism have become highly concep-
tualised and abstract, causing fissures between them and the social action research
that CRT writers and researchers support. Critical, political researchers generally
have one eye on the impact that their research has on various audiences. Often
the impact of researching and writing is rarely visited upon the authors, and as a
result ad hoc and piecemeal feedback become the best feedback many of us can
expect. In relation to issues where behaviour change is the *raison d'être* of the
research, the problem with not finding out efficiently can cause some frustration.

KH: Do you feel that your research has changed anything?
JL: I think most academics have to be honest that most of the time the
      differences they make are relatively small and marginal apart from
      one or two fortunate people. But there have been changes, yes. We
      wouldn't have been involved in the research, I don't think, otherwise.
      Clearly we do want to make a difference – one of the advantages I have
      is that I am seen to be fairly plausible by a wide range of policy
      interests. I don't think that I would get dismissed as a zealot despite
      my obviously passionate interest. I think you need to be alert to the

understanding that if you are constantly going in and beating people up you're not likely to get very far in terms of having an impact. Other than an adverse negative impact.

BW: . . . at times I feel thoroughly ineffectual, I get this westernised, first-world syndrome that everybody seems to be having, of, yeah, I'm a middle-class professional and it's like what are you going to do with it, or why can't we change the world, why can't we make some of the major impacts that we know probably need changing.

KH: So you're saying your lived politics helps to shake you out of your complacency?

BW: I would hope so.

JS: That's a great question and you know I think at this point of the game I anticipate resistance, overt resistance, direct resistance, as I continue along this path, as I have no plans in the years to come of letting up. I only plan to really intensify my focus on this important area . . . I just haven't really reflected upon it, as yet, but I do anticipate opposition in the days and the years ahead. Especially as I begin to really challenge the research status quo in our field and how it relates to education and often highly related sport management practice.

On reflection

Critical race theory encourages us in sport to challenge conventional methodologies, and this chapter does this through its reliance on researcher narrative to tell a story about 'doing research'. Hearing these researchers talking gives a sense of something novel and underused and yet it tells us much about the thought processes of academics involved in the practical application of theory to practice. More specifically, the responses to the questions can be viewed as 'everyday' pragmatic commentaries on the politics of having an agenda on 'race' and sport informed by personal politics, institutional influences and external pressures, especially where partners or contract work is being implemented. The situated nature of the politics of each researcher did not divert them from acknowledging a need to avoid 'race' neutral or colour-blind approaches to research that tended to ignore core issues where racialisation, racism and ethnic diversity need to be centred. Politics were in further evidence where researcher identities, bodies and reflections on 'multiple selves' necessitated an awareness of racial thinking amongst potential respondents. The tensions between anti-essentialism and the siginficance of different racialised bodies for 'average people' cannot be underestimated for researchers in this field. This needed to be managed in a way that would ease access into the field at the same time as recognising the reality of 'race' for many beyond the academy. These contradictions make up what Chong-Soon Lee described in Chapter 1 as the topography of 'race' and what McDonald and Birrell (1989: 292) use to illustrate the 'narratives that mark the body'.

These researchers are clearly aware of themselves as social beings who constitute part of the research process. All the researchers to varying degrees

incorporate an agenda for change that parallels many of the ideals emerging from CRT, and yet only one of the three researchers describes himself as a critical race theorist. This should not be problematic. CRT encourages transdisciplinarity and pragmatics in the hope that many interests converge in centring 'race' and transforming negative racial processes in sport. 'Race' is not centred consistently in leisure and sport analyses, although as stated earlier the development of a critical theory of 'race' in leisure and sport does mirror the sequence of development of CRT in the US as a result of the perceived weaknesses of dominant epistemologies. CRT writers would go further to argue that we need to centralise 'race' and racism in our analyses and research agendas. Where 'race' has been ignored, CRT would argue that we should include it; where it has been marginalised, CRT would argue that we should centre it; and where it has been problematised, CRT argues that we should theorise it. McDonald and Birrell (1989: 293) posit that *narratives are always already political* and so it is up to the reader to intepret the meanings to be gleaned from this collection of stories about researching 'race' and sport.

The Researchers

1   Professor Jonathan Long, Director of the Carnegie Research Institute
    Carnegie Faculty of Sport and Education
    Leeds Metropolitan University
    Headingley, Leeds.

2   John N. Singer PhD, Assistant Professor, Division of Sport Management
    Department of Health and Kinesiology
    Texas A&M University, College Station, Texas, US

3   Dr Beccy Watson, Principal Lecturer (Widening Participation)
    Carnegie Faculty of Sport and Education
    Leeds Metropolitan University
    Headingley, Leeds

Chapter 4

Whiteness and sport

Introduction

This chapter considers the complexities of how whiteness contributes to the formation of identities. The chapter draws mainly on contributions made by critical whiteness studies and critical race theory to develop our understanding of whiteness as process and plurality. In particular it explores the consequences of naming whiteness and embracing white identities, especially as the work of Ladson-Billings (1998), Parker *et al.* (1999), Crenshaw *et al.* (2001), Delgado and Stefancic (2001) and Gillborn (2005) challenges the efficacy of dominant liberal education as suitable processes for social transformation. Reins's (1998) argument that white privilege is the corollary to racism is explored here because of the rarely acknowledged link between the two. Further, many people involved in sport are viewed as problematic in being colour-blind and reproducing the inequalities that we experience in wider society. We are all racialised (Frankenberg 1999), and Harrison *et al.* (2004) are clear that 'race' is neglected in sport and physical education; they query the relative absence of a racial discourse in this academic arena.

Our need to reconsider racialisation in order to decide how to renegotiate whiteness as a tool for a transformative politics of difference has been encouraged by many (Giroux 1997; Lee and Lutz 2005a, b). Giroux (1997: 295) goes on to state that

> Analysing 'whiteness' as a central element of racial politics becomes useful in exploring how 'whiteness' as a cultural practice promotes race-based hierarchies, how white racial identity structures the struggle over cultural and political resources, and how rights and responsibilities are defined, confirmed, or contested across diverse racial claims.

It is necessary for any exercise around understanding whiteness and racialisation that explanations should be neither pedantic nor narrow (Giroux 1997). This chapter presents a context to understanding responses to white privilege, ethnic identities and identification with powerful discourses that themselves reinforce racism. This should comfort others contemplating going through this process in that they are not made to feel as though they are on trial because they are white unlike white discourses and codes (Leonardo 2002). The relationship between white people and whiteness is one that needs to be clarified further as there is a tendency to conflate people with processes. Frankenberg's (1999) view that whiteness is a *process* not a *thing*, *plural* and not *singular* in nature, begins the task of dismantling whiteness with white people complicit in its destruction. Leonardo (2002: 31) supports Frankenberg's skilful negotiation of these tensions between object and concept when he posits that '"Whiteness" is a racial discourse, whereas the category "white people" represents a socially constructed identity, usually based on skin colour'.

Writing on whiteness has been critically examined in a plethora of topical and disciplinary areas. There has been much interest in the legal, educational, political, historical and scientific ramifications of whiteness (cf. Delgado and Stefancic 1997). Whiteness and feminism have come in for consistent treatment by some, such as the seminal writer Ruth Frankenberg (1993, 1999); whiteness, power and resistance have had assorted treatment from Katz (1982) and Wellman (1993), as well as Kivel (2002) and Thompson *et al.* (2003) on white men challenging whiteness and its privileges; Roediger (1998) on black writers exploring whiteness; Ladson-Billings (2003) and Leonardo (2005) on whiteness, critical pedagogy and disciplinary ethics; and Giroux (1997) and Gabriel (1998) on whiteness and power relations in the media. Common themes that have emerged from such writings can be summarised as whiteness as *invisible*; whiteness as *privilege* or *resources*; whiteness as *norms*; and whiteness as *contingent* (Nayak 2005; Garner 2006).

Whiteness as (in)visible

In sport and related areas writers have adopted whiteness critiques as a framework to unpack and understand aspects of racialisation in sport (Long and Hylton 2002; Watson and Scraton 2001; King 2004; Erickson 2005; King 2007). They emphasise how sport incorporates dominant ideas and epistemologies whilst allowing others to be marginalised, rendering blackness visible and often the *a priori* object for debate where 'race' and racism are concerned, whilst whiteness and the power that is privileged by it remain untheorised, unexamined and invisible. The focus of this chapter is to demonstrate how a critical lens applied to whiteness can be used as a vehicle to enhance critical reflexivity in regards to rendering white identities visible and to examine and begin to dissemble negative power relations. Ladson-Billings (1998: 9) describes this process as a 'deconstruction of oppressive structures and discourses, reconstruction of human agency, and construction of equitable and socially just relations of power'.

Representations of 'black' crime, black entertainers, black sportsmen and sportswomen are commonplace while their 'white' equivalents go unremarked. Media reports rarely take the form: 'the white footballer David Beckham . . .', 'white muggers have today robbed . . .', 'white rock star Bon Jovi . . .'. In certain sports there are participants who have become conspicuous because of their racialised persona where previously a predominately white sport was left absent of any such discourse. Examples of these racialised representations appear in golf with Tiger Woods and Nancy Lopez, formula 1 racing has Lewis Hamilton and tennis has Serena and Venus Williams. Further comment which emphasises the absence of a whiteness discourse in these sports emerges from commentary on the changing spectator profile resulting from the draw of these players. Considering such a scenario makes more apposite Martin Luther King's parable in which he observed: 'Ten drunks, one black, the other nine white. "Look at that black drunk," says the indignant observer' (cited in Terkel 1992: 6). Giroux's (1997) critique of whiteness starts from the premise that 'race' structures social relations and fosters a differential experience of sport and leisure for those living either side of the infamous DuBoisian colour line. In an analysis of whiteness in sport (Long and Hylton 2002) we argue that much of the attention concerning the construction of 'racial' characteristics has examined features ascribed to black people. In relation to visibility whiteness has often been taken to signify 'raceless', normalised identities (cf. Frankenberg 1993, 1999; Brown 1997), or as Brown (1997) would suggest whiteness is a raceless paradigm for us to confront. The 'Other' is black, peripheral, while 'white' commands the centre, owing to a process of the 'normalisation' of whiteness. The discursive power that is embodied through the 'discourse of othering' (Riggins 1997) causes whiteness to be 'inside', 'included', 'powerful', the 'we', the 'us', the 'answer' as opposed to the problem, and most important of all, unspoken. Gabriel (1998) suggests that whiteness is reinforced through a series of discursive techniques that includes the power not to be named, 'exnomination' and 'naturalisation', where only whiteness can make sense of an issue. Even the universalisation of whiteness contributes to understanding white identity as it makes sense of 'our' news, 'our' television, important dates in 'our' calendar and 'our' sport. Where individuals associate themselves with social phenomena that represent them positively a process of identification will occur. The process of identity formation, and being identified, for white people becomes less problematic than for those consistently represented and treated more harshly owing to their racialised identities. Whiteness is not necessarily invisible to all but it is a luxury reserved for some and for many its presence and resistance to it constitute part of the everydayness of their world. Garner (2006: 259) argues that although whiteness is often invisible to white people it is visible to 'people of colour'. However, Frankenberg (1999: 37) completes this argument by adding that our varying abilities to 'see' whiteness are as much a result of critical consciousness as they are of 'race'.

White privilege and resources

For many the processes of whiteness are insidious and go unnoticed. The historical, conscious and unconscious privileging of whiteness finds its way into legal processes (Delgado and Stefancic 1995, 1997), education processes and knowledge production (Gordon *et al.* 1990; Ladson-Billings 1998), language and dominant discourses (Essed 2002; Gabriel 1998) and gender relations (Frankenberg 1993). It would be remarkable if these processes were not to extend to sport. These processes lead to what Maynard (1994: 20) has identified as the 'taken-for-granted everydayness of white privilege'.

In the past whiteness was not such a subtle issue but more a conspicuous resource in state-sponsored racial hierarchies. One drop of a black person's blood used to render individuals lesser beings under the law, and history has more recently evidenced this in apartheid South Africa where sport was subject to legal desegregation and benefits on condition of a person's racial status. The benefits of this are still being reaped today in a way that reflects colonial or slave legacies in other parts of the globe. However, it must be noted that there have also been points in history where whiteness boundaries have excluded fractions of what could be described as the white population. For example the Irish in America struggled to take advantage of the privileges of whiteness as new immigrants, and 'included' fractions of the black population have been made 'honorary whites' in South Africa. Racial privilege accrued through violence, overt force or structural coercion in law fundamentally means that although the privileges and resources of whiteness are more subtle today they still have sources in history that have made these social benefits possible.

Research in rugby league, cricket and grassroots football in the UK (Long *et al.* 1995, 1997, 2000) started the process of marking the absence of whiteness in soliciting self-definitions of ethnicity and through encouraging reflections on perceived characteristics of Asian and African Caribbean as well as white foot-ballers and cricketers. The relative awkwardness of the white respondents to what they struggled to see as a racialised self was congruent with the same respondents finding difficulties in recognising racism even where it did not affect them directly. The privilege of not having to deal with racism on the pitch, on sidelines, in leagues and on committees led Long *et al.* (2000) to identify indicators of white privilege in sport that even at a minimal level hint at the unremarked advantages of whiteness that many take for granted (see Table 4.1). Everyday white privilege in sport is taken for granted because it can take many forms. We tried to elaborate on this (Long and Hylton 2002) by adapting McIntosh's (1997) indicators of white privilege.

McIntosh (1997) identified 46 outcomes of privilege *vis-à-vis* her black colleagues that she could attach to her whiteness. She described her white privilege as an 'invisible package of unearned assets' that indicate this subtle but ultimately destructive process of power relations. McIntosh's reference to unearned assets resonates with the notion of whiteness as resources especially where insider status is granted for some to develop social capital where others' outsider status keeps them in deficit. Table 4.1 suggests ten parallels as default positions in which white people find themselves in sport. These largely unseen facets of whiteness illustrate the commonplace world of white privilege that

Table 4.1 Indicators of white privilege in sport

1 I can be fairly sure that wherever I go to play sport people will be neutral or pleasant to me where race is concerned.

2 I can go to any county or district association and find myself represented in its administration and management.

3 I can be fairly sure that when I go to the annual awards dance there will be refreshments that reflect my culinary preference.

4 I do not have to educate my team mates on the existence of institutional racism.

5 I can do well in sport without being presented as a role model to my 'race'.

6 I am never asked to speak for all of the people of my racial group.

7 I can be fairly sure that talking to the 'person in charge' will mean talking to someone of my own 'race'.

8 I do not have to worry about racist behaviour putting me off my game.

9 I can express myself in sport without people attributing it to my 'race'.

10 I can play in a single-'race' team without accusations of separation over integration.

reinforces difference and 'race' at the same time as normalising this advantaged position for white people in sport.

In each of the studies by Long *et al.* (1995, 1997, 2000) the privileges of whiteness emerged as the benefits of structures (teams, leagues and officials), actions, events, discourses, racism and spaces. The visibility and experience of racism in particular had a clear boundary between black and white players and officials as all of the black players had experienced racism and none of the white players had. It was also instructive that league officials had come through the grassroots playing system and these were also reflective of a structure viewed as white. Emphatic as the studies were, they were conducted *because* governing organisations were not aware of these issues. Some would go further to argue that the worst incarnation of white supremacy is where ignorance normalises whiteness (Gillborn 2005). White supremacy is used by Gillborn here to denote the recipients and outcomes of the privileges of whiteness rather than a reference to right-wing organisations. The need to problematise 'race', blackness and whiteness *and* to apply these concepts to sport renders white people visible in the racialisation process. It also means to name them and their part in reinforcing or challenging social relations. Where Dyer (1997: 1) provocatively states that 'other people are raced, we are just people', we can continue in this reflexive vein by providing supportive conditions for others to do just that. Table 4.1 develops

Flagg's (1997) argument that, where the transparency of whiteness is not disrupted as racelessness or 'race'-neutral, the ten points in the table are likely to remain as norms and be completely incomprehensible to many of those in sport.

Whiteness as norms

The profile of spectators in golf, tennis and formula 1 racing are changing owing to the prominence of Tiger, Venus, Serena and Lewis . . . but changing from what? Whiteness assumptions taken as norms have been interrogated and described by some as the absent centre from which everything else is judged (Lee and Lutz 2005a: 18; Nayak 2005). When commentators make the suggestions about the 'new audience' for their sports they rarely if ever comment on the profile of the 'old' audience; by this it is meant that rarely if ever is whiteness as the norm central to a discussion of 'race' or racialisation. Nayak's (2005) suggestion that many believe that racialisation is a 'black thang' leads only to a complex deception that white people do not lead racially structured lives, hence leaving norms undisturbed. Giroux's (1997: 307) analysis of the media encourages critical accounts of whiteness to embrace 'ethical and racial dilemmas that animate the larger racial and social landscape and how this [film] reworks or affirms their own intellectual and affective investments as organised through dominant racial ideologies and meanings at work'. This analysis of the film *Dangerous Minds* can be applied to others like the classic *White Men Can't Jump*. Whiteness can be exemplified in such media but often our experience of sport is less high-profile and subtle. Kivel (2002) has attempted to draw the salient aspects of Giroux's ideas out in his work where he has interrogated whiteness processes in the reinforcement of racial hierarchies in North America. The North American and western penchant for reifying differences to simple essentialising binaries has resulted in the conceptual whiteness and blackness mentioned earlier. The associations that this engenders have both a positive and a negative effect on social groups dependent upon how they are viewed by others. As well as reinforcing norms, this 'race' logic is but an aspect of the processes that disadvantage or privilege across our public and private domains. Another cluster of concepts and practices of whiteness occurs in sport, leisure and physical education as 'white', 'black', Latino/a, 'Asian', bringing with them a set of associations that advantage and disadvantage in racialised hierarchies that disproportionately affect each member of those classified without, surprisingly or not, affecting how whiteness prevails across all of the major sports researched over the years (Sports Council 1994, Back, Crabbe and Solomos 1999, Long *et al.* 1995; Long and Spracklen 1996; Long *et al.* 1997, Long *et al.* 2000, Carrington and McDonald 2001, Hylton 2003, Burdsey 2004b).

In sport what we often get are versions of conceptual whiteness or blackness that themselves signify notions of 'achievement', 'middleclassness', 'intelligence' and 'education' as normative characteristics of whiteness while 'gangs', 'basketball player', 'entertainer', 'sprinter' become the 'marginalised and delegitimated categories of blackness' (Ladson-Billings 1998: 9). More humorously, Coates's (2002) paper entitled 'I don't sing, I don't dance, and I don't play basketball!' emphasises that as a powerful social construct racialisation structures our sport and our biographies to the point that beneficiaries do not necessarily register the perks or 'privileges of whiteness'; neither do the dominant classifying discourses challenge the concepts that subtly racialise, marginalise and oppress large swathes of people. Many of our respondents (Long and Hylton 2002) found it difficult to recognise as racist the language and incidents around them. We argue that this is because of the process of normalisation that promotes a white privilege. Our findings are challenging as they restate what some would describe as fixed ideas of racial identities and boundaries. However these are not theorised findings, they are descriptions of experiences that when reported generate new knowledge for those unacquainted with such social dynamics while at the same time they challenge us to acknowledge that as much as we theorise identities as fluid and unfixed there are such phenomena that need critical examination because of their veracity and consistency (Watson and Scraton 2001). The processes are insidious, the outcomes so apparently natural that they go unremarked. Just as gender prompts us to react differently to baby boys and girls, so perceptions of 'race' steer daily interactions on a micro level (Wildman and Davis 1997).

King (1997) coined the phrase *dysconscious racism* as a way to focus attention on those who are willing to accept whiteness norms and privileges as unproblematic. These people could be those centre-left liberals, who abhor racism, just as easily as those viewed as supremacists, who are unwilling to disrupt the norms and assumptions that maintain the power of whiteness in society. By this King (1997) argues that, by being uncritical of their own whiteness or adhering to a view that 'race' is not an issue (post 'race') because they should be 'race'-neutral or colour-blind, individuals perpetuate norms and negative power relations. In the following section we will see that this normativity is both the product of power relations and a source of differential power. Frankenberg (1993: 237) notes that this process is 'fundamentally asymmetrical, for the term "whiteness" signals the production and reproduction of dominance rather than subordination, normativity rather than marginality, and privilege rather than disadvantage'.

Antiracism and whiteness

It has been remarked that whiteness processes have the capacity to defend and reinforce their place of power and prominence in sport (Walton and Butryn 2006, Denison and Markula 2005). This position is particularly emphasised where a 'crisis of whiteness' has been identified in sports where in the past elite winners were more often white. These spaces were previously perceived as white because, although the best runners came from different countries, they were white, coming from countries perceived as such owing to their colonising nation or settler colony histories (Frankenberg 1999). Middle and distance running has come in for recent treatment from Denison and Markula (2006), and Walton and Butryn (2005) who all argue that the (unacknowledged) centring of the white runner in the upper echelons of middle and distance running internationally has led to a back-lash that has depicted the white runner as the 'victim' to the superiority of the black runners. As in the Matt Shirvington versus Linford Christie case considered in Chapter 5, a 'great white hope' scenario often unfolds despite in many instances there being suitable home-grown black runners. Kincheloe and Steinberg (1998) suggest that the significance of the image of whiteness under siege is persuasive for many as it appeals emotionally to people susceptible to 'commonsense' expla-nations for the key issues of the day. Sport is no different from other important areas in people's lives where debates and experiences challenge attitudes, opinions and worldviews.

This penchant for the next great thing reinforces whiteness in a way that is unthreatening and often tied into a discourse of national identity and imagined community. The norm is therefore restated, strengthened and resurgent. Kusz (2001) illustrates this in his criticism of *Sports Illustrated* when it ran a report entitled 'Whatever happened to the white athlete' (*Sports Illustrated* 1997 cited Kusz 2001). Here the great white 'victim' was Kevin Little, a promising US sprinter who has had to suffer a loss of confidence and trauma of having to justify himself as a white sprinter. Here 'race' matters, the marking of whiteness matters and the public perception of white athletes in popular sports being less conspic-uous is interesting as it becomes a call for more successful white athletes in these sports and therefore for making whiteness less visible and more 'normal' again. Whiteness as victim still perpetuates white privilege as it reinforces insiderness, outsiderness, national identity and the privilege of being the 'we', the 'us' and the 'included'. Antiracists' engagement with these subtle processes is as imperative as reactions to overt racism because of the pervasive reach and subconscious impact of such discourses. Walton and Butryn (2006: 20) surmise that 'This focus on and unease with Black success in [distance] running, taken in conjunction with the deep-seated belief in the "American Dream" and sport as a meritocracy within the U.S. reveals how whiteness has provided the assumed norms'.

Essed's (2002) examination of everyday racism allows us to identify whiteness as a clear target for antiracism. Analyses of sports in the UK have depicted how racial hierarchies are constructed and perpetuated in the most mainstream of sports: football, rugby league and cricket (Long and Hylton 2002). The studies evidence how sport is a contested site of white racism, black resistance and whiteness processes that range from the casual racist behaviour by spectators to more institutional racialised processes and formations in governing administrative structures. A consistent recognition of the negative outcomes of racism in sport often leaves the privileges of whiteness ignored and firmly ensconced (Reins 1998). Essed (2002) explains how this everydayness emerges as racist notions inextricably link to the meanings that make actions manageable and under-standable. These practices become reified owing to their repetitive and recursive nature, and consequently Frankenberg's (1999) three reasons 'why our students should talk critically about whiteness' are particularly useful to start an antiracist agenda. Frankenberg (1999) urges us to 'displace the "unmarked marker" (cultural practice) and identify white status and the seeming transparency of white positioning. She states that we must consider a more thorough understanding of racial processes and formations and recognise opportunities for the analysis of white selves.'

This is always likely to generate personal stresses and anxieties associated with rethinking normative ideals and one's own identity at the centre of these. McIntyre (1997: 14) would support these points further as she establishes a position that the next generation of managers and teachers must be aware of, in order to reflect upon whiteness so as not to distance themselves from the individual, institutional and cultural forms of racism that have afflicted UK society. Jenkins (2004) suggests that, although we have more knowledge about ourselves than others, the knowledge of ourselves is at least as imperfect as our understanding of others. The reflexivity required can emerge from critical self-analysis and/or be facilitated through sites like education where young people can be encouraged in a supportive atmosphere to become critically introspective.

A critical awareness of whiteness offers the capacity to understand further how modalities of power are expressed in racialised sites, such as sport, leisure, education or even the media, where whiteness cannot only be considered but is implicated as a constituent element in forming racialised hierarchies (Westwood 2002). Further, white people become the focus of these studies because of their privileging in racial processes (Leonardo 2002), but, more, whiteness considerations must be examined even in benign contexts that are not overtly about 'race' (Kusz 2001). In sport it is more apparent than in other arenas owing to the public displays of racialisation and 'Othering' in traditional crude and newer more subtle forms of racism (Long et al. 2000; Long and Hylton 2002). In sport and leisure studies the work of MacClancy (1996), Carrington and McDonald (2001), Long and Hylton (2002), Andrews et al. (2002) and Burdsey (2004b) amongst others has sharpened the focus of 'race', ethnicity and identity to reinforce the privilege that whiteness appropriates to more advantaged white individuals whether they are conscious of it or otherwise. Andrews et al.'s (2002) analysis of repressive coercive power processes in the economic and demographic development of Memphis highlights the necessity of a transdisciplinary approach to understanding how sports become not only raced (whitened) but appropriated by class fractions (middle class). Andrews et al.'s (2002) analysis acknowledges the fluidity of racial identities as classed black and white identities are divided and become embodied through the pursuit of soccer. An understanding of this process, rather than fostering a threatened, apprehensive response, works to engender a moral enlightenment of oppressive historical processes and a desire for positive social transformation. Andrews et al.'s (2002) study is endorsed further by Giroux (1997), who urges teachers to approach student histories and the way they have shaped the spaces, practices and relationships that they have 'inherited'.

Whiteness as contingent

To describe whiteness in any way other than contingent would be to essentialise it in a way that would make it theoretically untenable. To reiterate earlier discussions on 'race', racialisation and racism, it has remained crucial to emphasise our differentiated experiences as for example, black, white, Asian, Latino/a, in addition to our classed and gendered bodies. Whiteness is something that affects us all in ways that enhance or negate our social, cultural and economic capital as it works dynamically with classed, gendered and raced beings. Kusz (2001) emphasises two key points in any analysis of whiteness: (1) whiteness is socially constructed and therefore is contingent upon dynamic and recurring changes in behaviour and discourses, and (2) we need also to consider the history and geography of the construction of whiteness so as not to universalise its properties or experiences. At any one time a number of different forms of whiteness will exist as gender, class, sexuality, age, nation and ethnicity intersect in a dynamic process of being and becoming (Kusz 2001). Whiteness discourses are also contradictory and multiply inflected, often defying a consistent logic as they resecure themselves (Kincheloe and Steinberg 1998). Garner (2006) also suggests that the most useful way for us to theorise whiteness is to see it as a contingent hierarchy.

Recent asylum seekers in the UK from Eastern Europe and the Irish and Italian settlers in the US illustrate Garner's (2006) view that we need to consider racialisation processes like whiteness more contextually especially as access to the privileges of whiteness is not equally distributed even amongst white people. Our positioning within racial hierarchies and our awareness of whiteness are also contingent on our degree of positioning or oppression at the hands of whiteness (Frankenberg 1999). Douglas and Jamieson's (2006) examination of the golfer Nancy Lopez demonstrates the tenuous, constructed nature of whiteness. Lopez's example demonstrates how parts of her identity were foregrounded whilst other aspects became less visible or marginal. For example, Lopez's Mexican identity was 'e-raced' because as a light-skinned Mexican she could 'pass for white' and so was portrayed as a white, middle-class American by the governing bodies of golf and the media rather than as a Mexican from a working-class background. This intersection of 'race' and class was clearly important for women's golf, which needed top golfers like Lopez to appeal to middle America through presenting her as 'one of them' or 'an honorary white'. Lopez became the norm in terms of her 'race' (whitened), class (middle), gender/sexuality (woman/heterosexual). Drawing on the work of Bonilla-Silva, Douglas and Jamieson (2006) attempt to describe this white-dominated racial hierarchy in the US as one that holds white people at the top with a sliding scale down to those perceived as black at the bottom. Their work led them to conclude that the (unacknowledged) standard of measure in professional sport was a predominantly white audience and media.

Whiteness and pedagogy

In CRT and critical whiteness studies there are bodies of work and activism that are successfully confronting the dominant ideals and assumptions that have underpinned established worldviews in the academy. But more profoundly they have gone further in destabilising the liberalism of those writers whose urgency towards social transformation has left the roots of racism undisturbed (Nebeker 1998). Apple's (2003) dialogues with Paulo Freire brought them to the conclusion that as educators they should centre a politics of exclusion and fix upon the power differentials and oppressive realities of social groups. For Apple (2003) the 'silences' of dominant groups needed to be examined rigorously if they were to be transformed, and a critical approach to pedagogy enabled him to challenge these issues. In pursuing a strategy of 'making whiteness strange' (Dyer 1997 cited Apple 2003: 115), CRT and whiteness pedagogies must promote a pragmatic, doctrine-free framework that encourages a critical scholarship that is plurivocal, anti-essentialist, 'race'-centred, transdisciplinary, transformatory and not dependent upon established paradigms. It is regularly argued that critical whiteness studies, like CRT, advocates counter-stories to the conventional voices heard in our research and teaching and therefore decentres privileged knowledge and power for 'other' accounts of social phenomena. Hence Crenshaw et al.'s (1995: xiii) view that 'Scholarship is inevitably political' ('due to the formal production, identification, and organisation of what will be called "knowledge"').

Considering white privilege and whiteness as (in)visible, I now examine findings from an exercise I conducted with students exploring whiteness and their own (predominantly) white identities. This exercise was chosen to challenge what Kincheloe and Steinberg (1998) call the white interpretative filter that has made sense of their education, relationships and their sport. Their reading of their experiences, identities and culture to this point has generally been uncritical of whiteness and for many of these students this was the first time that they had been introduced to the concept of whiteness even though in their final year of undergraduate study they had experienced three years of sociology. Sport for this group of students has been problematic where Others have been cast under the lens of sport's 'social issues'. Where the students have been sympathetic to these Others but have not located themselves in the nuanced processes that implicate them in a dominant hegemony, this process of learning about whiteness can be seen to have practical uses. This sociology module, accessed by sport students on social-science-underpinned courses, generally accepts that these students at this stage in their academic careers are able to think critically, reflectively and independently especially around social issues related to sport, leisure and physical education. The students selected for this study described themselves as white (92 per cent, n. 49); White British (86 per cent, n. 46), White English (4 per cent, n. 2) or White British Welsh (2 per cent, n. 1). In contrast 8 per cent of the students fell within the Black or Black British African category (2 per cent, n. 1), Asian Pakistani (4 per cent, n. 2) and Asian Indian (2 per cent, n. 1).

The work of Judy Katz was the foundation for the exercise with these sports studies students. Katz (1982) utilised a similar set of racialised qualities to those raised by Kivel (2002) to raise awareness of whiteness and for participants in her exercises to:

- Explore their White culture and develop a sense of positive identification of their Whiteness.
- Examine what it means to be White in a White society.
- Focus on the inconsistencies in their own attitudes and behaviour.
- Explore how they may be perpetuating racism.

(Katz 1982: 135)

The practical part of the session involved students completing an individual checklist based upon an adapted version of the Katz (1982) 'How I See Myself – My Whiteness' activity (Table 4.2). The students were asked to:

1   individually choose five (5) adjectives from the checklist to describe themselves
2   individually choose five (5) adjectives from the same checklist to describe themselves racially
3   discuss the difficulties or issues (facilitated by the seminar leader)
4   complete a simple survey (5 minutes) reflecting upon this process.

There are inherent difficulties in trying to describe oneself in five words, and this must be recognised at the start, although respondents were encouraged to identify any new words and to put them in their list if they felt something was missing. Given this caveat, the first question on the checklist encouraged students to begin the process of reflecting on their own identities before encouraging them in question 2 to look at themselves racially when they were asked to *select five (5) words from the list to describe yourself racially*. The students found question 1 on the checklist relatively easy to complete but struggled to identify the five words that could describe themselves racially. Figure 4.1 represents these views: 83 per cent of the group stated how problematic it was for them to see themselves racially. Another 11 per cent struggled to consider the issue of 'race'. The consensus was that the first question involved a personal opinion of themselves whereas the second question forced them to generalise beyond their own experiences and therefore to 'guess the correct response'. These responses were similar to the ones identified by Katz (1982) in her original work as this group of students found some difficulty because they generally saw themselves as 'raceless'. The invisibility of whiteness was embodied in the class's general inability to understand the requirements of the second question when applied to themselves. The subsequent discussion followed the theme of (1) white people being able to see themselves as individuals first and (2) black people generally seeing themselves as part of a social group first. For Katz (1982: 140), 'The important thing to stress here is that a

Table 4.2 Personal checklist

1. Select (5) words from the list below that best describe you:

accepted	disappointed	knowledgeable	schizophrenic
adaptive	dying	leader	scientific
afraid	easy	liberal	secure
alienated	emotional	limited	select
arrogant	employed	misunderstood	selective
assaulted	enraged	nice	sexual
average	exploited	normal	sharp
bad	flexible	oppressed	sister
beautiful	free	outraged	soft
better	friendly	paternal	soulful
big	good	patient	strong
blamed	happy	poor	supportive
brave	harsh	powerful	tight
brother	helpless	privileged	together
brutal	hopeful	proper	tokenised
chosen	humble	protective	tracked
citizen	hungry	protesting	true
confident	hurt	proud	undereducated
conservative	independent	pure	underemployed
controller	individual	puzzled	understanding
creative	inferior	religious	unemotional
denied	insulted	respected	up-tight
determined	intelligent	rich	validated
different	invisible	right	victimized
dignified	just	ripped-off	worthy

member of an oppressed group needs the support of a group first, whereas white people see themselves as individuals first.' Katz's (1982) view is that white people are less likely to see themselves as part of a group because they have that luxury, they have that privilege. People who are racially oppressed are more likely to see themselves as they are viewed by the system and so the reminders are always there for them from the moment they wake up in a subordinating and oppressive society.

Some of the comments representative of these students reinforced Katz's analysis as they included responses that pondered the novelty of the task or baulked at the sensitivity of issues by being evasive. In the feedback evaluations at the end of the class, narratives 1, 2 and 3 (below) summarise the dominant views. Some of the difficulties of naming racialised realities involve recognising difference and inequality; however this in itself was hard for some students to come to terms with. Similar 'discursive repertoires' were identified in Frankenberg's (1993) seminal study of white women where some of the women were particularly defensive when discussing 'race' and felt that discussing 'race' made an individual a racist, hence narratives 4, 5 and 6 lend some credence to this. Reins (1998: 92) suggests that such individuals may be confusing colour recognition with quality

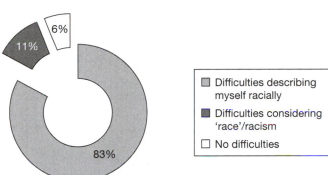

Whiteness study – student difficulties

6%

11%

83%

☐ Difficulties describing
myself racially

■ Difficulties considering
'race'/racism

☐ No difficulties

Figure 4.1 Whiteness study – student difficulties

of treatment because 'if they can't "see" colour they can't be guilty of treating people differently?' Other more critical students would be unsympathetic to these positions and would see these racial omissions or evasions as being racist in themselves. Clearly neither of these positions is particularly helpful in the consideration of whiteness; however recognition and understanding of these discourses are.

- White identity as novelty

  1 'Racially describing myself was difficult. Due to my lack of experience in answering the question.'
  2 'Racially identifying personal thoughts . . . never been asked to do it before.'
  3 'I found it difficult to describe myself from a racial viewpoint as I have never considered my race before.'

- White identity as evasion

  4 'Racism to me is not an issue and I see everyone as the same so it makes it difficult to discuss.'
  5 'Selecting a racial description . . . didn't want to offend anybody i.e. – choosing terms such as right/better.'
  6 'Describing myself racially, because in society whiteness is seen as the powerful race, however. . . . I didn't identify this as it could have been seen as being racist.'

On reflection

Looking at the student responses and listening to their comments in the classroom I was reminded of W.E.B. DuBois's regular return to the notion of 'the Veil' where the unspoken privileges of whiteness kept reminding him of his, and others', position within racial hierarchies. What DuBois wrote that resonated so well here was the recognition that where whiteness damages those on its margins it also must do damage to those who are inside. From my vantage point in the classroom, especially at the point of the pregnant pause where the majority of the class who were white were considering themselves racially, I felt able to answer Roediger's (2002) provocative question of 'When did white people become white?' because for this group I felt able to 'see them' *becoming white* (or visible?) that is, they were beginning to see themselves as part of a social group rather than just 'a man' or 'a woman'. I was able to see students acknowledging that they were 'inside', the 'we', the 'powerful', the 'privileged' which itself meant that, in entering this reflexive stage, a position of self-awareness was becoming apparent. The conscious engagement with whiteness challenged the 'hidden curriculum' identified by writers like Schick (2000) and Harrison *et al.* (2004). Harrison *et al.* (2004) posit that a hidden curriculum is made up of 'race'-based biases that emerge from uncritical formal teaching in addition to lessons learnt in the peer and home environment (Shick 2000). For students to start the process of challenge their histories and learning in relation to their relationship with others in a racialised society renders whiteness and their own identities visible as well as their own place in racialised power processes.

There was also some tentative movement for many in the group towards understanding the damage that whiteness was doing to them. In terms of student learning, the responses to the evaluation question in Figure 4.2, 'On reflection what did you learn about yourself (or others like you) having completed this exercise?', the most significant response again was that a third of the students learnt that they found the process of seeing themselves as raced beings a difficult task. However this question allowed students to identify a range of learning targets for the future: hence the ability to identify the need to improve their understanding of the experience of others as they felt that they were beginning to gain an insight into other biographies and other counter-stories from people in the same social space.

Marx and Pennington (2003) reassuringly suggest that a blame culture is unnecessary where individuals begin the process of 'unlearning racism', especially as this process can be wrapped in the inextricable guilt of acknowledging a person's status within a racial hierarchy. They go further to state that this stage of feeling guilt is a natural one that they sought to move past. The concept of 'whiteness as evasion' is symbolic of such a stage met by Marx and Pennington's (2003) pre-service teachers and is likely to be a staging post for further critical self-appraisals. Others identified an improved understanding of the impact of white privilege on society whilst some were simply able to identify that they now know of and are beginning to comprehend this new concept of whiteness. Across all students, 96 per cent acknowledged that they had an improved understanding of whiteness.

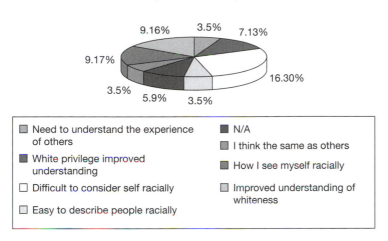

What did you learn about yourself?

9.16%   3.5%   7.13%

9.17%

3.5%

5.9%   3.5%

16.30%

- ▨ Need to understand the experience of others
- ■ White privilege improved understanding
- ☐ Difficult to consider self racially
- ☐ Easy to describe people racially

- ■ N/A
- ▨ I think the same as others
- ▨ How I see myself racially
- ▨ Improved understanding of whiteness

Figure 4.2 What did you learn about yourself? (multiple responses rounded to the nearest 1%

Conclusion

This exercise offered an opportunity for students to talk about whiteness as physiognomy, whiteness as lived experience and whiteness as process and whiteness as contingent. Here whiteness as practices and processes that reinforce racial hegemonies and invisible privileges were rendered visible (Dlamini 2002). It helped to further facilitate an examination of whiteness from students who had at least begun to see themselves as part of a racialised society, therefore challenging dominant paradigms within sport, leisure and physical education where policies are often colour-blind, where talk of 'race' and ethnicity is often 'black' and where 'the white mainstream' is the norm to aspire to. This process was one of discovery, and taken to its natural conclusion for many students it could occur at some personal, professional or emotional cost. Similarly, transplanting ideas from CRT and critical white studies is not likely to be a panacea either, as local circumstances are likely to dictate the nature of any interventions and this is likely to include the social background of the facilitator. In relation to this, Fishman and McCarthy (2005) found that tutors who are not reflexive of their own white biases (or their own blackness) are likely to reinforce racial differences. Fishman, in particular, found that his lack of reflexivity made it difficult for students to interrogate their own biases about 'race' issues. To reinforce this, Dlamini (2002: 52) outlines three predictable biases that may be carried into a classroom and affect the success of critical race pedagogy: (1) seeing antiracist education as a challenge to established teaching practices; (2) a conservative assimilationist Eurocentric starting point, which has been shown to be inadequate over the years; (3) antiracism as a catalyst for racist attitudes and practices.

Reflecting on my own blackness I remember a year when I shared with the equivalent group the feeling I have when a police car pulls up behind me at night, or for that matter what happens when I enter a country pub, in an effort to offer examples of racialised experiences and the white privilege identified in Table 4.1 from Long and Hylton (2002). In one case I told them how I expected to be pulled over because of my experience of the police. The interesting thing was that some students would not accept my version of events and would rather put my feelings down to individual than to collective issues. This is another example of whiteness being defended and resecured; but at the same time encouraging students to examine competing narratives on predicaments they have not lived is likely to add value to their learning: this for me is part of the process of examination and exploration with predominantly white student bodies. Dlamini (2002) argues that this is a process of student denial which she considers, when a person like her as a black woman (or me as a black man) is 'on the other side of the desk', to be teaching those who are privileged about their own power and the difficulties that ensue when these key moments arise. We must not forget, either, the sensitivity that must be practised by academics in not over-privileging our experiences for other forms of learning. The contested nature of our sport and leisure is further reified by a closer analysis of how we experience them both formally and informally. We should not forget the frustrations that can develop in debates about 'race' as identified by Patricia Williams in her Reith Lecture (1997). Williams (1997: 4) was keen to point out that

> Perhaps one reason that conversations about race are so often doomed to frustration is that the notion of whiteness as 'race' is almost never implicated . . . Exnomination permits whites to entertain the notion that race lives 'over there' on the other side of the tracks, in black bodies and inner city neighbourhoods, in a dark netherworld where whites are not involved.

Hytten and Warren (2003) warn us of the risks of reifying attitudes in attempting to engage students in considering whiteness during such seminars. Attempting to disrupt or displace whiteness however has much support, and there is much useful guidance in the literature and amongst colleagues who would argue that student responses like those above are clearly worth the effort. This process for each student represents a different kind of journey as they engage with other relations of power that cannot be subsumed under a racialised one. Gender, class and other intersecting identities need to be immersed in these analyses if we wish to fully acknowledge relations of power and the reification of oppression. For academics considering whiteness the way forward is clear, in so far as being critical of whiteness and its contingencies or a critical race pedagogy is not a 'one size fits all' affair. Rather, whiteness analyses or critical race pedagogy involve bespoke activity from a set of principles that have the potential to facilitate an effective transformatory antiracist politics amongst learners.

Chapter 5

'Race', sport and the media

with Ian Law

Introduction

Sport and its representation through media messages have proved a central site for the reproduction of dominant ideas concerning the racialisation of different groups. It has also been shown that the exposure of racist comments and incidents in sport has been a strong theme in race-related news (Law 2002). This chapter examines how the process works, particularly in relation to the process of racialisation. This is not to discount the significance of forms of anti-racism in sports media messages but to highlight the perpetuation of both overt and subtle forms of racially hostile representation. New evidence drawn from an analysis of two key sports media sources from the UK (*Observer Sport Monthly*) and the USA (*Sports Illustrated*) is analysed to assess the ways in which racialisation occurs. These data, from 2006, show how high-profile sports magazines can reinforce racialised notions of identities, whiteness, myths of difference and newer more subtle forms of enlightened racism to millions of readers across Europe and North America.

When the Greek runner Kostas Kenderis 'won' the Olympic 200 metre sprint in Sydney in 2000, Kevin showed a picture of him crossing the line to a group of sports studies students (see Figure 5.1). In showing them the picture he wanted to see if the students would find it difficult to challenge the myths and the stereotypes that they had grown up with and carried into the lecture theatre. When the image was projected he asked the leading question, 'What is *wrong* with this picture?' In a class of approximately eighty students consensus was reached that 'what was wrong' was that the white sprinter finished ahead of the black sprinters. This process has been repeated a number of times since then with similar results. What does this scenario tell us about how society prepares our young people to see the world? What does it tell us about the media's role in this process? What is the profound effect of the benign acceptance of these myths and stereotypes? Integrated with, and stemming from, this notion of differences between 'racial' groups is a racist media discourse that privileges a dominant white hegemony which perpetuates racial processes and formations in society. Some believe that the mass media deliberately influence their audiences by shaping biased accounts

Figure 5.1 Sydney Olympic Games 2000, 200 metre sprint

founded on a distorted construction of reality (Higgs and Weiller 1994). It could just as easily be argued that the media prepare versions of sport news that will appeal to commercial audiences who are comfortable and 'buy into' their dominant discourses and rhetoric. However, the compound effect of consistent racialised accounts across the media, whether biased, inadvertent or ad hoc, will have an overall impact upon all of us, especially those audiences critical of the media's influence and others whose politics are reinforced by favoured media sources.

It is generally accepted that sport is one domain where black people, so often the underdog, are often depicted as successful, heroic, winners (Campbell 1995). It could also be said that in these potentially neutral spaces ethnic identities are subservient to performances, winning and losing. The global media influence over sport is so powerful that the messages that emerge, from the television to the podcast, help us to understand what is happening in the world a little better than the day before. The reasons for this reside in the significance of sport as a social, cultural and political product of society. Our love for sport is such that often the success of the dominant sports teams can be an indicator of the state of the nation (Marqusee 2005). The significance of our mediated sport has not been lost on our social commentators who have explored this relationship (Hall 1990, Whannel 1992, Campbell 1995).

For most of us our identities have been constructed in a sense by who we think we are and how we think others view us. It is not purely as simple as this, as indicated previously in Chapter 1, in relation to our diversity and the dialectical nature of social processes, but still the media play an influential role in this formation of identities. To be a racialised sportsperson, the media imaginary presents for us images and conceptions that facilitate the categorisation of social groups, phenomena and events on a day-to-day basis. The media are key actors in constructing our ideas about what it means to be a racialised, gendered and classed body in society, and this dialogue is worked, reworked and transformed in the public domain of sport. This was recognised in 1998 when the independent think tank the Runnymede Trust (UK) established a Commission on the Future of Multi-Ethnic Britain and specified sport and the arts in addition to the media and other structural issues as key areas for study. In acknowledging the shifting and subtle nature of 'race' and racism, the Parekh Report, as it became known, concluded that UK media are always likely to be coloured by a dominant discourse acting as a lens from which to interpret our 'realities'. The Report goes on to argue that

> If the larger narrative is racist or more benignly representative of a 95/5 society then the story is likely to be interpreted in a racist or majority biased way, regardless of the conscious intentions of reporters, journalists and head-line writers.
>
> (Parekh Report 2000: 169)

It is a mark of a society and its media that, when the former Manchester United manager and football pundit Ron Atkinson resigned his job with the *Guardian* and also ITV Sport, it was due to his publicly denounced 'off-record' racist slurs on a live link to the Middle East (Howe 2004). Atkinson vented his spleen at the World Cup-winning and French international team captain Marcel Desailly, whom he described as a 'Fxxxing lazy thick nxxxer'. It is also the mark of a con-flicted institution that when Atkinson articulated his mitigation that 'I was responsible for putting Black players in the First Division when other managers wouldn't, so how can I be racist?' his mitigation was not accepted. In relation to Atkinson being part of a football culture there has been much made by cultural studies critics of the place of the media in how 'race', racism and ethnicity are portrayed or even re-presented to the public. Social critics like Darcus Howe (2004) would say that Atkinson's actions are commonplace and that his words were just the tip of the iceberg for football, professional sport and, by that token, the media. Given Atkinson's *faux pas* it is instructive to consider a similar incident explored by Campbell (1995: 60), who cites Ahmed Rashad, a former National Football League player commentator, making an observation about sports announcers:

> If you close your eyes and listen, you can tell whether a commentator is discussing a White or a Black athlete when he [sic] says that somebody is a 'natural', so fluid and graceful, you know he's talking about a Black performer. When you hear that this other guy's a hard worker, or that he comes to play

every day on the strength of guts and intelligence, you know that the player in question is White. Just open your eyes.

(Campbell 1995: 60)

Racism and the portrayal of 'race' in the media have been of some concern in sports studies owing to such explicit and implicit racist practices and policies that do little to tackle the regularity of incidents but, more damagingly, are often uncritical or reflective of the cumulative impact of racialised discourses on those 'reading' sport. Younge (2000) encourages us to read between the lines when we interpret media messages through something as innocuous as sport. The failure of the West Indies cricket team at Headingley in 2000 led Younge (2000) to illustrate how even in sport the politics of subjugation can be recreated. Here he is critical of the media excusing the thrashings meted out to the English team by putting defeat down to their not being able to compete against the natural abilities of the physical West Indians. However, for Younge one of the most enlightening things about these media messages appeared *after* England beat the West Indies. In this surprising turnaround Younge noted how these racialised arguments were demoted and became residual in cricket but transposed and renewed in football, athletics and other areas where there was more conspicuous black success. Younge posits that 'yesterday's "natural" cricketers are today's "natural" footballers . . . the switch is not in their genes but in our society' (Younge 2000: 25).

Younge's analysis locates a point in history where racism morphs not so much in terms of its targets but in context. Brookes (2002) contends that the media have been instrumental in renewing stereotypes based on ideologies of natural differences between socially constructed social groups. Processes of validation and the privileging of dominant ideas legitimate the commonsenseness of physical and psychological abilities and propensities for particular pursuits. Hall (1990) goes further to suggest that these stereotypes, views of a nation, xenophobia and knowledge of the black 'Other', can emerge from an overt racism which still erupts at key moments. Overt racism, encapsulated by Ron Atkinson, embraces openly racist opinions that could be evidenced in much of the early media coverage on black people in sport (Gordon and Rosenberg 1989). In examining this further, Hall (1990) states that the *inferential* racism of the media is worse than its *overt* racism. Hall (1990: 13) describes inferential racism as

Those . . . naturalized representations of events and situations relating to race, whether 'factual' or 'fictional' which have racist premises and propositions inscribed in them as a set of *unquestioned assumptions*. These enable racist statements to be formulated without ever bringing into awareness the racist predicates on which statements are grounded.

(Hall 1990: 13)

Gordon and Rosenberg's (1989) examination of a 1988 *Daily Mail* interview with the former England and Liverpool footballer John Barnes gives a clear indication of how inferential racism works in the media. The racism that Barnes suffered in the Merseyside Derby that year was the focus of the initial part of this article with the rest of the feature intent on arguing that racism was not a problem in Britain. The colour of Barnes's skin in the article was trivialised and equated to having a fat stomach or being different in some other superficial way. As Gordon and Rosenberg would argue, it is difficult to see journalists from this newspaper presenting an article based on the more political reflections of black athletes like Linford Christie, Thierry Henry or Les Ferdinand who have been less reticent or apologetic about their experiences of racism in sport and society. Eleven years after the Barnes interview the *Observer* (1999: 10) headlined one of its sports pages with 'Can White beat Black?' (see Figure 5.2) The piece presented us with an explanation about how the *Australian sports media* had built up the rivalry between *ageing black speed king* Linford Christie and *young white sprinter* Matt Shirvington. The aim of this article was an attempt to answer 'The most explosive question in sport . . . who runs the fastest: Blacks or Whites?' In this case Christie came out of retirement to run this race *because* he was so irritated by the racist premise of the false rivalry and putting his success down to hard work not natural

CAN WHITE BEAT BLACK?

Figure 5.2 Can white beat black?

Shirvington: Built up by the Australian media as the great white hope
Christie: It's not to do with colour, it's about how hard you work

The publisher would like to thank Guardian News and Media group for their permission to reprint title and captions from *The Observer*, and Getty for permission to use both images.

ability. However the *Observer* was keen to present a wealth of 'expertise' from discredited sport scientists who would argue that black sprinters have superiority over white sprinters. Over time black-white rivalry has been nurtured in the media and has not yet been satiated: the recursive nature of this debate means that until it no longer holds interest for the media or their audiences this phenomenon will have longevity. However, the media's role in this racialisation process must not go unquestioned.

We can see that Hall's (1990) analysis of the media is still relevant today even though some scholars have argued that recently the sports media have responded to criticisms and portray black and white athletes in the same light (Sabo *et al.* 1996). They have further argued that the media do not deliberately create a racialised discourse but their messages are a reflection of dominant discourses and hegemonic groups that reveal their racist assumptions 'in heat of the moment slippages' (Bruce 2004: 875). However, western culture is founded on racialised policies and practices, and racism is perpetuated by the (un)conscious support of these practices (Miles 1989). The challenge for media researchers, however, is not in ascertaining how media discourses differ from societal discourses, it is in identifying how and where the racial practices, racist views and hegemonic representations are reproduced and naturalised in the everyday messages created and consumed.

Framing a content analysis

Four categories for the analysis of sport content are outlined below as indicators of how a critical framing of media messages can be established to explore sport texts before being applied to the two sports magazines later in this chapter: (1) racialisation and mediated racial identities; (2) whitecentrism; (3) the myth of difference and mimetic accuracy; and (4) the myth of assimilation and enlightened racism. To examine these assumptions and practices in the media requires a critical interpretative analysis that unmasks invisible and unchallenged ideas that may lay deep below the surface. The protean nature of racism presents a number of challenges in establishing a theoretical framework from which to understand racialisation processes. In Chapter 1 racism was considered as a complex concept that can impact in completely different ways on what could be politically seen as the same social groups. The movement away from racialised groups as monoliths for the diversity of syncretic or hybrid identities has meant that analyses of 'race' in the media must be sensitive to the possibilities of their assumptions underpinning the fundamentals of the 'race' logic or racialisation processes that they aim to challenge (Bruce 2004).

Racialisation and mediated racial identities

Racialisation as outlined in Chapter 1 is a significant process to examine in the media as its many outcomes are often ignored or misunderstood (Law 2002).

However, the sticking point for Law (2002) in any exploration of 'race' in the media is an acceptable definition of racism that acknowledges the particularity of racisms without hindering a working definition for its analysis; Law's conceptualisation of racism in the media is one that essentialises humanities to biological explanations and portrayals. Hence racism here emerges from a concept of 'race' distinguished by 'race' characterising a collective identity; negative biological or cultural attributions associated with that group; boundaries that specify inclusion and exclusion; a variety of explanations from academic and political theses to fragmented viewpoints and representations; made good for many as a worthy lens through which to understand or 'make sense' of the world; and a capacity to privilege and form superficial identities amongst social groups.

Fanon (1986) points out that the black athletic body has become a key repository for contemporary desires, fantasies and fears about blackness. Carrington (2002b) concurs and argues that the photography of black athletes represents these fears and fantasies through the degree to which it has been sexualised, eroticised and transformed into an object of desire and envy. He posits that the black [male] torso is always heavily defined, shot with high-intensity film rendering it open and exposed to inspection (Carrington 2002b). In the same way the female athlete is photographed in such a way that sexualises and subordinates, the black male body is presented in a way that can be admired because it is portrayed as vulnerable and powerless (Mercer 1994). Carrington (2002b) demonstrates how this is achieved: black males are photographed naked or semi-naked, posed in animal-like positions, photographed in close-focus shots that highlight sweat and veins, and denied the opportunity to look into the camera. Throughout the analysis, awareness of these possible themes helps to ascertain dominant hegemonic representation of athletes. Little work has been conducted into the black female experience or portrayal in sport although the writings of Schultz (2005), Eastman and Billings (2002) and Thomas-Coventry (2004) are exceptions that make some headway in exploring these important issues.

Chapter 1 established that 'race' is not fixed and denotes the complex and contradictory nature of social identities and meanings. This view is informed by Hall (1981), whose argument that the meaning of a cultural symbol is produced by the social field it operates within and the practices it incorporates has merit. High-profile athletes within the sports media are important cultural symbols who provide and reproduce meanings (Kellner 1996). Andrews's (1996) analysis of the media coverage of Michael Jordan provides an example of this as he argues that 'Jordan's mediated racial identity is not stable, essential, or consistent; it is dynamic, complex, and contradictory' (Andrews 1996: 126). Similarly, Wilson (1997), like Kellner (1996), underpins her analysis of television and print media coverage of basketball with the concept of the floating racial signifier. She argues that the portrayal of black athletes in her sample are perceived as *good blacks and bad blacks*: good blacks represented in contradiction to traditional stereotypes and *bad blacks* negatively portrayed through stereotypical representations of deviance and lack of discipline. She illustrates how the 'race' of bad blacks was overtly used and how powerful and subtle associations with inner-city gangs, crime and other basketball players are made and yet 'race' is more notably absent from representations of *good blacks*. Kellner's analysis of Jordan's global popularity presents a more delicate and dynamic balance of racialised bodies as he is ostensibly portrayed as a 'good black' even though opportunities are taken to overdetermine his blackness through his penchant for gambling and other alleged nefarious past times. Kellner (1996), Wilson (1997) and Andrews (1996) all conclude that when black athletes are unthreatening and their potential to be a 'dangerous other' is minimal they lose their racial identity and become more universally acceptable.

As Andrews (1996) and Wilson (1997) posit, successful black athletes can be deracialised by the sports media who negate their ethnic background. The visibility of aracial sporting icons like Michael Jordan and footballer Ronaldinho allows society to apply a colour-blind rhetoric which removes white society from accusations of racism; if some black athletes can be successful then there is no societal structure holding others back. Leonard's (2004) media analysis of Kobe Bryant and accusations of rape made against him by a white woman highlights the process of racialisation and deracialisation and the fluid nature of mediated racial identities. Before the accusations, Leonard (2004) argues that the American media viewed Bryant differently from traditional stereotypes of black criminality and commentators located their surprise at his arrest in the context of a presumed difference between Bryant and the rest of the National Basketball Association (NBA). Like Michael Jordan he was seen as aracial, a good guy, an inspirational character for *all* our youngsters. Following the accusations however, Bryant's 'race' was highlighted and used to promote traditional racial stereotypes about black society, and transformed Bryant from the next Michael Jordan to yet another dangerous black 'brute' athlete (Campbell 1995, Lapchick 2000, Leonard 2004). Brookes (2002) also identifies how black sports stars can be seen as 'role models' and deracialised in contradiction to 'bad boys' who more closely resemble traditional stereotypes of the dangerous 'other'. Andrews (1996), Wilson (1997), Brookes (2002) and Leonard (2004) illustrate consistent characteristics of the aracial sporting icon: they are successful and unthreatening, and their potential to be a dangerous 'Other' is minimal. In addition, identifying deracialisation also involves checking for when the 'Other' is associated with whiteness, as well as when they are consciously disassociated from racial identities and groups.

A further theme to consider during this type of analysis is the relationship between racial representation and national identity. Cosgrove and Bruce (2005: 338) analyse how the New Zealand sailor Sir Peter Blake's death was covered by the print media, arguing that he was promoted to national hero in ways that obscured any racial dimensions. Using Blake as an expression of national identity allowed the media to reframe whiteness as superior and desirable, and the 'Other' as subordinate – just as Ben Johnson's rise and fall were analogous to his raised Canadian national status that quickly became residual to his Jamaican immigrant status after his demise through subsequent doping convictions (Jackson *et al.*

1998). Carrington (2004a) also identifies the close relationship between racial representation and national identity. Eric Moussambani's swim in the Sydney 2000 Olympic Games made him a universal representative for Black Africans, and allowed a 'reframing of the West's knowledge of the African other' in a way that Eddie the Eagle's hapless ski jumping was not reduced to biology (Carrington 2004a: 90). This was established by highlighting the differences between Moussambani and a normalised, unquestioned whiteness. Carrington (2004a) points out that Moussambani was referred to as 'the African', yet the laughable British ski jumper 'Eddie the Eagle' was never referred to as 'European'. When more successful black athletes are celebrated for their ability their promotion to national icon is often not forthcoming (Whannel 1992, Jackson 1998). Examining two sports magazines below we consider how national identity reinforces or obscures racial identities as part of a (de)racialisation process. The content analysis also identifies where successful black athletes are portrayed in relationship to national identity and whether this obscures their racial identity, and below we also consider how national identities have been used to reinforce dominant racial identities.

Whitecentrism

Law's (2002) media analysis framework draws on the work of Dyer (1997) and Gabriel (1998), who argue that there are a huge range of representations of whiteness commonly found in narrative structural positions and habits of perceptions as opposed to stereotypes. The implications of these ideas have their roots in the notion of racial hierarchies and the perceived location of individuals and groups reinforced through the narrative turn of media commentators. Gabriel (1998) refers to this as a reassertion of whiteness which ultimately maintains traditions and identities. The media play a central role in reaffirming white privilege and power in sport and society. Whiteness can be seen as a location of structural advantage or a way to see self and others (Frankenberg 2004). As considered in Chapter 4, whiteness can be viewed as an elaboration of unmarked and unnamed cultural practices and identities that can be seen as normal and invisible, and has no inherent but only socially constructed meanings (Long and Hylton 2002).

The analysis of whiteness in the media for this content analysis takes two forms (1) identifying whiteness that carries power and superiority and (2) uncovering the invisible whiteness that the racialised 'other' is marked against. The concepts of whitecentrism and Eurocentrism were originally separated by Law in his analysis of 'race' and the media (2002) but for the benefit of this study it is useful to marry them in one category for analysis. The process of privileging social groups because of perceived superior hegemonic cultural norms or whiteness is embraced under this heading. Underlying colonialist voices emerge here through a xenophobic Eurocentrism that merges with the positioning and privileging of whiteness in the media. Although Eurocentrism does not necessarily have a specific focus on whiteness processes, there is enough common ground in the repertoires of Eurocentrism and whiteness processes as they reify racial categories that regularly privilege whiteness over Others. In summary a critical whiteness analysis appears to identify powerful processes that privilege white voices, images or imagined communities whereas a critical approach to Eurocentrism identifies how power and the deficiency of the Other are embedded in all language; there is a close fit between the concept of whitecentrism and Eurocentrism. Shohat and Stam's (1994) understanding of Eurocentrism is very similar to other scholars' understanding of whitecentrism – it is an implicit positioning of domination. This content analysis considers how this domination is embedded in two sports magazines. Shohat and Stam's (1994) work has helped generate triggers of potential themes to be aware of: the dichotomous use of 'us' and 'them', the deficiency of the 'Other' who is presented in ways that oppose traditional Eurocentric white culture, and how hybrid identities recentre whiteness as the hegemonic group. Throughout this analysis consistent aspects of a hegemonic representation of a white majority emerge.

The myth of difference and mimetic accuracy

Campbell (1995) identifies a number of commonsense myths in media news that he merges into three broad categories and uses as a framework for media analysis: myth of marginality, myth of difference, and myth of assimilation. The basis for this section of the analysis of the two sports magazines centres on Campbell's (1995) framework for the myth of difference, and Law's (2002) concept of mimetic accuracy. On the basis of the work of Lévi-Strauss, Barthes, and Fiske, Campbell (1995: 14) provides a convincing argument for a more encompassing definition of 'myths'. He analyses cultural myths in semiotic terms, interpreting them as 'meaning-making systems that help explain societal attitudes, behaviours and ideologies'. Contemporary mythology about 'race', argues Campbell (1995: 15), contributes to the social order and has a significant role in belief formation in society. The mimetic accuracy that Law (2002) outlines considers how myths are generated when he explored the instrumental or exaggerated positioning of real life events portrayed as common, normal or typical of a social group. The first part of this category's focus involves identifying consistent patterns of mimetic representations that relate to race logic stereotypes, cultural stereotypes, the dangerous 'Other', and Hall's (1990) base images of 'race'.

The most researched stereotype in the sports media is that of black (male) physicality or athleticism. The success of black people in sport is explained by a commonsense assumption that the black athletes are better, because they are genetically different and physically superior to white athletes (Hoberman 1997, Younge 2000, Carrington and McDonald 2001, St Louis 2004). Genetically predisposed qualities like speed, strength and athletic ability are used to explain black sporting success, and this stereotype devalues black sporting achievement, and consoles the white athlete because they need to work harder to overcome this genetic deficiency (McCarthy and Jones 1997, McCarthy, Jones and Potrac

2003). Bizarrely, the covert suggestion is that white athletes are still superior, because the sporting successes they achieve are valued more highly, owing to the supposed natural disadvantage they have had to overcome (Younge 2000, Denham *et al.* 2002). Mercer (1994: 178) describes this stereotype as the most commonplace of all stereotypes: 'the black [man] as sports hero, mythologically endowed with a "naturally" muscular physique and an essential capacity for strength, grace and machinelike perfection'. Research into the covert reproduction of this stereotype has used quantitative content analysis methods to code the physical and cognitive descriptors of athletes. McCarthy and Jones (1997), Eastman and Billings (2001, 2002) and Rada and Wulfemeyer (2005) used this method to analyse television commentary and discovered that the stereotypes of black athleticism and white superior intellectual and cognitive qualities were reproduced. Denham *et al.* (2002), McCarthy *et al.* (2003) and Billings's (2004) similar analyses on the televised sports media support this research in demonstrating the reproduction of the black athleticism stereotype. Murrell and Curtis's (1994) analysis of the US print media indicates that the performance of black athletes was attributed to natural ability, and the performance of white quarterbacks was due to hard work, even if their sample was limited. Hardin *et al.* (2004) also investigated the print media when they analysed eight hundred photographs of US Olympic athletes, and they argue that black athletes are over-portrayed in strength sports, and white athletes overrepresented in aesthetic sports. Sabo *et al.* (1996) and Staurowsky's (2006) analysis of televised sports coverage in the US reveal how Asian and indigenous American athletes were unfairly framed in ways that drew on stereotypical descriptions as stoic conformists, excessively hard workers or profoundly inferior. The content analysis here considers the extent to which the racialised 'Other' is portrayed in relation to patterns of representation and historical stereotypes about culture.

The myth of assimilation and enlightened racism

Campbell's (1995) media analysis focuses heavily on the myth of assimilation and how it relates to enlightened racism. He suggests that by presenting the fictional or non-fictional success of black people the media can create an image that racism is a thing of the past and not a factor in stopping the majority of black people achieving similar success. He argues that the commonsense understandings of black people portrayed by the media 'serve to augment the notions of enlightened racism. White Americans can smugly argue that racial prejudice and discrimination are things of the past and point to successful African Americans as proof. But this is mythological thinking – the myth of assimilation.' Although Jhally and Lewis (1992) use the Cosby Show as an example of this, there are other examples across nations where the same can be said. They conclude that white viewers point to the social and economic success of a limited number of minorities in arguing that racism is not a factor in Others achieving success (Jhally and Lewis 1992: 110). McKay (1995) adapts this concept in her analysis of advertisements by multinational sports companies Nike, Puma and Reebok where the advertisements enable white audiences to deny the existence of institutional racism in sport or society because they mythologise individualism and meritocracy. Although not explicitly using the term 'enlightened racism', Juffer's (2002) analysis of the media coverage of Latino baseball players in the US contains similar underpinning arguments. She suggests that 'media coverage at times nostalgic for a more bounded sense of home and nation often emphasizes players' individual mobility, erasing the economic and political conditions that have brought Latin American players to the United States' (Juffer 2002: 337).

To analyse enlightened racism and the myth of assimilation, a content analysis should be cognisant of themes such as perceived levels of agency; trivialisation of social structures; colour-blindness; and the politics of racism. The visibility of black media analysts in the media portrays a message that the media fairly represents black and white athletes across their range of opportunities: for example how can a television station be racist if black ex-athletes are in the studio? Davis and Harris (1998) argue that despite black athletic dominance there is a disproportionate lack of black people working in the media. Thomas-Coventry (2004) discovered that black people who occupy media positions usually do so as studio analysts or competition-level reporters; and they are least likely to work as the play-by-play commentator or presenter. Although the analyst requires expertise, his or her position is peripheral, whereas the presenter and commentator occupy central positions and their narrative emits more authenticity and reliability (Thomas-Coventry 2004). Recently in the UK however there has been an increase in visible black media analysts, particularly on the BBC. A variety of black analysts are used (Efan Ekoku, Carlton Palmer, Ian Wright, Ruud Gullit, Leonardo); however it is interesting that the only black presenter – John Barnes – was removed from his presenting role and given a peripheral pitch-side analyst role. The few famous black former players and coaches who have become analysts and reporters also give viewers the impression that black people occupy a substantial number of jobs in the sports media industry (Eitzen and Sage 2003). This positioning of black people in the media can act as a token presence, portraying the appearance of opportunity, but not actually challenging the privileged status of those with power and influence in the institution (Murray 1998).

Jhally and Lewis (1992) base the term 'enlightened racism' on the subtle everyday practices by which the success or failure of African Americans was attributed to their ability or inability to take advantage of the American Dream. Similarly, Wilson (1997) identifies that, when black athletes are successful, their portrayal in the media reinforces the idea that they have made the right individual choices in taking advantage of opportunities. The media's culpability in this myth is clear for a number of writers (Jhally and Lewis 1992, Campbell 1995, Wilson 1997). This media analysis seeks to identify whether this individualism and invisibility of structure is prominent within the *Observer Sport Monthly* and *Sports Illustrated*. With a view to highlighting how media messages can contribute to a process of racialisation, whitecentrism, myths of difference and newer more subtle forms of enlightened racism, it is to an analysis of two significant representatives of the sports media in Europe (*Observer Sport Monthly*) and North America (*Sports Illustrated*) that we now turn.

Case studies: *Observer Sport Monthly* and *Sports Illustrated*

Observer Sport Monthly (OSM) was chosen as one of the sports papers in an analysis of sports news, partly because it was named for the second time as the best magazine at the sports industry awards in 2006. It has also been consistently praised by judges for its quality and range of sports coverage. OSM is a monthly publication issued with one of the major UK quality national Sundays, *The Observer*, which has an average readership of nearly 1.5 million. Part of the Guardian News and Media Group, the sports industry awards argue that *The Observer Sport Monthly* offers the finest sports writing and photography in Europe. Although OSM is a very popular sports magazine in the UK, its equivalent magazine in North America operates on a larger scale. *Sports Illustrated* (SI) was established in 1954 and is published by Time Inc.; its readership in 2008 was 21 million (Time Warner 2008). SI is a weekly sports magazine and therefore we chose issues near the first Sunday of every month to ensure a balance of content with OSM.

Because of SI's longevity and popularity in North America it has a higher profile and has attracted more attention than OSM, some wanted and some unwanted. In the recent past King *et al.* (2002) were extremely critical of a seven-page SI article concerning the use of indigenous American names and symbols in sport entitled 'The Indian wars'. They list a series of criticisms of the article and the problems of such inaccurate and inappropriate journalism, arguing that the article contains pronounced bias, misuses polling and representations of opinion, and decontextualises indigenous American sports mascots and the controversy surrounding them, leaving the impression on the audience that they are unproblematic (King *et al.* 2002). The authors argue that

> At a visual level, readers confront stereotype upon stereotype before the reporting begins . . . who would dare to point to the missing facts associated with the polling method, the bias of the SI article itself, or the more significant fact of white supremacy and privilege at the core of these images.
>
> (King *et al.* 2002: 383–4)

Conversely, SI publishes content that contradicts the position criticised by King *et al.*; for example writers such as Dyson *et al.* (2003) present an antiracist commentary on the sports media. Dyson *et al.* demonstrate how racism is ingrained within US sport by deploring the racist comments made on the American cable network Entertainment and Sports Programming Network (ESPN) by Rush Limbaugh, who suggested that black quarterbacks are overrated by the media *because they are black*, before commenting on how sport remains as racist as it ever was. These contradictions are considered further as the analysis of both magazines is conducted over the 2006 period.

Although there are journalistic differences in the style and presentation of each publication there remain consistencies that to varying degrees give some credence to the four themes outlined above. The number of magazines in each case meant that some of the themes outlined had a relatively low incidence (OSM no. = 12, SI no. = 12). A low presence or pattern should not dissuade the reader from the impact that one racist occurrence has on public perceptions as a result of the compound effect of similar such articles and discourses across the media and in wider society. Overall OSM tends to reflect a more studied and rounded style of writing, with more balance and depth than *SI*. *SI* articles tended to be shorter, with a greater use of statistics and data dissemination. The magazines differed also in their range of topics as *SI* had a consistent North American sport focus where the OSM was more willing to include athletes and sports in different countries.

Racialisation and mediated racial identities

A reading of the two magazines illustrates how the racialised 'Other' seems not to be a wholly valid member of a predominantly 'White/coloniser nation' and how two approaches were consistently used to do this devaluing. Some athletes were disassociated from their country as the reader was more likely to be told of the country of their familial origin than the one they represented. For example former England international Cyril Regis was referred to as French Guiana-born (OSM, January: 66). Regis was the only black player with four other players featured in a nostalgic look at Coventry City FC, and the only player with his country of origin identified. Similar occurrences appeared in the OSM in relation to heroes of French rugby, as Serge Betson was described as 'Cameroon-born' (OSM, February: 50); Serge Blanco's Venezuelan roots were highlighted (OSM, February: 51); Jonah Lomu, one of the most famous New Zealand rugby players, had his Tongan descent clarified for the reader (OSM, May: 77); and the US football player who scored the winning goal against England in 1950 is the 'Haiti born striker' Joe Gaetjens (OSM, July: 6). The significance of the roots of the Other being made clear is tantamount to stating that their identities are not redolent of the host nation but of an alien one instead. This pattern is what Gilroy (1987) identified as an alienating process in the identity formation of black people. The process of inclusion and exclusion is subtle but still active and effective in the way a disassociation process takes place in *SI*.

SI used the device of disassociation to link athletes to Other national identities. For example in the February 2006 issue, a Canadian Olympic bobsleigher is the 'Jamaican native Brown' (SI, February: 92); after winning a silver medal, Canadian Laselles Brown is described as 'a laid back Jamaican' (SI, February: 49); July's magazine is very explicit in its description of the runner Bernard Lagat the 'Kenyan who became a US citizen' (SI, July: 28). Similarly, June's preview of the

World Cup discusses four of America's most promising players . . . is it possible to spot the odd one out?

> Landon Donavon, a shy, lightning-quick forward, had grown up speaking Spanish with his Latino team-mates on the soccer fields of Southern California. DaMarcus Beasley, a gregarious African-American midfielder, had turned his back on basketball in hoops-mad Fort Wayne, Indiana, Oguchi Inyewu, a hulking defender from the suburbs of Washington D.C., was the son of Nigerian immigrants. And Bobby Convey, a flashy midfielder, had followed his sister, Kelly, a former All-American at Penn State, into the sport.

Convey stands out here because of the implicit status he holds as a white American. What is unquestioned here is Convey's Americanness, whereas the other players whose families are seemingly more recent arrivals to the US are more ambiguous in their location as 'American players'; a different reading of their position would be to interpret them as 'incomers', imposters or even mercenaries.

The second approach identified in the examination of the two sports magazines was a consistent hybridisation (or hyphenation) of athlete identities. The boxer Amir Khan is 'British-Muslim-Pakistani' (OSM, February: 23) whilst the cricketer Monty Panesar is a 'British-Indian' or 'British-Sikh' (OSM, November: 34). This phenomenon was evident also in the use of religion as a signifier of the racialised 'Other'. In both sports magazines the bifurcation of black and white athletes is consistent: even where athletes came from different countries the thread that linked them was often language using a crude racial reductionism in relation to nationality, ethnicity or culture. A cursory glance at the dominant descriptors for athletes in OSM demonstrates that white athletes are more likely to be described in relation to their Britishness (28 per cent), Europeanness (42 per cent) or other predominantly white nationality category (11 per cent) (see Table 5.1). (The figure of 28 per cent is inclusive of three categories (British, Welsh/Scottish/Irish, and English); the figure of 11 per cent is inclusive of the categories Other 'white nation' and white.)

It can be argued that this hybridisation of athletes recognises diversity and acknowledges differences and positively reinforces individual identities in a way that respects cultural heritage and national patronage. Where this is not done so thoughtfully with Other athletes, this hybridisation process is less positive owing to the privileging of national, ethnic or cultural labels or associations that have a racialising effect on the subject of the discussions, thus establishing a pattern or discourse to frame the context of each athlete. Exploring the SI content there was a similar set of descriptors although there was a more enthusiastic nationalistic centring of America in this magazine as an important identifier of the 'included' (17 per cent) (see Table 5.1).

European links were highly significant for white American athletes (56 per cent), and non-European but predominantly white nations were linked to 17 per

Table 5.1 Observer Sport Monthly and *Sports Illustrated* white athlete portrayals, number and (%)

Observer Sport Monthly			Sports Illustrated		
Other European nation	84	(41.8)	European nation	37	(56.1)
American	24	(11.9)	American	11	(16.7)
British	22	(10.9)			
Welsh/Scottish/Irish	18	(9.0)			
English	17	(8.5)			
Other 'white nation' (SA, NZ, Aus)	16	8.0	Other 'white nation' (SA, NZ, Aus)	11	(16.7)
Non-white nation	9	(4.5)	'Non-white' nation	7	(10.6)
Religious group	6	(3.0)	Religious group	0	(0.0)
White	5	(2.5)	White	0	(0.0)
Total	201	100	*Total*	66	100

cent of the athletes. In both magazines white athletes had a relatively low chance of a link being established with an Asian or African heritage as reporters chose to associate or disassociate athletes in a way that reinforced their insider or outsider status (OSM 4.5 per cent and SI 10.6 per cent – see Table 5.1). The context to the association or disassociation with a nation state, continent or imagined community can be further explained where reference is made to black athletes in the OSM and SI. A look at Table 5.2 indicates that in OSM about 12 per cent of the references to black athletes emphasised their Britishness in comparison to the 28 per cent for white athletes in Table 5.1, while white athletes were twice more likely to have their Britishness emphasised than black athletes. (The figure of 12.2 per cent is inclusive of the categories British Muslim, British Indian/Pakistani, English and British.)

Further there were less than 1 per cent of references associating black athletes to other European nations in comparison to about 42 per cent for white athletes (OSM). In Table 5.2 the pattern for SI was similar to that for OSM, as links to nations or continents perceived as black (African-American/Asian/Latin) for black athletes made up about 86 per cent of references in comparison to about 11 per cent for white athletes. As in the earlier case with OSM, white American athletes (17 per cent) were twice as likely as black athletes (8 per cent) to have their nationality emphasised. (The figure of 86 per cent is inclusive of the categories Asian country, African American, African country and black.)

Table 5.2 Observer Sport Monthly and *Sports Illustrated* black athlete
portrayals, number and (%)

Observer Sport Monthly			Sports Illustrated		
Non-white nation	55	(44.7)	Asian country	9	(25.0)
Religious group	15	(12.2)	African American	8	(22.2)
Asian	13	(10.6)	African country	7	(19.4)
Black	11	(8.9)	Black	7	(19.4)
British Muslim	7	(5.7)	American	3	(8.3)
African	5	(4.1)	Religion	1	(2.8)
British Indian/Pakistani	5	(4.1)	White nation	1	(2.8)
American	4	(3.3)			
African American	3	(2.4)			
English	2	(1.6)			
British	1	(0.8)			
Other European nation	1	(0.8)			
Other white nation (SA, NZ, Aus)	1	(0.8)			
Welsh/Scottish/Irish	0	0.0			
Total	123	100	*Total*	36	100

Whitecentrism

The second category for this analysis shows evidence of both magazines reinforcing racialised relations through the centring of the hegemonic white voice and
the privileging of whiteness. The privilege of being white in *SI* ultimately meant
that athletes were not linked with crime, drugs, physicality or educational failings.
In short white players were rarely presented as a problem or criminalised. This
constant repositioning of the status of whiteness tweaks the readers' views of the
'good', the 'bad' and the 'ugly'. Stereotypes are confirmed and egos satiated. *SI*
was highly Americancentric, and as a result a rereading of the magazine would
result in identifying a racial hierarchy in American sport that would see American
identity as central and beyond that American whiteness and then various shades
of American black culture. A number of countries are criticised in a derogatory
way that reinforces national stereotypes, imperialist or colonial legacies and racist
undertones. For example Germany's superior medal count to America at the
Winter Olympics is considered thus: 'it's as though the Germans are some sort of
perfect beings. Almost genetically superior in some respects. But I'm sure they
won't do anything with that knowledge' (*SI*, March: 18). Here hints of Nazism,
master races and Germany's nefarious past are dredged to reposition the might of

the US and those marked as American in a positive way. Similarly, in the Winter Olympics, *SI* suggests that Swedish success in the ice hockey was rigged and relied heavily on luck, it concludes that 'back home, Big Brother was watching' (*SI*, March: 47). The message the magazine portrays is that being American is not only desirable but the only acceptable identity. This makes the disassociation of black American athletes and their reassigned 'alternative national identity' even more pertinent.

In OSM there are particular aspects of articles that reassert an ideal hegemonic whiteness that suggests that to be British it is important to accept that all things 'imagined' as such must be assimilated and integrated to enhance tradition, culture and national identity. A feature on the boxer Amir Khan (OSM, February: 18–26) promotes him as an ideal type of Asian heritage citizen when it isolates Khan as an example of what Asians can be but are not 'The Khans are a British-Muslim-Pakistani family who are also "salt-of-the-earth" Lancashire. They are the perfect new fusion, exactly the blend *we* need' (emphasis added) (23). The obsession of idealising certain athletes as a way of demonstrating what British Muslims can achieve is continued in the August issue (48–51). The article, entitled 'Family affairs', is an occasional series into the home life of athletes. Amir Khan and cricketer Sajid Mahmood are portrayed as having and representing perfect British-Muslim families; the underlying message is again that 'this is what you should be like to fit in' as cultural markers of Asianness are diluted for commonly accepted signifiers of Britishness. Religious references become a large part of the way the Other is represented. Articles about Amir Khan and the Indian tennis player Sania Mirza (February: 54–61) are used to focus on religion and portray Islam and Asians as underdeveloped, extremist or old-fashioned in relation to British culture.

In July the feature article on the cricketer Imran Khan asks the question 'who should British Pakistanis, born and bred here, support, Pakistan or England?' (OSM, July: 22). Asking this question assumes that this is an inoffensive, innocuous question and that there are divergent views and perhaps a correct answer. However, there are also inconsistencies in the presentation of such issues in the OSM, which suggests that the OSM is not conscious of some of the messages emerging from its pages. The February issue (23) explores the complexities of multiethnic Britons who find the situational shift in identities from place of birth, family heritage, country represented and other variables a dynamic (and commonsense) development in the identity formation of multifaceted individuals, which of course usurp narrow, dogmatic nationalistic viewpoints. This more fluid reflection of a postmodern world is at odds with some of OSM's features. These inconsistencies litter the sports media and must constitute part of the explanatory landscape for any analysis of racialisation and the media.

The myth of difference and mimetic accuracy

Although there are contradictions, *SI* consistently reiterates stereotypes of black athleticism, white work ethics and psychological distinctions reinforcing the basic dualism underpinning a commonsense 'race' logic (St Louis, 2004). The stereotype of black physicality is also reproduced in OSM; however it is at worst inconsistent and at best inadvertent as regular inconsistencies in messages emerge. Where it could be evidenced that athletes were being reduced to mythical racial characteristics, others would argue something different. A piece on twelve young British athletes tipped to win medals at the 2012 Olympics (OSM, January: 30–41) outlines the hard work, commitment and willingness to make sacrifices that these athletes have to make to take them to Olympic medals. For Harry Aikines-Aryeetey, the black sprinter, the reader is offered a trivial quote about his hair, and his coach's comments 'we just need to develop his technique and keep him injury free', implying that he is a natural athlete who does not necessarily need to work hard for his success. In March the former Scottish sprinter Alan Wells compounds this stereotype that reinforces difference when he reflects on winning the 100 metres gold at the 1980 Olympics. Wells posits that he doubts that another white sprinter will ever equal his achievement in winning an Olympic 100 metres: 'Given a good black guy and a good white one, the black guy will always come in front because, basically, black athletes have an inherent natural ability, even if they're not all equal in that sense' (OSM, March: 55). As a sprinter with an Olympic gold medal, Alan Wells's voice has kudos and reflects that of the (White) institution, therefore carrying huge authority. When ex-athletes make such statements as insiders they bring a validity or spurious truth that adds to the myth of difference and stereotypes that reinforce racial processes and formations. The October issue (74) displays a photograph of the 'first Olympic final contested solely by black athletes', further exaggerating and reinforcing the message that sprinting is natural for black people and reaffirming Law's (2002) observations of mimetic accuracy in the media. The observation in a special issue on China that the five people who have gone under 13 seconds for the 110m hurdles 'are all black' (OSM, October: 52) apart from Chinese sprinter Liu who is 'our superman' (52) validates Wells's claim. Reading the message here it can be concluded that the only athlete able to compete with the black sprinters has to be extraordinary, a 'superman'. It must be reiterated that there were other articles similarly mentioning white athletes' lack of commitment and others featuring the mental abilities of Tiger Woods, Ronaldinho, Amir Khan, Monty Panesar and Imran Khan which sets them out and above their rivals. It remains to be seen if positive messages like these have the ability to counteract the excesses of the racialised coverage seen above.

Racialisation and mediated racial identities, whitecentrism and mimetic representations lead us to a more critical context for the myth of the 'dangerous Other'. From reading *SI* there would be no doubt that black people are significantly more dangerous and criminal than white people. Black athletes are consistently linked to crime and drugs. Fundamentally articles about black deviance appear randomly and therefore have an aggregate, compound effect; not once is a white person linked to crime or drugs. The lexical analysis of Table 5.3 summarises some of the commentary on black criminality in the magazine. To make sure the reader is in no doubt who is committing the crimes there is generally an accompanying photograph. There is no argument that these athletes have actually been in trouble with the law or even arrested but the decision to focus solely on black athletes illustrates the privilege that whiteness extends to white athletes. Black athletes are used to frame black society in a further example of mimetic accuracy, as deviant and dangerous. In these articles the 'race' of an athlete is not explicitly used in the text; instead the symbol is the photograph that accompanies the text. Because these events actually happened, are presented as 'facts' with little or no interpretation, they are near impossible for a reader to contend or ignore. Again, the approach that *SI* takes and its decision on what to include and exclude in the magazine is instructive. In *OSM* Leon and Michael Spinks are consistently linked to drugs and inner city street gangs in America during their childhood (*OSM*, March: 34–8), Chris Eubank 'moved to the Bronx' (May: 4), Asafa Powell is linked to gun crime (July: 36), Zidane is 'the hero of the lawless suburbs' (December: 39). This is definitely not an exclusive way to frame the racialised

Table 5.3 Black criminality in *Sports Illustrated*

Maurice Clarett's *arrest* and consequent missing of the Ohio State Championship. (Jan.: 21)

Andray Blatche - although no evidence or charges are against him, he is linked to *gun crime and car-jacking*. (Feb.: 110)

Marcus Vick - linked with *gun crime and poor discipline*. (March: 75)

The brother of Tyrone Carter is *imprisoned for 5 years* (to put this in perspective Tyrone Carter is not even a professional.) (April: 24)

Gilbert Arenas: '3 weeks after SI cover guy got booted from the playoffs, he *got arrested for disobeying police*'. (June: 30)

Hollywood Henderson - 'the former wild man struck lottery gold but beat even bigger odds by overcoming his *drug habit*'. (July: 122)

Michael Ray Robinson - '*Drugs* derailed a potential hall of fame career'. (July: 128)

An article writes 'at least 25 players on 17 of the league's 32 [NFL] teams had *brushes with the law*' - the accompanying photos are of five black players. (Aug.: 24)

Ramonce Taylor - '*charged with felony possession of Marijuana* in May'. (Sept.: 62)

'Most of what Kansas city heard about Johnson before this season was bad news. He was *charged twice with assault*'. (Sept.: 96)

Other – there are only isolated examples in OSM – however it is the childhood of these athletes that is used because they differ from an imagined or ideal white middle-class upbringing. As with SI, no white athlete was linked to gangs or crime. These unnecessary references to upbringing and family reinforce a deviant Other that is different and therefore subjugating as a result of any combination of racism, historical imperialism and xenophobia.

Similarly, in OSM an analysis of teams in the 2006 football World Cup incorporated a category used to highlight 'loose cannons' in specific teams. The only two white players out of the twelve teams are the Portuguese team and Gattuso of Italy. Table 5.4 illustrates how through using uncritical racialised descriptors OSM perpetuate racial processes. The myths and stereotypes of players from a massive range of backgrounds are signified in the use of the text italicised. In the article the Otherness of racialised players and teams is reinforced in a light-hearted and relatively non-threatening way that many will see as humorous and inoffensive. The underlying message likely to be imparted to readers is that the racialised Other at the World Cup is the player or team most likely to be emotionally fragile, mentally weak, deviant or unreliable.

The way whiteness and blackness are depicted can be illustrated further using the example of two ex-players profiled in the July issue of SI (see Figure 5.3). The first athletes interviewed in July's feature on 'Where are they now?' highlight the subtle differences between how the black and white person is allowed to be represented. An article on Lawrence Taylor consistently refers back to a previous drug habit (SI, July: 84–9):

Table 5.4 Racialised players in the World Cup (*Observer Sport Monthly*, June 2006)

Ecuador's Ivan Kaviedes 'famous for his temper . . . dropped by club and country for *indiscipline*' (45)

England's black defender Sol Campbell '*fragile mind-set*' (46)

Sweden's black forward Zlatan Ibrahimovich 'talented but unpredictable . . . half ballerina, half *gangsta*' (47)

Paraguay's black forward Nelson Cuevas (47)

Holland's '*tendency to implode*' (49) which is illustrated by the example of their black midfielder Edgar David's '*unpredictability*' (49)

Yamba Asha 'the Angolan *bad boy*' (51)

Iran's Ali Karimi and his '*volatile* streak' (51)

Ghana's Michael Essien and his '*over-exuberance* in the tackle' (55)

Brazil's black striker Adriano (56)

Togo's black striker Adebayor (59)

Portugal's '*lack of self-discipline*' (50) and Gattuso of Italy (54).

The Giants great who terrorized quarterbacks and battled a cocaine habit, his dark days chasing drugs and hookers, wrecking cars, drug arrests and stints in rehab . . . In the new millennium Taylor has taken the time and energy he used to put into scoring crack, plus the competitiveness and compulsiveness that made him the most feared defensive player of his era, and funnelled it all into his golf game.

The revelation that Taylor put his time and energy into drugs and not football suggests a further lack of professionalism. In comparison to the second athlete, Greg Norman (90–7), Taylor has still been extremely successful in business since retiring from sport. The article on Taylor consistently references his drug habit and gives the impression that he spends all day every day gambling while playing golf. There is no reference to the hard work he must put in to become successful in business. Norman however is presented with no aspersions on his character and is unchallenged as a hard worker, shrewd businessman and pillar of the community.

The myth of assimilation and enlightened racism

Previous references to Asian athletes in this chapter have heightened awareness of the myth of the assimilation imperative evidenced in OSM. Assimilation is an ideal to be striven for by new communities, and there are families such as the Khans and the Mahmoods working towards this 'integration' into their host communities. The myth of black success, fallen structural hurdles and assimilation into a host society has been clearly played out in OSM but less so in SI. However an interesting example of enlightened racism can be explored further in SI.

In July 2006 SI printed an article and a letter that presented racism as a problem that black people benefit from and seek to perpetuate where they can make personal gains. Two articles about the 'race card' give the impression that black people will use racism or a collective sense of subjugation as a way to gain an advantage in business. Although the article presents real issues from real cases, its backdrop is that it is printed in a sports magazine that considers racism in an ad hoc way and so the magazine's position on these issues is ambiguous. So in this case without any context to the professions under investigation or the story itself the reader is presented with 'Brother Beware, eagerly playing the race card, a few unscrupulous black financial advisers are hurting athlete-clients and legit minority businesses . . . this brand of black on black crime has victims beyond the ripped-off athletes' (SI, April: 20). The impression the article leaves is that black people are fully assimilated into US society and can forge successful careers without such aggressive or radical strategies – if they work hard they can succeed on their own merits. It further suggests that it is wrong for black people to use their collective experiences, backgrounds or social networks to gain a collective advantage. These messages are unproblematically stated as though these techniques are not already used by those who dominate sport business.

At one extreme this could be read from a covert enlightened racism perspective, as no real effort has been made to understand the wider context of employment issues, practices and patterns on racial or ethnic lines in the profession. This 'enlightened' view is likely to encourage readers' letters that reinforce these insider critiques. In the November issue of *SI* a letter forcefully argues that 'As a black man I am infuriated that, once again, some people are playing the race card to excuse bad behaviour' (*SI*, November: 12). Written by a black person, the letter achieves a number of things for the editors: (1) it confirms that black people argue that racism is present where there is none and that black people know it; (2) some black people succeed on their merits and do not choose to use the 'race' card and others use scare tactics (the 'race' card) to get their way; and (3) racism in society is not as bad as black people argue or they would not be using racism as an *excuse* in the first place! The decision to print the article and the letter leaves readers to make their own mind up about the issue. Some readers will attempt to understand the complexities of the two articles while others will accept the simple points and simple messages which add to their other 'enlightened' or assimilationist ideas about 'race' and racism. The approach that *SI* takes on these issues and the silence of alternative voices suggests that racism is a problem that impacts us all equally. This process supports the hegemonic whiteness considered in the earlier section as the commonsense majority voice is presented while the alternative challenging views of others are ignored.

Conclusion

The analysis of *Sports Illustrated* and the *Observer Sport Monthly* in 2006 illustrates the contradictions, ambiguities and ambivalence of media discourses previously considered in the analyses of Campbell (1995) and Law (2002). This examination of arguably the two highest-profile sports magazines in Europe and the United States provides further evidence of racialisation and its impact on identities, whitecentrism, difference and mimetic accuracy, and enlightened racism in the media. Power processes were revealed through who portrayed racialised entities and the nature of and balance of the representation, which consequently reinforced the location of social groups within racial hierarchies. The processes of association, disassociation and attribution and the power to echo these Othering discourses were commonplace across both magazines. The tendency to estrange athletes from their country was a practice that developed into a pattern too comfortably. Family origin was often the default association for those disassociated from their country of representation although Other nations were not beyond derogation. It is to these new cultural turns that we see racism and xenophobia reinventing and reinvigorating their discourse in such a matter-of-fact way that opposition to these devices may seem churlish to some. Should it be forgotten, we reiterate that this was not the only technique evidenced in this study, for in addition to the disassociation of athletes there were instances of athletes being realigned to Other national identities than to the one they represented. *SI* demonstrated this most explicitly and this was further exacerbated by the consistent hyphenation of athletes to reinforce their connection with collective Others rather than their being individual members of the 'we' or 'us' who are less likely to require an ethnic identifier.

This inferential racism witnessed here does little to change dated views of imagined communities and 'race' logic, and neither do they encourage readers to embrace the diversity of postmodern societies. What they are more likely to do is to re-present the stereotypes that limit aspirations and entrench myths about social groups, their behaviours and their desires. The (de)criminalisation of athletes and by association the criminalisation of racialised sports suggests that the power of the media remains strong and pervasive. We are in no doubt about the job of work to be done to turn the uncritical reporting of sports news around. Encouragingly, the contradictions in each magazine offered some hope of an antiracist agenda, even though consistent messages were lacking. It seems that these inconsistencies are points of both hope and disappointment where expectations are raised only for less enlightened views to be given equal credence. Further, the impact and power of these positive perspectives does not necessarily equate to the power of less informed views owing to the persuasiveness of everyday discourses on difference and the pernicious nature of everyday racial thinking in sport and the media.

Where the sport media can present a view of sport in a way that seems positive, they can still perpetuate social disadvantage, prejudice and stereotypes and catch us off guard. There are examples in the two sports magazines that could be construed as assimilationist or integrationist that emphasise the distance we have travelled to generate so many multiethnic sports stars. At the same time the burden of progress is placed firmly on the shoulders of those who have not been successful in management or business or politics especially as there are examples (role models?) of people just like those complaining that the system is flawed and disadvantages them. This enlightened racism is a variation on a theme that ultimately defends the status quo, power relations and racial hierarchies. Whether the media influence sport or sport influences the media remains part of the agenda for critical cultural analyses. Those concerned with the racialisation of sport must continue with more in-depth studies of the media and activism around their complicity in this process. 'Race' critical writers should view this chapter as a marker for a field worthy of further consideration.

Chapter 6 emphasises the futility of ambivalence where social justice in sport is the target. Antiracists are themselves challenged in the fight against racism because once they attempt to structure antiracism interventions they must struggle against profound philosophical and political dilemmas as considered next by Taguieff (2001), Woodward (2006) and Gilroy (1992). The contradictions in the media are likely to continue where commercial pressures trump social responsibilities. If the level of inconsistencies across just these two sports magazines offers an insight into other sports media then it reflects a value neutrality and colour-blindness that will not lead to the social transformation advocated by critical race theory writers.

Chapter 6

Antiracism and sport

Introduction

Antiracism is a common term with little consensus on what it entails. What is to be challenged? by whom? when? and for how long? remains a constant source of difficulty for many. Antiracism is as much a paradox as racism and as such the dangers of oversimplifying the causes of racism through poorly constructed interventions is ever-present. Reinforcing racial categories through the use of reductionist categories or through fixed or static views of racism are not uncommon in sport (Back, Crabbe and Solomos 2001, Garland and Rowe 2001). Antiracism in sport often focuses on explicit, high-profile concerns, and such initiatives are often seen as *the answer* to racism. Rugby league's 'Tackle It' or awareness-raising campaigns like Thierry Henry and Nike's 'Stand Up Speak Up' cannot be viewed in isolation as they are often historically located and resource-led with some form of political or ideological position to uphold (Gilroy 1992, Solomos and Back 1995, Bhavnani *et al.* 2005, Swinney and Horne 2005). This becomes even more transparent where public organisations like local authorities or non-governmental bodies fall under a critical lens where equal opportunities and antiracism are often conflated. This final chapter draws together many of the theoretical and conceptual tensions stemming from the ambiguous and transitory nature of racism as it explores the pragmatics of theory, policy and practice. The implications of the assumptions that underpin antiracist behaviour are explored through a consideration of the work of Beneton (2001), Taguieff (2001), Essed (2002) and Solórzano and Yosso (2005), whose work has interrogated some of what amount to essential problematics for antiracists in sport today in terms of how critical lenses applied to antiracism can facilitate more rigorous cutting-edge transformatory activities. Beneton's (2001: 83) suspicion of racism and antiracism leads him to conclude that 'One has to maintain firmly the two following propositions: (1) racism is a false idea; (2) all forms of antiracism are not valid'.

The antiracism problematic

By 'valid' Beneton is not saying that antiracism is worthless but he is arguing that there is no one answer to racism as this would be a reductionist proposition in itself and therefore antiracism(s) as the battle against racism(s) must take part on many fronts. 'Whoever calls into question *the correct version of antiracism* deserts the good camp . . . in other words there are antiracisms' (emphasis added). Taguieff (2001) makes salutary, bold and critical points in relation to antiracism as he argues that the logic of antiracism as the antithesis to racism is not as unambiguous as originally thought (See Figure 6.1). He does this through identifying two dominant positions that at one and the same time can be occupied by racists and antiracists, thus presenting a paradox rarely given critical consideration. These discourses he calls heterophobia (which in its most extreme form could be translated into a fear of difference) and heterophilia (in its extreme form a love of difference). Heterophobia is more recognised in sport as a defence of a sovereign culture which might range from a national culture to a local community. Eurocentrism or other forms of ethnocentrism are terms used to typify this type of activity. Similarly heterophilia is most commonly recognised as the political discourse that recognises diversity and acknowledges difference in sport and other public pursuits but at its extreme could be a form of apartheid as seen in South Africa or the deep south of the US. These two discourses are both dynamic and tenuous in that both can be advocated by the same people or by racist and antiracist organisations at the same time. Taguieff argues that these ambiguities can present antiracists with analogous racist consequences. By this he means that an antiracist response might stem from the same ideological root as a racist intervention. For example as commentators on new racism have argued, both racists and antiracists are likely to agree on the principle of recognising diversity and difference for vastly differing reasons (Cohen 1999). Further, an antiracist discourse that recognises cultural differences could expediently meet invidious racist demands for the acceptance of divided cultures to the detriment of a harmonious society. This kind of anomaly Taguieff (2001: 19) admits 'presents an obstacle to any attempt at cold and careful analysis'.

Taguieff (2001) goes on to simplify the two discourses into two key forms of racialisation. The first is the racism of inclusion which involves an assimilation of the Other or even a fusion of opposites: this he calls heterophobia. An ideal context for heterophobia would be a homogeneous sovereign population where culturally and traditionally people initiate from the 'same stock'. Here differences either real or perceived are denied, ultimately through conflict, until the social and perceived (biological, intellectual or cultural) differences become acceptable for the majority dominant hegemonic population. This we often experience in politics when there are heightened debates on immigration and in sport at times of intense international competition. Terrorism has hastened these discussions, just as in the UK the '7/7' bombings have made the discourse of 'us' and 'them' commonplace. France has recently been engaged in these debates in many areas of its social policy, in particular where religion is concerned, and the constitution of its football team is under debate.

The second form of racialisation, which he calls heterophilia, is a racism of exclusion, an extreme version infamously evidenced in South Africa's apartheid

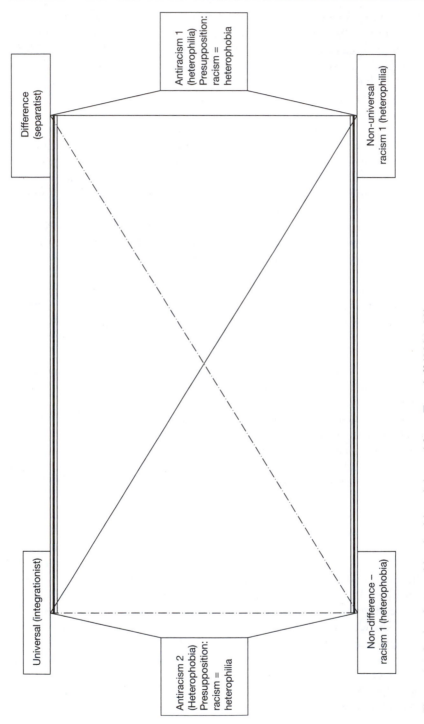

Figure 6.1 Antiracism and its doubles. Adapted from Taguieff (2001: 28)

regime. This essentialising of difference is again both real and imagined but sinisterly is still defended to fix the outcomes of racialising processes. Another significant implication of such beliefs is the reiteration of naturalising categories of 'races' and racial differences as separateness is valorised and justified. The vocabulary of racial science is based upon such sinister foundations and so are the harrowing actions of militants and nation states over recent years that have informed death and destruction according to related ideological canons. The starting point for heterophilia is that *difference is good* and in pushing beyond this point its racism occurs as it is moved to its most extreme position. As with heterophobia, difference is never difference for those on the 'inside' difference is lauded where it keeps the Other at a distance and clearly distinguishable from the 'insider' group – 'the threat of non-differentiation' (Taguieff 2001: 26). The threat of non-differentiation impinges on the 'good differences' between individuals or groups, and the threat of a 'universal' politics from opponents becomes the real enemy and racist in itself, as in its defence any challenge to it shifts heterophiles from a heterogeneous group (albeit differentiated) to one homogenised and monocultural group.

Taguieff juxtaposes two forms of antiracism that are at one and the same time polar opposites, therefore emphasising the ambiguities in the discourse of antiracism. The racism of heterophilia is countered by the antiracism of heterophobia and the racism of heterophobia is countered by the antiracism of heterophilia: both antiracisms intended to expose, devalue and challenge the destructive social processes of the racism that they were developed to counter. So in each case the antiracist strategy is defined by its racism. The antiracism for heterophobia (heterophilia) becomes the antithesis of a homogenising, assimilationist and universalising racism. On the other hand the antiracism to heterophilia must challenge a differentialist, divisive majoritarian version of multiculturalism that would ultimately lead to segregated communities. The value in the case of each antiracism has to be emphasised to promote credible alternatives to that which is destructive and clearly warranting an ethical alternative to the racism being practised. Taguieff (2001: 28) contends that

> There is, on the one hand, an antiuniversalist and differentialist antiracism (*heterophilia*) and, on the other hand, a universalist and antidifferentialist antiracism (*heterophobia*) – an interlacing of antiracisms that echoes the chiasmus of their respective racisms. [emphasis added]

Acknowledging only certain forms of racism in sport, such as chanting, physical abuse on and off the field of play or reactions to events or incidents, is likely to deny the less obvious incarnations of racism in sport. Cohen adds to the relative disarray of antiracists as he suggests that antiracism is also limited by the biography and situatedness of each actor. Just as cultural workers might use a cultural lens to critique racism, Cohen (1999) suggests that others facing institutions such as housing or law (or sport) will see their approach as requiring a more structural institutional focus. To these complexities Armstrong and Ng (2005: 39) add that in the fight against racism other social forces require consideration at the same time where smart antiracism is to be the outcome:

> An integrative anti-racist approach would acknowledge explicitly that we are all gendered, racialised, and differently constructed subjects who do not participate as equals in interactional settings. It recognises that racism as well as sexism and other forms of oppression are systemic and that we therefore cannot cleanse ourselves of racism through good will.

The implications for antiracism in sport means a need for more sophisticated strategies that are not limited to challenging overt racism at events or in the media. The more subtle nuanced versions of antiracism have to challenge the behaviour and policies of individuals as well as institutions so that discrimination and prejudice do not result from the cultural stereotyping and divisive discourse of this inadvertent racism (Cohen 1999). Consequently, the types of racism that have been described as institutionalised, discursive or processual are as much a site of resistance for antiracists as are the more overt incarnations of racism. Those who consider themselves 'antiracists' must be wary of the lure of high-profile initiatives as a reactive response to racism. Essed (2002) urges us to contest the everyday circumstances of racism or 'invisible' racist events if a real challenge is to be mounted against the insidious practices of racism in sport.

Antiracist assumptions

Essed (2002) is clear that one of the key sites of struggle for antiracists is the conceptual terrain hinted at by the work of Taguieff (2001) previously, and this need for a critical consciousness in the arsenal of antiracists is more evident where assumptions are explored that underpin antiracism. Bowser (1995) draws out two concerns with antiracists or policy makers: (1) they are often willing to assume that racism does not exist where it is not observable and (2) others would prefer to see racism as an organisational malfunction that can be effectively adjusted through regulation. Both of these assumptions accept views of racism that are static, ahistorical and individualistic rather than socially constructed and dynamic. Critical race theorists Solórzano and Yosso (2005) acknowledge the imperative of understanding the root cause of antiracism as all antiracist practice is simply not the same, not based on sound principles, not necessarily positive and not necessarily undertaken for the good of those subject to racism. Solórzano and Yosso examine these anomalies further to facilitate a clearer semblance of types of resistance, critical consciousness and motivations toward social justice that goes some way to explaining why some examples of antiracism in sport are spurious whilst others are more rigorous. Drawing on the early work of the influential and radical educator Paulo Freire, their model (Figure 6.2) is a useful device for a

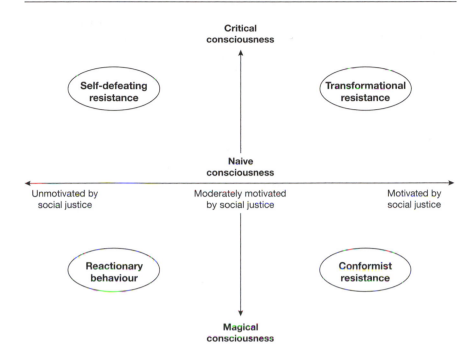

Figure 6.2 Models of antiracism. Adapted from Solórzano and Yosso (2005)

simple reading of complex intersections of critical antiracisms, motivation and resistance. Using Solórzano and Yosso's model the y axis represents levels of consciousness which we all have, to varying degrees, on a continuum from the top (1) critique of the system (or critical consciousness), in the centre (2) naive consciousness and at the bottom (3) magical consciousness (or no critique of the system). A magical consciousness can be identified in sport by those whose perceptions of powerlessness lead them to do little or nothing about the racism they or others encounter because of its apparent inevitability. Capitulation or resignation are useful verbs to describe the character of those who fall into this category. Fate is a likely belief system for groups like these as they are more determined by social processes than determining.

A self-blame system is associated with those occupying the middle ground of this continuum labelled 'naive'. Responses to racism by those with a naive pre-disposition might involve urging communities, individuals or themselves, rather than the system, to change to speed up integration or assimilation into dominant cultures or communities. A policy of disassociation from their own community might be a practice attractive to those naively hoping that this type of behaviour might ensure that the system and institutions might treat them better where they assume the identity, behaviour or share the expectations of hegemonic others. In sport this type of behaviour characterises responses to racialised social unrest that offers a political 'band aid' effect to much wider and deeper social ills. The palliative effect of such interventions is typified by tokenism, time limitations and short-term resources.

Critical consciousness reflects the highest state of political awareness, as knowledge of systems and structures reveals the strategies for change for those disempowered by historical inequities. The systematic oppression caused by the failings of an unfair social system are understood and become the target for radical challenges to established philosophies and practices. In sport and other public settings this level of critical practice has rarely been seen although there are examples in the work of the Greater London Council in the 1980s, the post-apartheid quota system in South African sport and organisations like Sport Against Racism in Ireland (SARI). In 1997 SARI was founded to support cultural integration and social inclusion in Ireland by using sport as a medium to combat racism, xenophobia, sectarianism and other forms of discrimination. SARI's mission also reflects the findings from a large body of international research that supports the proposition that sport, along with the arts and broader cultural activities, can serve as a medium for addressing racism and enhancing social inclusion (National Action Plan Against Racism – NAPAR, (Department of Justice, Equality and Law Reform, 2005)). The social context for SARI is that an influx of new communities has been the backdrop to many of the antiracism initiatives in Ireland. Since SARI's inception Ireland has become a country of net inward migration for only the second period in its history, and much of this is bound up with its new membership of the European Union and the expansion of the Union over the recent past. The racism that has become the focus for SARI and the NAPAR in Ireland is manifest through racism experienced by Travellers; racism experienced by recent migrants, including labour migrants, refugees and asylum seekers; racism experienced by black and minority ethnic people; racism experienced by Jews and Muslims in the form of anti-Semitism and Islamophobia; the intersection of racism with other forms of discrimination.

The main aims for SARI are to present sporting and cultural events that bring together people from different cultures and backgrounds; to produce materials for use in schools and sports clubs to help educate young people on issues of racism; to promote a positive attitude towards people from different ethnic backgrounds; to work with local sports clubs encouraging equality for all people regardless of colour, religion or any other form of discrimination; integrating minority ethnic groups through sport. Since it was established SARI has been involved in the development of a series of European and international initiatives. As early as 1997, SARI represented Ireland at the Madrid conference of the EU Year Against Racism and participated in the International Conference in Stockholm during which the Charter of Practice in European Sport was established. In 1999 SARI became one of the founders of Football Against Racism in Europe (FARE), which is supported by every national football federation in Europe and featured very prominently in the 2006 World Cup in Germany. In 2000, SARI was invited by the Council of Europe and British Council to contribute to a major conference in

Strasbourg on the Social Responsibility of Sport which led to the Bratislava Agreement (see NPAR). SARI was also an active partner in the 2004 European Year of Education through Sport and in January 2005 hosted two high-profile workshops at Croke Park as a part of that initiative.

SARI incorporates a community development philosophy underpinned by an integrationist ethic. SARI cites the Brian Kerr Intercontinental league as an exemplar of the work that it carries out. This league, endorsed by the high-profile former national team manager Brian Kerr, invites 'new communities' to establish football teams (male and female). Each team is encouraged to work within its own community to network, empower and build capacity for a sustainable and successful club or community. As part of this process of intra-cultural community development the teams play each other as part of an inter-cultural process of mutual respect and integration. Further, mainstream teams are invited by SARI to actively 'poach' and play against the Intercontinental teams as part of this process of inter-cultural détente and integration. The Standing Conference for Community Development (2001: 5) posits that

> A community development approach starts with people in communities coming together to address themes. It supports the connections that exist between them and the fact that individuals, groups and organisations need to learn from each other and co-operate if consistent and sustainable change is to be achieved. Community development spans the traditional boundaries of organisations in a way which is flexible and responsive to the priorities and concerns of communities.

The important aspect for SARI is the building of social capital as the key to social inclusion and integration into Irish society. SARI can boast working with and bringing together Palestinians and Israelis, clans from the Ivory Coast, factions from Poland, Nigerians and Chinese. SARI staff are aware of the accusations that they might be reinforcing separatism through this initiative but are willing to accept that this is part of a process of establishing confidence and respecting identities as they work towards wider integration. SARI's workers would also argue that some of its work is too radical and challenging for mainstream funding organisations like local authorities who prefer more liberal initiatives and perhaps less controversial endeavours such as the campaigning organisation Show Racism the Red Card. SARI regularly argues that its work is not just about what happens in the stadium but also about wider issues than sport, on the street – which sometimes takes SARI into highly charged or politically sensitive arenas with immigration departments, the police, and law courts because for SARI individuals suffering racism need support regardless of whether it is limited to sport. Given this backdrop SARI's work has still been acknowledged and supported by a number of mainstream organisations, not least the National Action Plan Against Racism which used SARI as an example of good practice (Department of Justice, Equality and Law Reform 2005: 143). Also, in 2005 SARI was awarded two years' funding from Social Entrepreneurs – Ireland to enable one of the founder three members to devote his energies full-time to the future development of the organisation. The organisation's founders believe that this funding represents a watershed in the development of the organisation and are now determined to transform it from an all volunteer endeavour with a limited organisational capacity to a fully professional entity whose operations exemplify best practice for voluntary organisations. SARI's critical consciousness, situatedness and reflexivity make it an antiracist organisation aware of wider social, economic and political forces in which its work is set and as a result it strategically works to consciously challenge itself and others to work in a way to counter the racism(s) pertinent to its clients.

Antiracism philosophies

Crossing Solórzano and Yosso's (2005) y axis (levels of consciousness) is their x axis which represents a continuum of motivations. From the extreme left, there are (1) those unmotivated by social justice; in the centre (3) those moderately motivated by social justice and change; and those on the right of the continuum, (3) those who are openly motivated by social justice and its incumbent rewards. The intersection of the two axes reveals the four quadrants of the model, three intriguing forms of antiracism that few would wish to be associated with and one which is most popular in the rhetoric of antiracism: a transformational resistance informed by critical activists motivated by social justice. Each of the other three has at least one weakness likely to make any antiracist intervention unsuccessful. For example a Self-Defeating Resistance describes those with a critical knowledge of social structures and inequalities but with little or no motivation for social justice. Similarly, uncritical antiracist agents can be identified in the two lower half quadrants, describing those who are at worst unmotivated by social justice (Reactionary Behaviour) or, where they are motivated by social justice, embody at best a liberal conformist agenda resulting in slow incremental or piecemeal change (Conformist Resistance). Each of the weakened quadrants to varying degrees perpetuates the status quo and to greater or lesser degrees the racialised power relations that typify our popular sports. The fourth quadrant illustrates an ideal position of thoughtful and informed activism intent on social justice in sport. Antiracism that falls into this category is likely to make significant impacts into the racisms perpetrated by those established processes and practices in sport. The acid test for Solórzano and Yosso (2005) posed in the shape of a question for antiracists is *how can you be confident that your work falls into this ideal category?* Any antiracist intervention needs to be clear about the racism(s) it is tackling; it must also be evident in its aims and related objectives. Taguieff's (2001) understanding of critical consciousness with reference to antiracism encourages us to heed the traps of rhetoric and ideology as he raises questions that many feel weaken the position of antiracists owing to the often uncritical but compelling moral and ethical arguments for there to be antiracism.

Models of antiracism philosophies are useful conceptual tools; however, practice tends to deviate from these neat views of how things ought to be. What happens in practice tends to require a sensitive and critical application of these ideas. By far one of the most high-profile examples of antiracism in sport was the Thierry Henry/Nike Stand Up Speak Up campaign (Sterkenberg *et al.* 2005). As a Europe-wide campaign it encouraged fans and organisations to show their displeasure of racism by acting in concert on the terraces by speaking out against it, through implementing change through funded initiatives, or to contribute donations and subsequently show support by wearing the interlocking black and white wristbands depicting the antiracist politics of the wearer. Over five million bands were sold and the funding administered by the King Baudouin Foundation, which distributed the funds to national partners to fund antiracism initiatives in 2005–6. The Stand Up Speak Up campaign can be used as an example of the anomalies experienced in sport's antiracism interventions. The campaign funded a number of initiatives that ranged from charter initiatives to multi-network Europe-wide initiatives like Football Against Racism in Europe and Eurofan. However, today we are able to buy the black and white bands on eBay now that they have become fashion accessories. However, the value of this intervention raises a number of serious question for antiracism in sport. If we use Solórzano and Yosso's (2005) model to explore this campaign further, the interlocking bands in isolation do little more than suggest that the purchasing of these bands and the raising of the profile of racism in sport is likely to succeed in tackling racism. The message that racism exists because people in sport lack awareness of its odious outcomes trivialises a highly complex set of processes (conformist resistance). In effect the campaign could have done more harm than good as good people may be lulled into a false sense of security and complacency because of the simplicity of the messages emerging from the campaign. Antiracism is reduced to tokenism and so with it is the daily racism that it was established to counter. On another level the funding generated by the donations has been distributed across Europe to established and newly formed antiracism initiatives in sport that have scored many successes in the fight against racism. This campaign embodies how the battle against racism is never fully won or lost. However, a critical lens applied to antiracism is more likely to reduce the possibilities of wasted resources, weak assumptions and negative outcomes in antiracism in sport.

Informal antiracism: resistance through sport

It has been documented that sport can be used as a form of resistance or antiracist vehicle for individuals and communities affected by the systemic racism in their daily lives. Sport as antiracism in these cases is often implied and assumed by those involved. Carrington (1999), Williams (1994) and Westwood (1990) suggest that sport can be used as a site of resistance and demonstrate so through their work. Often sport acts as an arena in which groups can restate their identities and positions of power that are being negated by racism in other areas of their lives. Westwood's (1990) argument is that spaces themselves become racialised and become appropriated by groups through a form of 'neighbourhood nationalism'. Westwood (1990) goes further to emphasise that spaces are defended against outsiders who represent oppressors and those who are privileged in some way. Williams's (1994) case study of Highfield Rangers, a predominantly African Caribbean team, evidences how it was established as a response to the exclusion and discrimination that its founder members experienced in the 1970s. The Highfield club was seen as a site of empowerment and resistance against the collective experience of racism in sport and wider society for its members, fans and community. Williams describes this process as a form of community politics. This is a process considered by Carrington (1999) at the Caribbean Cricket Club (the first black cricket club formed in Britain). Williams posited that Highfield Rangers, like the Fforde Grene (see Long et al. 2000) and the Caribbean Cricket Club, 'inhabited a social space where symbolic victories can be achieved as a means of alleviating wider community tensions or of responding to perceived community injustices' (Williams 1994: 171).

It is debatable what the measured impact is of these community actions beyond a feeling of enhanced self and community worth. Beyond the intuitive feelings of worth born out of necessity there is rarely any sense, or demand, for harder measures of success for these informal activities. These antiracist interventions are often ambiguous and vague but united by a challenge to the institution of sport that reproduces the hegemony of *the system* that symbolically alienates and disempowers them, not because of the multivariate differences across black communities but because of the superficial fact of their blackness or other related ethnic characteristics.

Britton (1999) explains how a racialisation of a sporting community acted as a unifying process for a black voluntary sector group. This process is mirrored in my ethnographic study of a black sports pressure group (BEMSport) in the north of England (Hylton 2003, 2008). For Britton's and my group blackness itself indicated membership and a foundation for resistance for their shared experiences of racialised exclusions. BEMSport is the acronym for the Black and Ethnic Minority Sports Forum. It is committed to equality of opportunity and antiracism in sport and recreation for black people in a county in the north of England. Its commitment was in recognition of the disparity in the representation of black people as administrators and managers in sport as opposed to purely participants (Hylton/ ILAM 1999, Jarvie 1991, Long et al. 2000). BEMSport is made up of executive members who are all experienced full-time black sports development professionals, drawn from areas in the county that have the highest black and culturally diverse populations. Each member has worked for their authority and/or their local community for over ten years and yet significantly none at a senior (principal) officer level. The members of BEMSport were conscious of the institutional structures that have systematically and summarily excluded black people from the policy-making and implementation processes in sport, and why black people in this county in the north of England have felt it necessary to resist this.

BEMSport occupied a space in a regional sport policy network that was paradoxical. BEMSport's existence clearly contested the notion of sport as the great leveller, or even as a domain for race equality. The discourse of equality within the public sector, which presents local government sport as equitable in terms of the development and implementation of sports policy or practice, was the target of the business of BEMSport. BEMSport's story is a counter-story, a competing discourse, an alternative paradigm that situates the black experience of sport in a process that constrains as it liberates, empowers as it disempowers, includes as it excludes (Delgado and Stefancic 2000, Goldberg 1993, Ladson-Billings 1998, Nebeker 1998). Delgado's (2000) argument that 'in-groups' create their own stories applies here to the public commitments by local authorities to the equality that they often fail to deliver in sport. 'Outgroups' like BEMSport aim to subvert that reality, hence BEMSport's forceful objectives (see Table 6.1) that place racism and equality of outcome in local authorities as two of their primary concerns. According to Hain (1976), an organisation with the social and community drives of BEMSport draws towards it individuals who in the past have been isolated by the organisation and structure of their working or personal

Table 6.1 BEMSport's Nine Objectives, 2003

To promote sport and physical recreation in Northshire for Black and Ethnic Minorities (BEM)

To promote the development of sport for local Black and Ethnic Minority groups in the region.

To bring together BEM community representatives, recreation and leisure services officers, community sports development officers and officials of sports governing bodies to discuss sports race equity issues and other related matters in the context of BEM participation

To enhance consultation processes between sports providers and representatives of Black and Ethnic Minorities.

To promote equality of opportunity and outcome for Black and Ethnic Minorities in:
• Sports participation including administration officiating and coaching.
• The pursuit of excellence.
• Representation in sports management and administration in local authorities, governing bodies and the voluntary sector.
• Media coverage.

To encourage the provision of educational and training opportunities in sport and recreation for Black and Ethnic Minorities.

To raise the awareness and develop an understanding among sports providers of racism in sport and its impact on the ability of members of Black and Ethnic Minorities to access opportunities in sport.

To give participants the opportunity to share experiences of good practice.

To oppose racism in sport at all levels.

experiences. He suggests that organisations like these enable people to take some control of their own destiny by affecting and effecting change. This was clearly the case for the black professionals linked to the emergent pressure group as they saw the sum of BEMSport becoming far more influential than its parts. Consequently the forum members have made a point to those established organisations in the sports policy network that they are failing and it is time that there was a critical black voice amongst them. Whatever the motivation for the forum members to be involved, the increased level of agency achieved by volunteers in community or pressure groups is an important factor for them to join such a group. The key members demonstrated that their ability to influence policy makers and practitioners in their new position as BEMSport executive members was a common reason for them to become involved.

As we saw in Chapter 3, by opening up alternative lines of inquiry that include these often undervalued sources of data, BEMSport produces an oppositional story that rejects the claims of progress in public-sector sport. Instead it produces contradictions that count as caveats for more complacent local authorities and incentives for more forward-looking ones. Similarly, the work of Hylton (2003), Horne (1995) and Swinney and Horne (2005) has evidenced how the colour-blindness, tensions and confusions behind equality policies in local government sport have reproduced these hegemonic assumptions. Hylton's (2003) work in particular highlights how the assumptive worlds of senior officers and policy makers in local government subvert and bypass policy where their 'real world pressures' dictate a reprioritisation of policy for everyday practices. The institutionalised hierarchy of liberal opinions, attitudes and ideologies meant that equality initiatives and transformations for social justice failed to influence them without a shattering of hardened ideologies or worldviews. Liberal approaches ensure a minimal position from which to tackle inequality. However, this minimalist state intervention fails to actively reduce the gap between those who are advantaged by the system and those who are not. Cunningham (1992) supports this view that holders of a minimalist ideology base equality on merit and on the removal of barriers to achievement. Here the market offers individuals the chance to compete to be unequal, procedure-led policies are adopted which are 'race'-blind and gender-blind, and rewards are awarded on merit alone. Jewson and Mason (1986, 1992) aligned the minimalist view with New Right ideologies and Conservative politics. Conversely, Jewson and Mason's (1992) conception of a radical approach requires an increased role for the state from a regulator to a facilitator. The views expressed by Gilroy (1987), Solomos (1989), Anthias and Yuval-Davis (1993), Edwards (1995), Jones (1996) and Mason (2000) that we are living in an unequal racist society means for radicals that direct intervention is required by the state to contest the traditional way in which resources have been distributed in relation to outcomes in sport. The liberalist ideal of the market being the arbiter of moral values and equality is called into question by the more radical view that members of society are not in a position to know who is privileged or underprivileged owing to their inability to ascertain starting points.

Organisations such as the GLC and Lambeth Council are high profile examples of this radical, highly politicised stance towards equality and antiracism in local government provision. In summary, aspects of liberalism in this context exacerbate inequality. Radicals further argue that inequality must be challenged on any agenda and so must any emphasis on a reduced role for the state in such matters (Henry 1993).

The need for external and informal antiracists is emphasised by the policy gaps in professionalised networks. The Home Office report on community self-help reiterates how community groups like BEMSport are in fact a paradox (Home Office 1999). They are necessary because of the actions or inactions of public authorities. Their emergence occurs as a response to the perceived need of a black community that sees a disparity in the quality and quantity of sports facilities and services available to it. As noted earlier, the emergence of BEMSport in itself sends a message to local authorities and other sports governing agencies that others in their network need to go beyond documented affirmations of inequality and racism in sport, and that black people are taking action to address the imbalances.

Antiracist practice

Bhavnani et al. (2005) rightly suggests that we know very little about the efficacy of antiracism interventions as we are often prepared to accept anecdotal testimonies regarding the success of activities against what we know is a very ambiguous and slippery concept of 'racism'. Although Bhavnani et al. (2005), Taguieff (2001) and Solórzano and Yosso (2005) would strongly advocate that where racism has been identified it would be wrong to do nothing. They would posit that any starting point for antiracist interventions must be critically informed, must be underpinned by sound and ethical motives for social justice and from a practical viewpoint must be SMART. SMART principles are simply an acronym for specific, measurable, achievable, realistic and time-limited. It is not suggested by this that racism is somehow measurable, nor that we can accurately measure the impact of racism on groups or individuals from an arbitrary starting point of 10 down to 0. There are clearly conceptual and practical complexities and difficulties that must be overcome even to begin to make a statement about the impact of antiracist interventions. This is further blurred by the economic framework that many professional antiracism organisations find themselves, which naturally forces a deviation or dilution of their original goals as they attempt to ensure longevity and continued employment. The Football Unites Racism Divides (FURD) director reinforces this notion in relation to the identity that FURD presents to funding organisations and by that token the antiracism intervention that is proposed for specific funding opportunities: 'The language of diversity? Whether you say ethnic minorities or minority ethnic or what . . . that's for funding, for bids. Now, we have to say the right things for European funding, Government funding' (cited Woodward 2006: 8).

However there are ways of measuring success using 'softer', more qualitative indicators in addition to more positivistic measures. Researching and evaluating antiracism interventions take some creativity and pragmatism, and therefore whatever 'measurements' are made from organisational rationales and practice through to community perceptions of racist incidents are reliable indicators of progress and success for critical researchers and practitioners. The range of initiatives that fall under the umbrella of antiracism is vast in terms of scale, organisation and goals. Many professional interventions emerge out of the public sector with its historical discourses of multiculturalism, equal opportunities and more recently social exclusion, social cohesion and social capital. These organisations generally have a public duty to promote racial equality and therefore have a much longer record of successes and failures than within sporting circles where antiracism has tended to be incidental, ad hoc and piecemeal. My multiple-site case study (Hylton 2003) of three local authorities in the north of England is an example of how organisations that recognise inequality in sport on the basis of 'race' can fail to meet the ethos of their own rhetoric and policy promises. Similarly Thierry Henry and Nike's Stand Up Speak Up campaign emphasises how a range of disparate organisations can fall under the same label of antiracism and yet clearly raise more questions than they solve in terms of the claims they make in accepting funding to promote what some could argue to be a superficial high-profile token gesture.

Antiracism and cosmopolitanism

The speed and accessibility of communications across a shrinking world ensure that universal sympathy is generally felt for good causes and traumatic incidents. Such has been the case in Spain, where everyone from *The Times* to the *China Daily* and ESPN were simultaneously reporting about the collective outrage of incidents in the country. The Spanish football team manager's racist outbursts against Thierry Henry is not an isolated case, as the matches between Spain and England in 2004, and Zaragoza and Barcelona in 2006, which nearly entailed a pitch walk-off by Samuel Eto'o, are indicative of the endemic racism in the Spanish game. Carlos Ferreyra Nunez, co-ordinator of Spain's United Against Racism group, believes the problem is widespread. 'Racism is a cancer that has touched every aspect of football . . . racist behaviour could be seen every week and all over the country' (BBC Sport 2004). As images of war and famine all over the globe draw sympathy and attention then so does the sport we experience and our collective desire to shape it because of the influence it has on a daily basis.

According to Beck (2006) cosmopolitanism is the definitive feature of a new era of reflexive modernity. Where our traditional national borders – and by that token our differences – are fast disappearing then a new world order needs to be reflected by new world politics and governance. If our social realities are such that the onset of global markets and the globalisation of politics, communications, media and culture changes the ways that we experience our sport, then that requires our sports to reflect the imperatives of a cosmopolitan world. Cosmopolitan sport has been described as an activity that projects an ideal of world sporting governance and citizenship (Jarvie 2006). A weakness of traditional views of antiracist politics has been the narrow focus on the nation as the central organising factor. Beck urges us to go beyond this 'self-centred narcissism' and the constraints that this form of thinking puts upon our ability to think beyond national borders and our local or global realities. Beck would argue that, unlike campaigns such as the Thierry Henry/Nike initiative, antiracism interventions are doomed to failure as they tend to adopt a 'local' nationalism that represents a local view on human rights, equality or racism. In many ways they offer an 'aggressive intolerance' to others beyond their borders. The international response to the Spanish football team manager's comments about Thierry Henry are a case in point where the local football association response was one of indifference to outside perspectives, denying the virtual proximity that globalisation affords us in the 'global village'. Antiracism interventions constitute part of a cosmopolitan politics or outlook in sport that symbolises a global community, citizenship and a collective resistance to all forms of racism wherever it occurs.

Beck (2006) posits five principles of a cosmopolitan outlook. First, our collective experience of world events has ensured a sense of co-dependence or interdependence which dissolves the borders between 'internal/external', 'us and them', and 'national/international'. Second, owing to the everydayness of lived differences and a cosmopolitan lived state we are more tolerant of new people and less curious. Third, owing to shared 'instant experiences' cosmopolitan empathy has developed where citizens tend to have a perspective on more immediate world events than in previous eras. The fourth principle encourages a healthy scepticism against those wishing to maintain national borders in a global society. The final principle is one that recognises the social, cultural and political interconnectedness that accepts pride in the local as long as the global is not forgotten, as this is likely to be narrow-minded and possibly likely to ignore a larger, more complex view. Hall (2002) develops this further with a view of cosmopolitanism that raises the notion of the 'cosmopolitan self'. The cosmopolitan self argues for attachments to multiple cultures, but importantly those imagined cultures that form key social structures such as religious, family or national cultures. Hall disagrees with organisations that suggest that types of racism are acceptable in a particular culture in isolation from others in a globalised world, as has been suggested in Spain (BBC Sport 2004). Pragmatically, Hall suggests that our state of 'natural cultural embeddedness' is one that we cannot easily throw off, and so socially and culturally cosmopolitanism has to accept these conditions. Where the politics and governance of antiracism in sport are concerned, these points are essential to consider as cultural differences and/or similarities must be skilfully negotiated, hence the need for governing bodies. This does not allay the need for a global governance system that reflects these antecedents. Hall's fear of an assimilationist discourse pervading governance systems is one that needs to be reiterated here but more importantly even the most basic equality structures have awoken to the fact that governing body neutrality will lead to the dis-advantaging of individuals and communities without effective tailored responses to local problems. Antiracist interventions must take into account these social, historical, political, cultural, economic and global issues.

Conclusion

Being critical of antiracism is a necessary evil: it forces an engagement with uncomfortable questions akin to asking which of your children you favour. Taguieff's (2001) problematisation of antiracism presents a compelling argument for a reassessment of how we view the boundaries between racism and antiracism and effectively illustrates the mutual philosophical starting points for both racism and antiracism. Heterophobia and heterophilia symbolise types of antiracism and racism that warrant care especially in light of the subtleties argued by authors of new racism and cultural racism theses. The invidious rhetorical devices that can sabotage antiracist interventions as well as spurious antiracist thinking that reinforce racisms are hailed as possible outcomes of weak thinking in relation to conceptualising racisms and their subsequent antiracism interventions. Anti-racism is defined by its racism, which means that one approach does not suit all and antiracism(s) remain of their day, situated and as dynamic as the racism(s) they seek to challenge.

Antiracism as a concept remains slippery because of its nascent forms. To understand antiracism is to understand racism, and to comprehend antiracist practice is to comprehend the conscious motivations and capacity for resistance that constitute any interventions that pertain to sport. In informal circumstances the success of antiracism can be judged adequately where sport has been deemed anecdotally to adjust the felt racialised power relations in favour of those previously disadvantaged or less powerful than the systems they wish to desta-bilise. Sport as antiracism, or antiracism in informal sport, is rarely negative in outcome as bespoke community interventions often demonstrate immediate felt results. These successes must not be underestimated in sport even if their paucity in the sport literature means that their impacts are poorly documented. More formal antiracism interventions have to aspire to higher standards and duties of care; however there is consistency in the literature on the complacency and underachievement of the institution of sport regarding challenging racism. The deficiency in critical consciousness and reflexivity in policy practice advocated by Horne (1995), Hylton (2003), Swinney and Horne (2005) and Solórzano and Yosso (2005) is apparent in analyses of sport and racism, and sport and racial equality.

Jarvie's (2006) summation of the way forward for sport using a cosmopolitan outlook involves accepting a federal structure of sporting bodies over a repre-sentative one where the world's sporting issues can be prioritised like a United Nations of antiracism in sport. From a political perspective, individuals will have a desire to belong and identify with something local which in governance terms would be the national governing bodies. Operating within a single global structure this may present some difficulties for some cross-national organisations, but that is not to say it is impossible or unworkable. The conceptual or ideological has always to be translated into the practical, and for this there are no apologies! Racism is abhorrent, shifting but complex, and the responses to it must also be malleable in order to tackle racism's various incarnations politically, in practice, and philosophically. If antiracists hope to make gains towards transformational resistance, the gaps between reflexive consciousness, policy and practice must diminish so that the dynamism of racism is met by dynamic responses.

References

Aitchison, C. (2000) 'Poststructural feminist theories of representing Others: a response to the "crisis" in leisure studies discourse'. *Leisure Studies*, 19, 127–144.

Alexander, C. (1996) *The Art of Being Black*, Oxford: Clarendon Press.

Alexander, C. and Knowles, C., eds (2005) *Making Race Matter: Bodies, Space and Identity*, Basingstoke: Palgrave Macmillan.

Anderson, B. (1991) *Imagined Communities*, London: Verso.

Andrews, D., Pitter, R., Zwick, D. and and Ambrose, D. (2002) 'Soccer's racial frontier: sport and the suburbanization of contemporary America'. In G. Armstrong and R. Giuliannoti, eds, *Entering the Field: New Perspectives on World Football*, Oxford: Berg.

Andrews, D.L. (1996) 'The facts of Michael Jordan's blackness: excavating a floating racial signifier'. *Sociology of Sport Journal*, 13(2), 125–158.

Anthias, F. (1998) 'Rethinking social divisions: some notes towards a theoretical framework'. *The Sociological Review*, 505–535.

Anthias, F. and Yuval-Davis, N. (1993) *Racialized Boundaries*, London: Routledge.

Appiah, K.A. (1992) *In My Father's House: Africa in the Philosophy of Culture*, London: Methuen.

Apple, M. (1996) 'Introduction'. In P. Carspecken, ed., *Critical Ethnography: A Practical Guide*, London: Routledge.

Apple, M. (2003) 'Freire and the politics of race in education'. *International Journal of Leadership in Education*, 6(2), April–June, 107–118.

Armstrong, J. and Ng, R. (2005) 'Deconstructing race, deconstructing racism'. In J. Lee and J. Lutz, eds, *Situating 'Race' and Racisms in Space and Time and Theory: Critical Essays for Activists and Scholars*, London: McGill-Queens University Press.

Back, L. (2004) 'Writing in and against time'. In M. Bulmer, and J. Solomos, eds, *Researching Race and Racism*, London: Routledge.

Back, L., Crabbe, T. and Solomos, J. (1999) 'Beyond the racist/hooligan couplet: race, social theory and football culture'. *British Journal of Sociology*, 50(3), Sept., 419–442.

Back, L., Crabbe, T. and Solomos, J. (2001) *The Changing Face of Football*, Oxford: Berg.

Bains, J. (2005) *Asians Can Play Football; Another Wasted Decade*, Leicester: Asians in Football Forum.

Bains, J. and Johal, S. (1998) *Corner Flags and Corner Shops: The Asian Football Experience*, London: Phoenix.

Bains, J. and Patel, R. (1996) *Asians Can't Play Football*, Solihull: ASDAL.

Banton, M. (1998) *Racial Theories*, Cambridge: Cambridge University Press.

Barot, R. and Bird, J. (2001) 'Racialization: the genealogy and critique of a concept', *Ethnic and Racial Studies*, 24(4), 601–618.

Barth, F. (1969) *Ethnic Groups and Boundaries: The Social Organization of Cultural Difference*, London: George Allen & Unwin.

Basu, D. (2001) 'The colour line and sociology'. In P. Ratcliffe, ed., *The Politics of Social Science Research: 'Race', Ethnicity and Social Change*, Basingstoke: Palgrave.

BBC Sport (2004) http://news.bbc.co.uk/go/pr/fr/-/sport2/hi/football/4019621.stm.

Beck, U. (2006) *Cosmopolitan Vision*, Cambridge: Polity Press.

Beneton, P. (2001) 'On the corruptions of antiracism', *Culture and Society*, Nov./Dec., 83–88.

Ben-Tovim, G., Gabriel, J., Law, I., Stredder, K., eds (1986) *The Local Politics of Race*, London: Macmillan.

Ben-Tovim, G., Gabriel, J., Law, I., Stredder, K., eds (1992) 'A political analysis of local struggles for racial equality'. In P. Braham *et al.*, eds, *Racism and Anti-racism: Inequalities, Opportunities and Policies*, London: Sage.

Bhavnani, R., Mirza, H. and Meetoo, V. (2005) *Tackling the Roots of Racism*, Bristol: The Policy Press.

Bhopal, K. (2000), 'Gender, "race" and power in the research process'. In C. Truman, D.M. Mertens and B. Humphries, eds, *Research and Inequality*, London: UCL Press.

Billings, A.C. (2004) 'Depicting the quarterback in black and white: a content analysis of college and professional football broadcast commentary'. *Howard Journal of Communications*, 15(4), 201–210.

Billings, A. and Eastman, S. (2002) 'Selective representation of gender and ethnicity, and nationality in American television coverage of the 2000 summer Olympics'. *International Review for the Sociology of Sport*, 37(3–4), 351–370.

Birrell, S. (1989) 'Racial relations theories and sport: suggestions for a more critical analysis'. *Sociology of Sport*, 6, 212–227.

Bonilla-Silva, E. (2002) 'The linguistics of color blind racism: how to talk nasty about blacks without sounding "racist"'. *Critical Sociology*, 28(1–2),

Bowser, B. (ed) (1995) *Racism and Antiracism in World Perspective*, London: Sage.

Britton, N.J. (1999) 'Racialised identity and the term "black"'. In S. Roseneil and J. Seymour, eds, *Practising Identities Power and Resistance*, London: Macmillan.

Brookes, R. (2002) *Representing Sport*, London: Arnold.

Brown, E. (1997) 'Confronting racelessness'. In R. Delgado and J. Stefancic, eds, *Critical White Studies*, Philadelphia: Temple University Press.

Bruce, T. (2004) 'Marking the boundaries of the "normal" in televised sports: the play-by-play of race'. *Media, Culture and Society*, 26(6): 861–879.

Brunsma, D. and Rockquemore, K. (2002) 'What does black mean? Exploring the epistemological stranglehold of racial classification'. *Critical Sociology*, 28(1–2), 101–121.

Bulmer, M. and Solomos, J., eds (1999) *Ethnic and Racial Studies Today*, London: Routledge.

Bulmer, M. and Solomos, J., eds (2004) *Researching Race and Racism*, London: Routledge.

Burdsey, D. (2004a) 'Obstacle race? "race", racism and the recruitment of British Asian professional footballers'. *Patterns of Prejudice*, 38(3), 279–299.

Burdsey, D. (2004b) '"One of the lads"? Dual ethnicity and assimilated ethnicities in the careers of British Asian professional footballers'. *Ethnic and Racial Studies*, 27(5), 757–779.

Campbell, C. (1995) *Race Myth and the News*, London: Sage.

Cantle, T. (2002) *Community Cohesion: A Report of the Independent Review Team*. London: Home Office.

Carrington, B. (1998a) 'Sport masculinity and black cultural resistance'. *Journal of Sport and Social Issues*, 22(3), 275–298.

Carrington, B. (1998b) '"Football's coming home": but whose home? And do we want it? Nation, football and the politics of exclusion'. In A. Brown, ed., *Fanatics! Power, Identity and Fandom in Football*, pp. 101–123, London: Routledge.

Carrington, B. (1999) 'Cricket, culture and identity: an ethnographic analysis of the significance of sport within black communities'. In S. Roseneil and J. Seymour, eds, *Practising Identities Power and Resistance*, London: Macmillan.

Carrington, B. (2002a) 'Masculinity and black cultural resistance'. In S. Scraton and A. Flintoff, eds, *Gender and Sport: A Reader*, pp. 141–155. London: Routledge.

Carrington, B. (2002b) 'Race, representation and the sporting body'. In CUCR'S *Occasional Paper Series*. Brighton: University of Brighton.

Carrington, B. (2004a) 'Cosmopolitan Olympism, humanism and the spectacle of "race"'. In J. Bale and M.K. Cristensen, eds, *Post-Olympism? Questioning Sport in the 21st Century*, Oxford: Berg.

Carrington, B. (2004b) 'Introduction: race/nation/sport'. *Leisure Studies*, 23(1), 1–3.

Carrington, B. and McDonald, I. (2001) *'Race', Sport and British Society*, London: Routledge.

Carroll, R. (2001) 'Racist, violent, corrupt: welcome to Serie A', OSM, May, 38–45.

Cashmore, E. (1982) *Black Sportsmen*, London: Routledge and Kegan Paul.

Cashmore, E. and Troyna, B., eds (1982) *Black Youth in Crisis*, London: Routledge and Kegan Paul.

Chong-Soon Lee, J. (1995) 'Navigating the topology of race'. In K. Crenshaw, N. Gotanda, G. Peller and T. Kendall, eds, *Critical Race Theory: The Key Writings that Formed the Movement*, pp. 441–449. New York: New Press.

Clarke, J. and Speeden, S. (2000) *Measuring Up: Report of a Study of the Adoption and Implementation of Racial Equality Means Quality, the CRE's Standard for Local Government*. Liverpool: Centre for Local Policy Studies, Edge Hill College.

Coakley, J. (2001) *Sport in Society: Issues and Controversies*, London: McGraw Hill.

Coalter, F. (1998) 'Leisure studies, leisure policy and social citizenship: the failure of welfare or the limits of welfare?' *Leisure Studies*, 17, 21–36.

Coalter, F. (2000) 'Leisure studies, leisure policy and social citizenship: a response to Rosemary Deem'. *Leisure Studies*, 19, 37–44.

Coates, R. (2002) 'I don't sing, I don't dance, and I don't play basketball! Is sociology declining in significance, or has it just returned to business as usual?' *Critical Sociology*, 28(1–2), 255–279.

Cohen, P., ed. (1999) *New Ethnicities, Old Racisms*, New York: St Martin's Press.

Collins, P. (1990) *Black Feminist Thought*, London: Routledge.

Collins, P. (2000) *Black Feminist Thought*, 2nd ed., London: Routledge.

Commission for Racial Equality (1995) *Racial Equality Means Quality*, London: CRE.

Commission for Racial Equality (1999) *Auditing for Equality*, London: CRE.

Cornell, S. and Hartmann, D. (1998) *Ethnicity and Race*, London: Pine Forge Press.

Cosgrove, A. and Bruce, T. (2005) 'The way New Zealanders would like to see themselves: reading white masculinity via media coverage of the death of Sir Peter Blake'. *Sociology of Sport*, 23(2), 336–355.

Crenshaw, K., Gotanda, N., Peller, G. and Kendall, T., eds 1995 *Critical Race Theory: The Key Writings that Formed the Movement*, New York: New Press.

Crompton, R. and Jones, G. (1988) 'Researching white collar organisations: why sociologists should not stop doing case studies'. In A. Bryman, ed. *Doing Research in Organisations*, London: Routledge.

Cronin, M. and Mayall, D., eds (1998) *Sporting Nationalisms: Identity, Ethnicity, Immigration and Assimilation*, London: Frank Cass.

Cross, M. and Keith, M., eds (1993) *Racism, the City and the State*, London: Routledge.

Cunningham, S. (1992) 'The development of equal opportunities theory and practice in the European Community'. *Policy and Politics*, 20(3), 177–189.

Darder, A. and Torres, R. (2003) 'Shattering the "race" lens: toward a critical theory of racism'. In A. Darder, M. Baltodano and R. Torres, eds, *The Critical Pedagogy Reader*, London: RoutledgeFalmer.

Darder, A. and Torres, R. (2004) *After Race*, London: NYU Press.

Darder, A., Baltodano, M. and Torres, R., eds (2003) *The Critical Pedagogy Reader*, London: RoutledgeFalmer.

Davis, L.R and Harris, O (1998) 'Race and ethnicity in US sports media'. In L. Wenner, ed., *MediaSport*, pp. 154–169. London: Routledge.

Deem, R. (1999) 'How do we get out of the ghetto? Strategies for research on gender and leisure for the twenty-first century'. *Leisure Studies*, 18, 161–177.

Delgado, R. and Stefancic, J., eds, (1995) *Critical Race Theory: The Cutting Edge*, Philadelphia: Temple University Press.

Delgado, R. and Stefancic, J. (1995b) 'Why do we tell the same stories? Law reform, critical librarianship, and the triple helix dilemma'. In R. Delgado and J. Stefancic, eds, *Critical Race Theory: The Cutting Edge*, pp. 206–216. Philadelphia: Temple University Press.

Delgado, R. and Stefancic, J., eds (1997) *Critical White Studies*, Philadelphia: Temple University Press.

Delgado, R. (2000) 'Storytelling for oppositionists and others: a plea for narrative'. In Delgado, R. and Stefancic, J., eds, *Critical Race Theory: The Cutting Edge*, second ed., Philadelphia: Temple University Press.

Delgado, R. and Stefancic, J. (2001) *Critical Race Theory: An Introduction*, New York: NYU Press.

Denham, B., Billings, A. and Halone, K. (2002) 'Differential accounts of race in broadcast commentary of the 2000 NCAA men's and women's final four basketball tournaments'. *Sociology of Sport*, 19(4), 315–332.

Denison, J. and Markula, P. (2005) 'The press conference as a performance: representing Haile Gebrselassie'. *Sociology of Sport*, 22, 311–335.

Denzin, N. and Lincoln, Y.S., eds (1994) *Handbook of Qualitative Research*, pp.175–188. Thousand Oaks, CA: Sage Publications.

Denzin, N. and Lincoln, Y.S., eds (1998) *The Landscape of Qualitative Research*, London: Sage.

Department of Justice, Equality and Law Reform (2005) *Planning for Diversity: National Action Plan against Racism – 2005–2008*, Dublin: Department of Justice, Equality and Law Reform.

Dines, N., Cattell, V., Gesler, W. and Curtis, S. (2006) *Public Spaces, Social Relations and Well-Being in east London*, York: Joseph Rowntree Foundation.

Dixon-Gottschild, B. (2005) 'Whoa! Whiteness in dance'. *Dance Magazine*, June, 46–47.

Dixson, A. and Rousseau, C. (2006) 'And we are still not saved: critical race theory in education ten years later'. In A. Dixson and C. Rousseau, eds, *Critical Race Theory in Education: All God's Children Got a Song*, New York: Routledge.

Dlamini, S. (2002) 'From the other side of the desk: notes on teaching about race when racialised'. *Race, Ethnicity and Education*, 5(1), 51–66.

Dockery, G. (2000) 'Participatory research: whose role, whose responsibility'. In C. Truman, D.M. Mertens and B. Humphries, eds, *Research and Inequality*, London: UCL Press.

Douglas, D. and Jamieson, K. (2006) 'A farewell to remember: interrogating the Nancy Lopez farewell tour'. *Sociology of Sport*, 23, 117–141.

DuBois, W.E.B. (1994) *The Souls of Black Folk*, New York: Dover Publications.

Durrheim, K. and Dixon, J. (2001) 'The role of place and metaphor in racial exclusion: South Africa's beaches as sites of shifting racialization'. *Ethnic and Racial Studies*, 24(3), May, 433–450.

Dyer, R. (1997) *White: Essays on Race and Culture*, London and New York: Routledge.

Dyson, M., Kennedy, K. and Bechtel, M. (2003) 'Some pain some gain'. *Sports Illustrated*, 29 December, 33.

Eastman, S. and Billings, A. (2001) 'Biased voices of sports: racial and gender stereotyping in college basketball announcing'. *Howard Journal of Communications*, 12(4), 183–204.

Eastman, S. and Billings, A. (2002) 'Selective representation of gender, ethnicity, and nationality in American television coverage of the 2000 summer Olympics'. *International Review for the Sociology of Sport*, 37(3/4), 351–370.

Edwards, J. (1995), *When Race Counts*, London: Routledge.

Eitzen, D. and Sage, G. (2003) *Sociology of North American Sport*, 7th edition, Boston: McGrawHill.

Erickson, B. (2005) 'Style matters: explorations of bodies, whiteness, and identity in rock climbing'. *Sociology of Sport*, 22, 373–396.

Eriksen, T. (1997) 'Ethnicity, race and nation'. In M. Guibernau and J. Rex, eds, *The Ethnicity Reader: Nationalism, Multiculturalism and Migration*, Cambridge: Politiy Press.

Essed, P. (2001) 'Multi-identifications and transformations: reaching beyond racial and ethnic reductionisms'. *Social Identities*, 7(4), 493–509.

Essed, P. (2002), 'Everyday racism'. In P. Essed and D. Goldberg, eds, *Race Critical Theories*, Oxford: Blackwell.

Essed, P. and Goldberg, D., eds (2002) *Race Critical Theories*, Oxford: Blackwell.

Fanon, F. (1986) *Black Skin White Masks*, London: Pluto.

Fawcett, B. and Hearn, J. (2004) 'Researching others: epistemology, experience, standpoints and participation'. *International Journal of Social Research Methodology*, 7(3), 201–218.

Fenton, S. (2003) *Ethnicity*, Cambridge: Polity Press.

Fetterman, D. (1989) *Ethnography: Step by Step*, London: Sage

Fishman, S. and McCarthy, L. (2005) 'Talk about race: when student stories and multi-cultural curricula are not enough'. *Race, Ethnicity and Education*, 8(4), 347–364.

Flagg, B. (1997) 'Anti-discrimination law and transparency: barriers to equality?' In R. Delgado and J. Stefancic, eds, *Critical White Studies*, Philadelphia: Temple University Press.

Fleming, S. (1991) 'Sport, schooling and Asian male culture'. In G. Jarvie, ed., *Sport, Racism and Ethnicity*, London: Falmer Press.

Floyd, M. (1998) 'Getting beyond marginality and ethnicity: the challenge for race and ethnic studies in leisure research'. *Journal of Leisure Research*, 30(1), 3–20.

Forst, R. (1996) 'Justice, reason and critique: basic concepts of critical theory'. In D. Rasmussen, ed., *The Handbook of Critical Theory*, pp. 138–162. Oxford: Blackwell.

Frankenberg, R. (1993) *White Woman, Race Matters: The Social Construction of Whiteness*, London: Routledge.

Frankenberg, R., ed. (1999) *Displacing Whiteness*, Durham and London: Duke University Press.

Frankenberg, R. (2004) 'On unsteady ground: crafting and engaging in the uncritical study of whiteness'. In M. Bulmer and J. Solomos, eds, *Researching Race and Racism*, London: Routledge.

Fredman, S. (2001) 'Combating racism with human rights: the right to equality'. In S. Fredman, ed., *Discrimination and Human Rights: The Case of Racism*, Oxford: Oxford University Press.

Gabriel, J. (1998) *Whitewash: Racialised Politics and the Media*, London: Routledge.

Gardiner, S. and Welch, R. (2001) 'Sport, racism and the limits of "colour-blind" law'. In B. Carrington and I. McDonald, eds, *'Race', Sport and British Society*, pp. 133–149. London: Routledge.

Garland, J. (2004) 'The same old story? Englishness, the tabloid press and the 2002 football World Cup'. *Leisure Studies*, 23(1), 79–92.

Garland, J. and Rowe, M. (2001) *Racism and Anti-racism in Football*, Basingstoke: Palgrave.

Garner, S. (2006) 'The uses of whiteness: what sociologists working on Europe can draw from US research on whiteness'. *Sociology*, 40(2), 257–275.

Gates, H., ed. (1986) *Race Writing and Difference*, Chicago: University of Chicago Press.

Geertz, C. (1994) 'Primordial and civic ties'. In J. Hutchinson and A. Smith, eds, *Nationalism*, Oxford: Oxford University Press.

Gellner, E. (1994) 'Nationalism and high cultures'. In J. Hutchinson and A. Smith, eds, *Nationalism*, Oxford: Oxford University Press.

Gillborn, D. (2005) 'Education policy as an act of white supremacy: whiteness, critical race theory and education reform'. *Journal of Education Policy*, 20(4), July, 485–505.

Gilroy, P. (1987) *There Ain't No Black in the Union Jack*, London: Routledge.

Gilroy, P. (1992) 'The end of antiracism'. In P. Braham, A. Rattansi and R. Skellington, eds, *Racism and Antiracism: Inequalities, Opportunities and Policies*, London: Sage.

Gilroy, P. (1993) *Small Acts: Thoughts on the Politics of Black Culture*, London: Serpent's Tail.

Gilroy, P. (2000) *Against Race: Imagining Political Culture beyond the Colour Line*, Cambridge, MA: Harvard University Press.

Giroux, H. (1997) *Pedagogy and the Politics of Hope: Theory, Culture and Schooling: A Critical Reader*, Boulder: Westview.

Goldberg, D. (1993) *Racist Culture*, Oxford: Blackwell.

Goldberg, D. (2002) *The Racial State*, Oxford, Blackwell.

Gordon, P. and Rosenberg, D. (1989) 'Daily racism: the press and Black people'. In P. Gordon and D. Rosenberg, eds, *Daily Racism: The Press and Black People in Britain*. London: Runnymede Trust.

Gordon, W., Miller, F. and Rollock, D. (1990) 'Coping with communicentric bias in knowledge production'. *Educational Researcher*, 19(3), 14–19.

Gramman, J. and Allison, M. (1999) 'Ethnicity, race, and leisure'. In E. Jackson and

T. Burton, eds, *Leisure Studies: Prospects for the Twentieth Century*, pp. 283–297. State College, PA: Venture Publishing.

Gramsci, A. (1971) *Selections from the Prison Notebooks*, London: Lawrence and Wishart.

Guardian, (2007) 'I'm Asian and different – it's good', 27 January, http://www.guardian.co.uk/g2/story/0,,1991894,00.html#article_continue.

Guillaumin, C. (1995) *Racism, Sexism, Power and Ideology*, London: Routledge.

Gunaratnam, Y. (2003) *Researching 'Race' and Ethnicity: Methods, Knowledge and Power*, London: Sage.

Habermas, J. (1987) *The Theory of Communicative Action*, Boston: Beacon Press.

Hain, P. (1976) *Community Politics*, London: Calder.

Hall, S. (1981) 'Notes on deconstructing the popular'. In R. Samuel, ed., *People's History and Socialist Theory*, London: Routledge and Kegan Paul.

Hall, S. (1990) 'The whites of their eyes: racist ideologies and the media'. In M. Alvarado and J. Thompson, eds, *The Media Reader*, London: BFI.

Hall, S. (1997) 'The spectacle of the "Other"'. In S. Hall, ed., *Representation: Cultural Representations and Signifying Practices*, London: Sage.

Hall, S. (2000) 'Conclusion: the multi-cultural question'. In B. Hesse, ed., *Un/settled Multiculturalisms: Diasporas, Entanglements, Transruptions*, London: Zed Books.

Hall, S. (2002) 'Political belonging in a world of multiple identities'. In S. Vertovec and R. Cohen, eds, *Conceiving Cosmopolitanism: Theory, Context and Practice*, Oxford: Oxford University Press.

Haney-Lopez, I. (2000), 'The social construction of "race"'. In R. Delgado and J. Stefancic, eds, *Critical Race Theory: The Cutting Edge*, pp. 163–175. Philadelphia: Temple University Press.

Hardin, M., Dodd, J., Chance, J. and Walsdorf, K. (2004) 'Sporting images in black and white: race in newspaper coverage of the 2000 Olympic Games'. *Howard Journal of Communications*, 15(4), 211–227.

Hargeaves, J. (1986) *Sport, Power and Culture*, Cambridge: Polity Press.

Hargreaves, J. (1994) *Sporting Females: Critical Issues in the History and Sociology of Women's Sports*, London: Routledge.

Harris, A. (1999) 'Building theory, building community'. *Social and Legal Studies*, 8(3), 313–325.

Harris, A. (2003) 'Race and essentialism in feminist legal theory'. In A.K. Wing, ed., *Critical Race Feminism*, pp. 34–41. London: NYU.

Harrison, L., Azzarito, L. and Burden, J. (2004) 'Perceptions of athletic superiority: a view from the other side'. *Race Ethnicity and Education*, 7(2), July, 159–166.

Harvey, L. (1990) *Critical Social Research*, London: Unwin-Hyman.

Hatfield, D. (1996) 'The Jack Nicklaus syndrome', *Humanist*, July–August, 1.

Hemingway, J. (1999) 'Critique and emancipation: toward a critical theory of leisure'. In E. Jackson and T. Burton, eds, *Leisure Studies: Prospects for the Twentieth Century*, pp. 487–506. State College, PA: Venture Publishing.

Hemingway, J. and Wood Parr, M. (2000) 'Leisure research and leisure practice: three perspectives on constructing the research-practice relation'. *Leisure Sciences*, 22, 139–162.

Henderson, K. (1988) 'The need for critical theory in the study of leisure and minority groups'. *Leisure Information Quarterly*, 15(3), 1–3.

Henderson, K. (1998) 'Researching diverse populations'. *Journal of Leisure Research*, 30(1), 157–174.

Henry, I. (1993) *The Politics of Leisure Policy*, London: Routledge.

Higgs, C. and Weiller, K. (1994) 'Gender bias and the 1992 Summer Olympic Games: an analysis of television coverage'. *Journal of Sport and Social Issues*, 18(3), 234–246.

Hoberman, J. (1997) *Darwin's Athletes: How Sport has Damaged Black America and Preserved the Myth of Race*, Boston: Houghton Mifflin Company.

Hobsbawm, E. (1992) *Nations and Nationalism since 1780*, Cambridge: Cambridge University Press.

Home Office (1999) *Policy Action Team 9: Community Self-Help*, London: Home Office.

hooks, b. (1990) *Yearning: Race, Gender and Cultural Politics*, Boston: South End Press.

hooks, b. (1998) 'Representation of whiteness in the black imagination'. In D. Roediger, ed., *Black on White: Black Writers on What It Means to Be White*, New York: SChocken Books.

hooks, b. and West, C. (1991) *Breaking Bread: Insurgent Black Intellectual Life*, Boston: Southend Press.

Horne, J. (1995), 'Local authority black and ethnic minority provision in Scotland'. In M. Talbot, S. Fleming and A. Tomlinson, eds, *Policy and Politics in Sport, Physical Education and Leisure*, LSA Pub. 95, pp. 159–176. Edinburgh: Moray House Institute/ Heriot-Watt University.

Howe, D. (2004) 'It was not a lapse: Atkinson was up to his neck in football's endemic racism'. *The New Statesman*, 3 May, 11.

Humphries, B. (2000) 'Premises of emancipatory research'. In C. Truman, D.M. Mertens and B. Humphries, eds, *Research and Inequality*, London: UCL Press.

Husband, C., ed. (1984) *'Race' in Britain: Continuity and Change*, London: Hutchinson University Library.

Hutchinson, J. and Smith, A., eds (1994) *Nationalism*, Oxford: Oxford University Press.

Hylton, K. (1995) 'A "Lived Experience"'. In J. Long, ed., *Nightmares and Successes: Doing Small Scale Research in Leisure*, Leeds: LMU.

Hylton, K. (2003) *Local Government 'Race' and Sports Policy Implementation*, Unpublished PhD Thesis, Leeds Metropolitan University.

Hylton, K. (2005) '"Race", sport and leisure: lessons from critical race theory'. *Leisure Studies*, 24(1), January, 81–98.

Hylton, K./ILAM (1999) 'Where are the black leisure managers?' *Leisure Manager*, September, 32–34.

Hytten, K. and Warren, J. (2003) 'Engaging whiteness: how racial power gets reified in education'. *Qualitative Studies in Education*, 16(1), 65–89.

Ismond, P. (2003) *Black and Asian Athletes in British Sport and Society: A Sporting Chance?* Basingstoke: Palgrave Macmillan.

Jackson, S. (1998) 'A twist of race: Ben Johnson and the Canadian crisis of racial and national identity'. *Sociology of Sport*, 15(1), 21–40.

Jackson, S., Andrews, D. and Cole, C. (1998) 'Race, nation and authenticity of identity: interrogating the "everywhere" man (Michael Jordan) and the "nowhere" man (Ben Johnson)'. In M. Cronin and D. Mayall, eds, *Sporting Nationalisms: Identity, Ethnicity, Immigration and Assimilation*, London: Frank Cass.

Jarvie, G. (1991a) *Sport, Racism and Ethnicity*, London: Falmer.

Jarvie, G. (1991b) 'There ain't no problem here?', *Sport and Leisure*, Nov./Dec., 20–21.

Jarvie, G. (2006) *Sport, Culture and Society*, London: Routledge.

Jarvie, G. and Maguire, J. (1994) *Sport and Leisure in Social Thought*, London: Routledge.

Jarvie, G. and Reid, I. (1997) 'Race relations, sociology of sport and the new politics of race and racism'. *Leisure Studies*, 16(4), 211–219.

Jenkins, R. (1994) 'Rethinking ethnicity: identity, categorization and power'. *Ethnic and Racial Studies*, 17(2), 197–223.

Jenkins, R. (1997) *Rethinking Ethnicity: Arguments and Explorations*, London: Sage.

Jenkins, R. (2004) *Social Identity*, London: Routledge.

Jewson, N. and Mason, D. (1986) '"Race" employment and equal opportunities: towards a political economy and an agenda for the 1990s'. *Sociological Review*, 42(4), Nov.

Jewson, N. and Mason, D. (1992), 'The theory and practice of equal opportunities policies: liberal and radical approaches'. In P. Braham, A. Rattansi and R. Skellington, eds, *Racism and Anti-racism: Inequalities, Opportunities and Policies*, London: Sage.

Jhally, S. and Lewis, J. (1992) *Enlightened Racism: The Cosby Show, Audiences, and the Myth of the American Dream*, Boulder: Westview Press.

Jones, R. (2002) 'The black experience within English semi-professional soccer'. *Journal of Sport and Social Issues*, 26(1), February, 47–65.

Jones, T. (1996) *Britain's Ethnic Minorities*, London: PSI.

Juffer, J. (2002) 'Who's the man? Sammy Sosa, Latinos, and televisual redefinitions of the "American Pastime"'. *Journal of Sport and Social Issues*, 26(4), 337–359.

Katz, J. (1982) *White Awareness: Handbook for Anti-racism Training*, Norman: University of Oklahoma.

Kellner, D. (1989) *Critical Theory, Marxism and Modernity*, Baltimore: Johns Hopkins University Press.

Kellner, D. (1996) 'Sports, media culture and race – some reflections on Michael Jordan'. *Sociology of Sport Journal*, 13, 458–467.

Kew, S. (1979) *Ethnic Groups and Leisure: A Review for the Joint Panel on Leisure and Recreation Research*, London: Sports Council.

Kincheloe, J. and Steinberg, S. (1998) 'Addressing the crisis of whiteness'. In J. Kincheloe, S. Steinberg, N. Rodriguez and R. Chennault, eds, *White Reign*, New York: St Martin's Griffin.

King, C. (2004) 'Race and cultural identity: playing the race game inside football'. *Leisure Studies*, 23(1), 19–30.

King, C.R. (2007) 'Staging the Winter White Olympics: or why sport matters to white power'. *Journal of Sport and Social Issues*, 31, 89–94.

King, C., Staurowsky, R., Ellen, J., Baca, L., Davis, L. and Pewewardy, C. (2002) 'Of polis and race prejudice, *Sports Illustrated* errant Indian wars'. *Journal of Sport and Social Issues*, 26(4), 381–401.

King, J. (1997) 'Dysconscious racism: ideology, identity, and miseducation'. In R. Delgado and J. Stefancic, eds, *Critical White Studies*, Philadelphia: Temple University Press.

Kivel, P. (2002) *Uprooting Racism: How White People Can Work for Racial Justice*, Gabrioloa Island, New Society Publishers.

Kusz, K. (2001) 'I want to be the minority: the politics of youthful white masculinities in sport and popular culture in 1990s America'. *Journal of Sport and Social Issues*, 25(4), November, 390–416.

Lacy, K. (2004) 'Black spaces, black places: strategic assimilation and identity construction in middle-class suburbia'. *Ethnic and Racial Studies*, 27(6), 908–930.

Ladson-Billings, G. (1998) 'Just what is critical race theory and what's it doing in a nice field like education?' *Qualitative Studies in Education*, 11(1), 7–24.

Ladson-Billings, G., ed. (2003) *Critical Race Theory: Perspectives on Social Studies*. Greenwich: Information Age Publishing.

Lapchick, R. (2000) 'Crime and athletes: new racial stereotypes'. *Society*, March/April.

Lapchick, R. (2001) *Smashing Barriers: Race and Sport in the New Millennium*, London: Madison Books.

Lather, P. (1991) *Getting Smart: Feminist Research and Pedagogy with/in the Postmodern*, London: Routledge.

Law, I. (1996) *Racism, Ethnicity and Social Policy*, London: Prentice Hall/Harvester Wheatsheaf.

Law, I. (2002) *Race in the News*, Basingstoke: Palgrave.

Layder, D. (1994) *Understanding Social Theory*, London: Sage.

Lee, J. and Lutz, J., eds (2005a) *Situating 'Race' and Racisms in Space and Time and Theory: Critical Essays for Activists and Scholars*, London: McGill-Queens University Press.

Lee, J. and Lutz, J. (2005b) 'Introduction: toward a critical literacy of racism, antiracism and racialisation'. In J. Lee and J. Lutz, eds, *Situating 'Race' and Racisms in Space and Time and Theory: Critical Essays for Activists and Scholars*, London: McGill-Queens University Press.

Leeds Metropolitan University (LMU) (2003) *Raising the Standard: An Evaluation of Progress*, Leeds: Coachwise.

Lefebvre, H. (1991) *The Production of Space*, Oxford: Blackwell.

Lenzo, K. (1995), 'Validity and self reflexivity meet poststructuralism: scientific ethos and the transgressive self'. *Educational Researcher*, 24(4), 17–23.

Leonard, D. (2004) 'The next M.J or the next O.J.? Kobe Bryant, race, and the absurdity of colourblind rhetoric'. *Journal of Sport and Social Issues*, 28(3), 284–313.

Leonardo, Z. (2002) 'The souls of white folk: critical pedagogy, whiteness studies, and globalization discourse'. *Race, Ethnicity and Education*, 5(1), 29–50.

Leonardo, Z., ed. (2005) 'Foreword'. In *Critical Pedagogy and Race*, Oxford: Blackwell.

Lewis, G. (1998) 'Welfare and the social construction of "Race"'. In E. Saraga ed., *Embodying the Social Construction of Difference*, pp. 92–138. London: Routledge.

Local Government Association (LGA) (2001) *Promoting Racial Equality Through Sport: A Standard for Local Authority Sport and Leisure Services*, London: LGA.

Lomax, M. (2004) '"Curt Flood stood up for us": the quest to break down racial barriers and structural inequality in major league baseball'. In J. Mangan and A. Ritchie, eds, *Ethnicity, Sport, Identity: Struggles for Status*, London: Frank Cass.

Long, J. (2000) 'No racism here? A preliminary examination of sporting innocence'. *Managing Leisure*, 5(3), 121–133.

Long, J. and Hylton, K. (2002) 'Shades of white: an examination of whiteness in sport'. *Leisure Studies*, 21, 87–103.

Long, J. and Spracklen, K. (1996) 'Positional play: racial stereotyping in rugby league'. *The Bulletin of Physical Education*, 32, 18–22.

Long, J. and Wray, S. (2003) 'It depends who you are: on asking difficult questions in leisure research'. *Loisir et Société*, 26(1), 169–182.

Long, J., Hylton, K., Dart, J. and Welch, M. (2000). *Part of the Game? An Examination of Racism in Grass Roots Football*. London: Kick It Out.

Long, J., Nesti, M., Carrington, B. and Gilson, N. (1997). *Crossing the Boundary: A Study of the Nature and Extent of Racism in Local League Cricket*, Leeds: Leeds Metropolitan University.

Long, J., Tongue, N., Spracklen, K. and Carrington, B. (1995a) '"Asians cannot wear turbans in the scrum": explorations of racist discourse within professional rugby league'. *Leisure Studies*, 16 249–259.

Long, J., Tongue, N., Spracklen, K. and Carrington, B. (1995) *What's the Difference: A Study of the Nature and Extent of Racism in Rugby League*. Leeds: RFL/CRE/LCC/LMU.

Lorde, A. (1979) 'The master's tools will never dismantle the master's house'. In C. Lemert, ed., (1999) *Social Theory: The Multicultural and Classic Readings*, Boulder: Westview Press.

Lynn, M., Yosso, T., Solorzano, D. and Parker, L. (2002) 'Critical race theory and education: qualitative research in the new millennium'. *Qualitative Inquiry*, 8(1), 3–6.

MacClancy, J., ed. (1996) *Sport, Identity and Ethnicity*, Oxford: Berg.

McCorkel, J. and Myers, K. (2003) 'What difference does difference make? Position and privilege in the field'. *Qualitative Sociology*, 26(2), 199–231.

McDonald, I. (2002) 'Critical social research and political intervention: moralistic versus radical approaches'. In J. Sugden and A. Tomlinson, eds, *Power Games: A Critical Sociology of Sport*, pp. 100–116. London: Routledge.

McDonald, I. and Ugra, S. (1999) 'It's just not cricket! Ethnicity, division and imagining the other in English cricket'. In P. Cohen, ed., *New Ethnicities, Old Racisms*, New York: St Martin's Press.

McDonald, M. and Birrell, S. (1999) 'Reading sport critically: a methodology for interrogating power'. *Sociology of Sport Journal*, 16, 283–300.

McIntosh, P. (1997) 'White privilege and male privilege: a personal account of coming to see correspondence through work in women's studies'. In R. Delgado and J. Stefancic, eds, *Critical White Studies: Looking Behind the Mirror*, Philadelphia: Temple University Press.

McIntyre, A. (1997) *Making Meaning of Whiteness: Exploring Racial Identity with White Teachers*, New York: SUNY.

McKay, J (1995) '"Just do it:" corporate sports slogans and the political economy of enlightened racism in discourse studies'. *The Cultural Politics of Education*, 16(2), 191–201.

Macpherson, Sir William, of Cluny (1999) *Report of the Stephen Lawrence Inquiry* (Cm4262-I), London: The Stationery Office.

Malik, K. (1996) *The Meaning of Race*, London: Macmillan Press.

Marqusee, M. (1994) *Anyone But England: Cricket and the National Malaise*, London: Verso.

Marqusee, M. (2003) 'Racism – one step forward'. *The Guardian*, 18 December, 32.

Marqusee, M. (2005) *Anyone But England: An Outsider Looks at English Cricket*, London: Aurum Press.

Marx, S. and Pennington, J. (2003) 'Pedagogies of critical race theory: experimentations with white preservice teachers'. *Qualitative Studies in Education*, 16(1), 91–110.

Mason, D. (1990) 'Competing conceptions of "fairness" and the formulation and implementation of equal opportunities policies'. In W. Ball and J. Solomos, eds, *Race and Local Politics*, London: Macmillan.

Mason, D. (2000) *Race and Ethnicity in Modern Britain*, Oxford: Oxford University Press.

Mason, J. (1996) *Qualitative Researching*, London: Sage.

Maynard, M. (1994) '"Race", gender and the concept of "difference" in feminist thought'. In H. Afshar and M. Maynard, eds, *The Dynamics of Race and Gender*, London: Taylor and Francis.

Maynard, M. (2002) '"Race", gender and the concept of "difference" in feminist thought'. In S. Scraton and A. Flintoff, eds, *Gender and Sport: A Reader*, pp. 111–126. London: Routledge.

McCarthy, D. and Jones, R. (1997) 'Speed, aggression, strength, and tactical naïveté: the portrayal of Black soccer players on television'. *Journal of Sport and Social Issues*, 21(4), 348–361.

McCarthy, D., Jones, R. and Potrac, P. (2003) 'Constructing images and interpreting realities: the case of the Black soccer player on television'. *International Review for the Sociology of Sport*, 38(2), 217–238.

Mercer, K. (1994) *Welcome to the Jungle: New Positions in Black Cultural Studies*, London: Routledge.

Messner, M. (1992) *Power at Play: Sports and the Problem of Masculinity*, Boston: Beacon.

Miles, R. (1989) *Racism*, London: Routledge.

Mirza, H. (1997) *Black British Feminism: A Reader*, London: Routledge.

Mirza, Q. (1999) 'Patricia Williams: inflecting critical race theory'. *Feminist Legal Studies*, 7, 111–132.

Modood, T. (1988) '"Black" racial equality and Asian identity'. *New Community*, 14, 397–404.

Modood, T. (1994) 'Political blackness and British Asians'. *Sociology*, 28(4), 859–876.

Modood, T. (1997) 'Difference, cultural racism and anti-racism'. In P. Werbner and T. Modood, eds, *Debating Cultural Identity*, London: Zed Books.

Modood, T. (1998) 'Ethnic diversity and racial disadvantage in employment'. In T. Blackstone *et al.*, eds, *Race Relations in Britain: A Developing Agenda*, London: Routledge.

Modood, T. (2005) *Multicultural Politics: Racism, ethnicity and Muslims in Britain*, Edinburgh: Edinburgh University Press.

Montagu, A. (1997) *Man's Most Dangerous Myth: The Fallacy of 'Race'*, London: Sage.

Montoya, M. (2002) 'Celebrating racialized legal narratives'. In F. Valdes, J. McCristal Culp and A. Harris, eds, *Crossroads, Directions and a New Critical Race Theory*, Philadelphia: Temple University Press.

Morgan, D., ed. *Men, Masculinities and Social Theory*, London: Unwin Hyman.

Murji, K. and Solomos, J., eds (2005) *Racialization: Studies in Theory and Practice*, New York: Oxford University Press.

Murray, R. (1998) *Social Closure: The Theory of Monopolisation and Exclusion*, New York: Oxford University Press

Murrell, A. and Curtis, E. (1994) 'Casual attributions of performance for black and white quarterbacks in the NFL: A look at the sports pages'. *Journal of Sport and Social Issues*, 18(3), 224–233.

Nanton, P. (1989) 'The new orthodoxy: racial categories and equal opportunity policy'. *New Community*, 15(4), 549–564.

Naples, A. (1997) 'A feminist revisiting of the insider/outsider debate'. In R. Hertz, ed., *Reflexivity and Voice*, London: Sage.

Nayak, A. (2005) 'White lives'. In K. Murji and J. Solomos, eds, *Racialization: Studies in Theory and Practice*, Oxford: Oxford University Press.

Nebeker, K. (1998) 'Critical race theory: a white graduate student's struggle with this growing area of scholarship'. *Qualitative Studies in Education*, 11(1), 25–41.

Observer (1999) (Mackay, D. and Campbell, D.) 'Can white beat black?', (28 March), 10.

Observer (2004) 'Top award for OSM', 7 June, 3.

Observer (2006) 'Observer scoops top sports award', 30 April, 30.

Ohri, S. and Faruqi, S. (1988) 'The politics of racism, statistics and equal opportunity:

towards a black perspective'. In A. Bhat, R. Carr-Hill and S. Ohri, eds (1988) *Britain's Black Population*, Aldershot, Gower.

Omi, M. and Winant, H. (1994) *Racial Formation in the United States: From the 1960s to the 1990s*, London and Boston: Routledge.

Omi, M. and Winant, H. (2002) 'Racial formation'. In P. Essed and D. Goldberg, eds, *Race Critical Theories*, Oxford: Blackwell.

Ouseley, H. (2001) *Community Pride Not Prejudice: Making Diversity Work in Bradford*, presented to Bradford Vision by Sir Herman Ouseley. Bradford: Bradford Vision.

Outlaw, L. (1990) 'Toward a critical theory of "race": a need for rethinking'. In D. Goldberg, ed., *Anatomy of Racism*, Minneapolis: University of Minneapolis.

Owusu, K., ed. (2000) *Black British Culture and Society*, London: Routledge.

Parekh, B. (2000) *The Future of Multi-ethnic Britain*, London: Runnymede Trust.

Parker, L. (1998) '"Race is race ain't": an exploration of the utility of critical race theory in qualitative research in education'. *Qualitative Studies in Education*, 11(1), 43–55.

Parker, L. and Lynn, M. (2002) 'What's race got to do with it? Critical race theory's conflicts with and connections to qualitative research methodology and epistemology'. *Qualitative Inquiry*, 8(3), 7–22.

Parker, L., Deyhle, D. and Villenas, S., eds (1999) *Race Is . . . Race Isn't: Critical Race Theory and Qualitative Studies in Education*, Boulder: Westview Press.

Peters, M. (2005) 'Editorial – critical race matters'. In Z. Leonardo, ed., *Critical Pedagogy and Race*, Oxford: Blackwell.

Polley, M. (1998) *Moving the Goalposts: A History of Sport and Society Since 1945*, London: Routledge.

Rada, J. and Wulfemeyer, T. (2005) 'Color coded: racial descriptors in television coverage of intercollegiate sports'. *Journal of Broadcasting and Electronic Media*, 49(1), 65–85.

Ratcliffe, P., ed., (1994) *'Race', Ethnicity and Nation: International Perspectives on Social Conflict*, London: UCL Press.

Ratcliffe, P. (1999) '"Race", education and the discourse of "exclusion": a critical research note'. *Race Ethnicity and Education*, 2(1), 149–155.

Ratcliffe, P. (2001) 'Sociology, the state and social change: theoretical considerations'. In P. Ratcliffe, ed., *The Politics of Social Science Research: 'Race', Ethnicity and Social Change*, Basingstoke: Palgrave.

Rattansi, A. (2005) 'The uses of racialization: the time spaces and subject-objects of the raced body'. In K. Murji and J. Solomos, eds, *Racialization in Theory and Practice*, New York: Oxford University Press.

Raymond, L. (1995) *Doing Research on Sensitive Topics*, London: Sage.

Reinharz, S. (1997) 'Who am I? The need for a variety of selves in the field'. In R. Hertz, ed., *Reflexivity and Voice*, London: Sage.

Reins, F. (1998) 'Is the benign really harmless?' In J. Kincheloe, S. Steinberg, N. Rodriguez and R. Chennault, eds, *White Reign*, New York: St Martin's Griffin.

Riggins, S. (1997) *The Language and Politics of Exclusion: Others in Discourse*, London: Sage.

Roediger, D., ed. (1998) *Black on White: Black Writers on What it Means to be White*, New York: Schocken Books.

Roediger, D. (2002) *Colored White: Transcending the Racial Past*, London: UCL.

Roithmayr, D. (1999) 'Introduction to critical race theory in educational research and praxis'. In L. Parker, D. Deyhle and S. Villenas, eds, *Race Is . . . Race Isn't: Critical Race Theory and Qualitative Studies in Education*, Boulder: Westview Press.

Rojek, C. (1989) *Leisure for Leisure: Critical Essays*, London: Macmillan.

Rowe, M. (1998) *The Racialisation of Disorder in Twentieth Century Britain*, Aldershot: Ashgate.

Rushton, J. (1996) *Race, Evolution and Behaviour: A Life History Perspective*, London: Transaction Publishers.

Sabo, D., Jansen, S., Tate, D., Duncan, M.C. and Leggett, S. (1996) 'Televising international sport: race, ethnicity, and nationalistic bias'. *Journal of Sport and Social Issues*, 21(1), 7–21.

Saggar, S. (1992) *Race and Politics in Britain*, London: Harvester Wheatsheaf.

Sailes, G. (1993) 'An investigation of campus stereotypes: The myth of Black athlete superiority and the dumb jock stereotype'. *Sociology of Sport Journal*, 10(1), 88–97.

St Louis, B. (2004) 'Sport and common sense racial science'. *Leisure Studies*, 23(1), January, 31–46.

Schick, C. (2000) '"By virtue of being white": resistance in anti-racist pedagogy'. *Race, Ethnicity and Education*, 3(1), 2000, 83–102.

Schultz, J. (2005) 'Reading the catsuit: Serena Williams and the production of blackness at the 2002 U.S. Open'. *Journal of Sport and Social Issues*, 29(3), August, 338–357.

Scraton, S. (2001) 'Reconceptualising race, gender and sport: the contribution of black feminism'. In B. Carrington and I. McDonald, eds, *'Race', Sport and British Society*, pp.170–187, London: Routledge.

Seidman, S. (2004) *Contested Knowledge: Social Theory Today*, Oxford: Blackwell.

Shohat, E. and Stam, R. (1994) *Unthinking Eurocentrism: Multiculturalism and the Media*, London: Routledge.

Shropshire, K. (1996) *In Black and White: Race and Sports in America*, London: New York University Press.

Silverman, D. (1993) *Interpreting Qualitative Data*, London: Sage.

Singer, J.N. (2005a) 'Addressing epistemological racism in sport management research'. *Journal of Sport Management*, 19(4), 464–479.

Singer, J.N. (2005b). 'Understanding racism through the eyes of African American male student-athletes'. *Race, Ethnicity, & Education*, 8(4), 365–386.

Skellington, R. (1996) *'Race' in Britain Today*, London: Sage in association with Open University.

Solomos, J. (1989) *Race and Racism in Contemporary Britain*, London: Macmillan.

Solomos, J. (1995) 'Racism and anti-racism in Great Britain: historical trends and contemporary issues'. In B. Bowser, ed., *Racism and Anti-racism in World Perspective*, London: Sage.

Solomos, J. and Back, L. (1995) *Race, Politics and Social Change*, London: Routledge.

Solomos, J. and Back, L. (2001) 'Conceptualizing racisms: social theory, politics and research'. In E. Cashmore and J. Jennings, eds, *Racism: Essential Readings*, London: Sage.

Solórzano, D. and Bernal, D. (2001) 'Examining transformational resistance through a critical race and LatCrit theory framework: Chicana and Chicano students in an urban context'. *Urban Education*, 36(3), May, 308–342.

Solórzano, D. and Yosso, T. (2001), 'Critical race and Latcrit theory and method: counter-storytelling'. *Qualitative Studies in Education*, 14(4), 471–495.

Solórzano, D. and Yosso, T. (2005) 'Maintaining social justice hopes within academic realities: a Freirean approach to critical race/LatCrit pedagogy'. In Z. Leonardo, ed., *Critical Pedagogy and Race*, Oxford: Blackwell.

Song, M. (2004) 'Introduction: who's at the bottom? Examining claims about racial hierarch'. *Ethnic & Racial Studies*, 27(6), Nov., 859–877.

Spencer, N. (2004) 'Sister act VI: Venus and Serena Williams at Indian Wells: "sincere fictions" and white racism'. *Journal of Sport and Social Issues*, 28(2), May, 115–135.

Sports Council (1994) *Black and Ethnic Minorities and Sport: Policy Objectives*, London: Sports Council.

Sports Illustrated (1999) '*Sports Illustrated* and IMG partner with American General, Chrysler, Compaq and Motorola for multi-million dollar sponsorship of *Sports Illustrated*'s 20th Century Sports Awards', available online at http://sportsillustrated. cnn.com/about_us/news/1999/11/04/20thCentury_sponsors/index.html.

Sports Illustrated (2003) 'Welcome to rush week', 13 Nov., 22–23.

Sterkenberg, J., Janssens, J. and Rijnen, B., eds (2005) *Football and Racism: An Inventory of the Problems and Solutions in Eight West European Countries in the Framework of the Stand Up Speak Up Campaign*, Brussels, King Baudouin Foundation.

Standing Conference for Community Development (2001) *Strategic Framework*, Sheffield: Community Development Foundation

Stanfield II, J. (1993) *Race and Ethnicity in Research Methods*, London: Sage.

Staurowsky, E. (2006) 'Getting beyond imagery: the challenge of reading narratives about American Indian Athletes'. *The International Journal of the History of Sport*, 23(2), 190–212.

Steier, F. (ed) (1995) *Research and Reflexivity*, London: Sage.

Sterkenberg, J., Janssens, J. and Rijnen, B., eds (2005) *Football and Racism: An Inventory of the Problems and Solutions in Eight West European Countries in the Framework of the Stand Up, Speak Up Campaign*, Brussels: King Baudouin Foundation.

Stodolska, M. (2000) 'Looking beyond the invisible: can research on leisure of ethnic and racial minorities contribute to leisure theory?' *Journal of Leisure Research*, 32(1), 156–160.

Stoecker, R. (1991) *Evaluating and Rethinking the Case Study*, London: Routledge.

Stovall, D. (2005) 'A challenge to traditional theory: critical race theory, African-American organizers, and education'. *Discourse Studies in the Cultural Politics of Education*, 26(1), March, 95–108.

Sugden, J. and Tomlinson, A. (2002) *Power Games: A Critical Sociology of Sport*, London: Routledge.

Swinney, A. and Horne, J. (2005) 'Race equality and leisure policy: discourses in Scottish local authorities', *Leisure Studies*, 24(3), July, 271–289.

Taguieff, P. (2001) *The Force of Prejudice: On Racism and Its Doubles*, London, University of Minneapolis Press.

Tate IV, W. (1999) 'Conclusion'. In L. Parker, D. Deyhle and S. Villenas, eds, *Race Is . . . Race Isn't: Critical Race Theory and Qualitative Studies in Education*, Boulder: Westview Press.

Terkel, S. (1992) *Race: How Blacks and Whites Feel About the American Obsession*, New York: Free Press.

Thomas, H. (2000) *Race and Planning: The UK Experience*, London: UCL Press.

Thomas, H. and Piccolo, F. (2000) Best value, planning and racial equality'. *Planning Practice and Research*, 15(1), Feb.–May, 79–95.

Thomas, J. (1993) *Doing Critical Ethnography*, London: Sage.

Thomas-Coventry, B. (2004) 'On the sidelines: sex and racial segregation in television sports broadcasting'. *Sociology of Sport Journal*, 21(2), 322–341.

Thompson, C., Schaefer, E. and Brod, H. (2003) *White Men Challenging Racism: 35 Personal Stories*, Durham and London: Duke University Press.

Time Warner (2008) http://www.timewarner.com/corp/newsroom/pr/0,20812,785743,00.html.

Truman, C., Mertens, D.M. and Humphries, B., eds (2000) *Research and Inequality*, London: UCL Press.

Twine, F.W. and Warren, J., eds (2000) *Racing Research Researching Race: Methodological Dilemmas in Critical Race Studies*, London: New York University Press.

UNESCO (1978) *Declaration on Race and Racial Prejudice*, Paris: UNESCO.

Valdes, F., McCristal, C. and Harris, A., eds (2002) *Crossroads, Directions, and a New Critical Race Theory*, Philadelphia: Temple University Press.

Van Ingen, C. (2003) 'Geographies of gender, sexuality and race: reframing the focus on space in sport sociology'. *International Review for the Sociology of Sport*, 38(2), 201–216.

Verma, G.K. and Darby, J. (1994) *Winners and Losers: Ethnic Minorities in Sport and Recreation*. Manchester University, School of Education, London: Falmer Press.

Villalpando, O. (2004) 'Practical considerations of critical race theory and Latino critical theory for Latino college students'. *New Directions for Student Services*, 105, Spring, 41–50.

Wallman, S. (1988) 'Ethnicity and the boundary process in context'. In J. Rex and D. Mason, eds, *Theories of Race and Ethnic Relations*, Cambridge: University of Cambridge.

Walton, T. and Butryn, T. (2006) 'Policing the race: US men's distance running and the crisis of whiteness'. *Sociology of Sport*, 23, 1–28.

Ward, J. and Lott, T. (2002) *Philosophers on Race*, Oxford: Blackwell.

Watson, B. and Scraton, S. (2001) 'Confronting whiteness? Researching the leisure lives of South Asian mothers'. *Journal of Gender Studies*, 10(3), 265–277.

Weber, M. (1997) 'The concept of ethnicity: what is an ethnic group?' In M. Guibernau and J. Rex, eds, *The Ethnicity Reader: Nationalism, Multiculturalism and Migration*, Cambridge: Polity Press.

Wellman, T. (1993) *Portraits of White Racism*, Cambridge: Cambridge University Press.

Werbner, P. (1996) '"Our blood is green": cricket, identity and social empowerment among British Pakistanis'. In J. MacClancy, ed., *Sport, Identity and Ethnicity*, pp. 87–111. Oxford: Berg.

West, C. (1989) 'Black culture and postmodernism'. In B. Kruger and P. Mariani, eds, *Remaking History: Discussions in Contemporary Culture*, pp. 87–96 Seattle: Bay Press.

West, C. (1995) 'Foreword'. In K. Crenshaw, N. Gotanda, G. Peller and T. Kendall, eds, *Critical Race Theory: The Key Writings that Formed the Movement*, New York: New Press.

Westwood, S. (1990) 'Racism, black masculinity and the politics of space'. In J. Hearn and D. Morgan, eds, *Men, Masculinities and Social Theory*, London: Unwin Hyman.

Westwood, S. (2002) *Power and the Social*, London: Routledge.

Whannel, G. (1992) *Fields in Vision: Television Sport and Cultural Transformation*, London: Routledge.

Whannel, G. (2002) *Media Sports Stars: Masculinities and Moralities*, London: Routledge.

White, J. and Adams, G. (1994) 'Making sense with diversity: the context of research, theory and knowledge development'. In J. White and G. Adams, eds, *Public Administration*, London: Sage.

Wieviorka, M. (1995) *The Arena of Racism*, London: Sage.

Wildman, S. and Davis, A. (1997) 'Making systems of privilege visible'. In R. Delgado and

J. Stefancic, eds, *Critical White Studies: Looking Behind the Mirror*, Philadelphia: Temple University Press.

Williams, B. (2004) 'The truth in the tale: race and "counterstorytelling" in the classroom'. *Journal of Adolescent and Adult Literacy*, 48(2), October, 164–169.

Williams, J. (1994) 'Rangers is a black club'. In R. Giuliannoti and J. Williams, eds, *Game without Frontiers: Football, Identity and Modernity*, Popular Culture Studies 5, Aldershot: Arena Publications.

Williams, P. (1997) *Seeing a Colour-blind Future: The Paradox of Race – The 1997 Reith Lectures*, London: Virago Press.

Williams, R. (1977) *Marxism and Literature*, Oxford: Oxford University Press.

Wilson, B. (1997) 'Good blacks and bad blacks: media constructions of African American athletes in Canadian basketball'. *International Review for the Sociology of Sport*, 37(2), 177–189.

Winant, M. (2001) *The World Is a Ghetto: Race and democracy since World War II*, New York: Basics Books.

Witkin, S. (2000) 'Integrative human rights approach to social research'. In C. Truman, D.M. Mertens and B. Humphries, eds, *Research and Inequality*, London: UCL Press.

Woodward, K. (2004). 'Rumbles in the jungle: racialization and the performance of masculinity'. *Leisure Studies*, 23(1), 5–17.

Woodward, K. (2006) 'Here we go – but where? The possibilities of diaspora in the field of sport'. Milton Keynes: Open University working paper.

Wray, S. (2002) 'Connecting ethnicity, gender and physicality: Muslim Pakistani women, physical activity and health'. In S. Scraton and A. Flintoff, eds, *Gender and Sport: A Reader*, London: Routledge.

Younge, G. (2000) 'White on black'. *Recreation*, November, 24–25.

Index

Spinks, Michael 100
Sport Against Racism in Ireland (SARI)
    112–14
sport literature 11, 20–1, 56, 122
sport management employment practices
    32, 33; resistance to 116
sports club culture 13
Sports Council 69
Sports Illustrated 71, 81, 93–4; myth of
    assimilation and enlightened racism
    102–3; myth of difference and mimetic
    accuracy 99–100; racialisation and
    mediated racial idenitites in 94–7;
    whitecentrism 97–8
Spracklen, K. 69
St Louis, B. 3, 4, 90, 99
Stam, R. 90
'Stand Up Speak Up' campaign 106, 115,
    120, 121
Standing Conference for Community
    Development 113
Stanfield II, J. 23, 25, 30, 38, 43
Staurowsky, E. 91
Stefancic, J. 22, 30, 31, 32, 33, 34, 35, 41,
    43, 55, 56, 64, 65, 67, 117
Steinberg, S. 71, 73, 74
stereotypes 3–4, 18, 20–1, 69, 90–1, 104;
    affecting team positions 7; of Asian
    and indigenous American athletes 91;
    of 'bad blacks' 87–8; black male
    athleticism ix, 90–1, 99; contradicting
    1, 87; destabilising 56; media renewal
    of 81–2, 84, 91, 93, 97, 99, 101, 104;
    mimetic representations relating to 90;
    national 97–8; and sports club culture
    13; of sprinters 81–2, 99; of white
    people in sport 3–4, 69, 90–1; of
    women in sport 20
Sterkenberg, J. 115
Stodolska, M. 39
Stoecker, R. 44
storytelling and counter-storytelling
    55–6
Stovall, D. 22
Sugden, J. 4, 37, 38
swimming 89
Swinney, A. 11, 24, 32, 43, 106, 118, 122

Taguieff, P. 104, 106, 107–9, 108, 110,
    114, 119, 122
Tate IV, W. 26, 30
Taylor, Lawrence 101–2

teams: national 17; playing positions 7;
    supporting 13, 14, 98
'Tebbit test' 14
television: black employment in 92; sports
    commentary 91
tennis 8, 31, 66, 69, 98
Terkel, S. 5, 66
terrorism 107
There Ain't no Black in the Union Jack 18
Thomas-Coventry, B. 87, 92
Thomas, H. 5, 7, 36, 37, 59
Thompson, C. 65
Tomlinson, A. 4, 38
Torres, R. 8, 34, 35
transdisciplinarity 24, 34–5, 36, 41, 63,
    72
transformational resistance 33, 114
Troyna, B. 11
Truman, C. 47, 61
Turtletaub, John 3
Twine, F.W. 25, 42, 47

Ugra, S. 13
UNESCO 5

Valdes, F. 26
Van Ingen, C. 7, 8
Verma, G.K. 5
Villalpando, O. 34

Wallman, S. 15
Walton, T. 70, 71
Warren, J. 25, 42, 47, 80
Watson, B. 20, 24, 37, 40, 43–4, 65, 70
Weber, M. 12
Weiller, K. 82
Welch, R. 23, 24, 31, 43
Wellman, T. 65
Wells, Alan 99
Werbner, P. 36
West, Cornel 2, 26, 29, 33, 37, 38, 42, 43,
    51, 52, 59
Westwood, S. 72, 115, 116
Whannel, G. 82, 89
white athletes 90–1, 100
White, J. 59
White Men Can't Jump 3–4, 69
white privilege 66–8, 70, 74, 78; media
    role in 89; whiteness as victim 71
white supremacy 68
whitecentrism 65–6, 69, 89–90, 97–8
whiteness 56, 64–80; antiracism and 70–2;

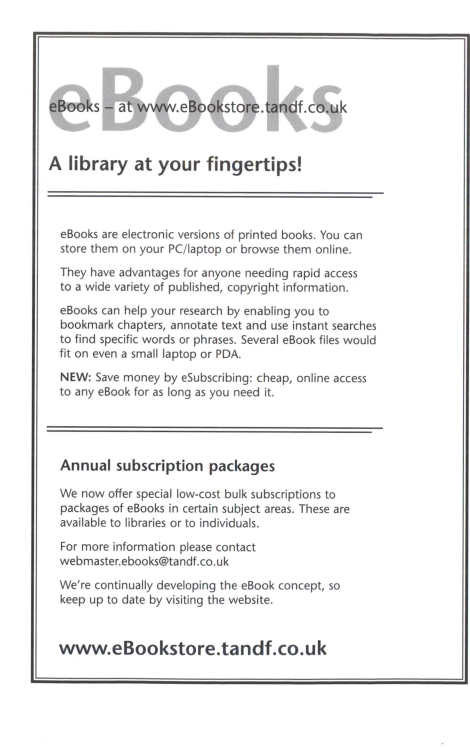

eBooks

eBooks – at www.eBookstore.tandf.co.uk

A library at your fingertips!

eBooks are electronic versions of printed books. You can store them on your PC/laptop or browse them online.

They have advantages for anyone needing rapid access to a wide variety of published, copyright information.

eBooks can help your research by enabling you to bookmark chapters, annotate text and use instant searches to find specific words or phrases. Several eBook files would fit on even a small laptop or PDA.

NEW: Save money by eSubscribing: cheap, online access to any eBook for as long as you need it.

Annual subscription packages

We now offer special low-cost bulk subscriptions to packages of eBooks in certain subject areas. These are available to libraries or to individuals.

For more information please contact webmaster.ebooks@tandf.co.uk

We're continually developing the eBook concept, so keep up to date by visiting the website.

www.eBookstore.tandf.co.uk

LIBRARY, UNIVERSITY OF CHESTER